Skiing and Snowboarding Fitness

Reach your potential on the slopes

Mark Hines

FIREFLY BOOKS

A FIREFLY BOOK

Published by Firefly Books Ltd. 2007

First printing

Publisher Cataloging-in-Publication Data (U.S.)

Hines, Mark, 1978-
  Skiing & snowboarding fitness : reach your potential on the slopes / Mark Hines.
[144] p. : col. ill. ; cm.
Includes index.
Summary: Provides a fitness program specifically designed for the rigors of skiing and snowboarding at all levels.
ISBN-13: 978-1-55407-323-8 (pbk.)
ISBN-10: 1-55407-323-5 (pbk.)
1. Skis and skiing—Training. 2. Snowboarding—Training. I. Title.
796.93 dc22   GV854.85.H56 2007

Library and Archives Canada Cataloguing in Publication

Hines, Mark, 1978-
  Skiing & snowboarding fitness : reach your potential on the slopes / Mark Hines.
Includes index.
ISBN-13: 978-1-55407-323-8
ISBN-10: 1-55407-323-5
    1. Downhill skiing—Training. 2. Snowboarding—Training. 3. Physical fitness. I. Title. II. Title: Skiing and snowboarding fitness.
GV854.85.H55 2007   796.93   C2007-902275-8

Published in the United States by
Firefly Books (U.S.) Inc.
P.O. Box 1338, Ellicott Station
Buffalo, New York 14205

Published in Canada by
Firefly Books Ltd.
66 Leek Crescent
Richmond Hill, Ontario L4B 1H1

Design: James Watson
Cover Image: Corbis

Printed in China

Contents

Acknowledgments

I would like to thank a number of people for making this book possible. Firstly, I would like to thank both of my parents for teaching me to ski from a young age, and for taking me to a number of beautiful places around the world where I could practice.

On a technical level, I would like to thank my dear friend John Hardy, as an authority on all matters relating to biomechanics and exercise prescription. It is through the existence of John that I have always had somebody at hand that I can phone up and argue with about many issues surrounding exercise science and kinesiology. Most importantly, it is good to have somebody to agree with when we find ourselves challenging the status quo.

Also on a technical level, I would like to thank Dr. Mike Langran for his input on the sports injuries section. I am most grateful that he allowed me to use some of the statistics and information from his website; www.ski-injury.com

Finally, I would like to thank my two models, Emily and Stephen, for their help in making this book happen. They have both been wonderful colleagues and are good friends. I have enjoyed training with them in the past, and am grateful for the time and commitment that they put in to getting the photographs right for this book.

Introduction

Skiing and snowboarding are becoming more accessible to a greater range of people all over the world. Downhill sports have spread from their origins in Scandinavia to just about anywhere that has a hill and sees some snow. With the growing sophistication of artificial indoor and outdoor slopes, skiing and snowboarding are not only available to more people but can also be practiced to a greater standard than on older dry slopes. Despite the growing numbers of practitioners, the increasing number of ski lifts and trails means that there are many places that can be enjoyed free from the crowds.

With more people skiing and riding on- and off-trail, it is important to ensure that everyone is appropriately physically conditioned. For those who ski or ride all year round, this can be a good opportunity to improve muscle and joint function, and apply it directly to improve technical skills. For those who hit the slopes only once or twice a year, being physically conditioned will enable them to get the most pleasure and development from their trips.

The purpose of this book is to introduce you to the most effective exercises for downhill sports. Indeed, the exercises will develop the body of anyone, regardless of how adept they are. The plan is to treat the body as a functional unit, developing that unit for the specific tasks required of it when on the hill or mountain so as to improve technique and fitness. While this is not a book about developing technical skills – something best learned on the slopes – it does set out to train the individual to be better able (from a specific fitness perspective) to develop technical skills.

As an exercise scientist specializing in biomechanics, my work involves studying the way people move and then finding ways to improve their movement and reduce their risk of injury or pain. You may be surprised to learn that there are very few top athletes with fantastic biomechanics. This is not to say that moving badly is good because these people are likely to pick up muscle injuries (we've all heard of soccer players and sprinters tearing their hamstrings) and may suffer from even more problems later in life.

Regardless of what skill level you are – whether an absolute novice or a gold medallist – you can improve your abilities on the slopes and decrease your risk of injury. I have never met anybody who suffered from a *slight* injury, or was only *slightly* sore the day after their first day on the slopes. So, we shall begin at the beginning. We will get you moving properly first, to ensure your joints are doing what they are supposed to, and then we will start increasing the demands of the training over the course of several weeks. This will have the effect of developing the body specifically for the rigors of skiing and riding while maintaining optimal joint positioning. In short, you will be moving properly and performing what I believe to be the best training programs ever devised. I write that because most exercise programs tend to train the legs and arms, which is interesting but not specific enough to do much good, but more on that later.

From a safety perspective, the fitter someone is, the less likely that person is to have an accident. There are, however, many types of fitness. Although we tend to have a preconceived idea of what we would describe or recognize as fitness, we can quite easily miss out on some important factors. We could describe a marathon runner as fit, and we could describe an Olympic power-lifter as fit, and although we would be correct both times, they are clearly very different types of fitness, and one type is by no means more important than the other. Someone who plays chess could be described as mentally fit, and could 'train' to improve mental fitness, but this in itself would not make the chess player fitter for any physical function.

Flexibility, strength, endurance, power, cardiovascular ability, balance, proprioception (detailed later), stability and nervous function are all important and independent types of fitness. When all these factors that contribute to overall fitness are developed, physical and mental fatigue can be offset or prevented, thereby improving all-round ability to perform to the best standard that your technique will allow. Technique itself can then be developed far better than if the body lacks sufficient levels of fitness in any of the factors mentioned.

Most importantly, 'fitness,' in whatever guise, can be improved through developmental training. This means starting from whatever exercising background – whether novice, beginner, intermediate, advanced or professional – and improving ability through small but significant steps. The exercises included in this book make up a course of different programs. They are intended not just to take the beginner to an advanced stage, but to take anybody from any level and allow them the opportunity to make natural and comfortable progressions far beyond those that might be derived from other programs.

Skiing and snowboarding are highly technical sports, and although technical ability can be nurtured through an appropriate exercise program, actual technical skills are best improved when on the hill. What improvements depend upon, however, is the body's ability to recover from bouts of skiing or riding (even down to an individual turn), as well as the body's ability to react and move accordingly in relation to speed and the to nature of the surface beneath it. Exercise training can be used to prevent fatigue, to ensure muscles have energy for developing power when needed, and to allow the body to react to maintain posture and balance regardless of the demands of the terrain. This can all be brought together to give the individual the supporting tools required to make the most out of their specific sport.

Fitness for downhill sports has to include a number of factors. Most importantly, regardless of the starting point, everybody can benefit from specific training. The problem is that few people really understand what 'specific' means, and the abundance of contradictions and misconceptions in the exercise industry could bewilder the most seasoned professional from any background. By the end of this book, however, you should have improved your knowledge of skiing and snowboarding fitness to the point of being an expert on the subjects. The goal, therefore, is not only to improve your overall fitness and ability, but also to increase your understanding of how the body works, and how this relates to what is essentially an original approach to training for two of the most exciting sports in the world.

The History of Hitting the Slopes

As a skier or snowboarder, you are one of more than 200 million downhill enthusiasts in the world today. Not only that, but you are also part of one of the oldest winter traditions. It was around 5000 years ago that people first started strapping skis to their feet. The Norwegians were the first, using skis as they were hunting across the snow-covered Nordic landscape. Skiing then spread across Scandinavia and Russia, initially as a mode of transportation, and eventually as a sport similar to modern cross-country skiing.

Alpine (downhill) skiing was the next stage in the evolution of winter sports. That is not to suggest that cross-country skiing was made redundant, rather that skis were developed that were engineered according to the precise nature of the skiing activity. The first Alpine skiing competition was held in Oslo in the 1850s. A few decades later, skiing spread to the rest of Europe and the United States, where miners entertained themselves with skiing competitions during the winter months. The first slalom was held in Mürren, Switzerland, in 1922, and in 1924 it became the first Olympic Alpine event.

Alpine skiing underwent a huge renaissance in the 1990s with the development of carving skis. There are now more than 70 million snowboarders in the world, with emerging sports such as skiboarding and telemark skiing growing in presence on the slopes. Ski lifts have become faster and increased in number. Together with the expansion and development of ski areas, and improved snow-making facilities, the number of winter sports enthusiasts has grown.

People may hit the slopes for the challenge, for sport, for the release it brings or simply because it is fun. Whatever the reason, downhill sports are superb for all-over body strength, particularly for the lower back and legs. They also improve muscular endurance and power, both of which are important as we grow older. Mountain air has health benefits too. It is much less polluted than the air found in cities and has lower oxygen levels. This is why mountain air may cause less free radical damage to the body's cells, which is linked to disease, including cancer.

In addition to the physical benefits, skiing and snowboarding take the individual to an environment far removed from the stress of everyday life. The contrasts in surroundings offer a monumental release from the mundane, while rekindling and nurturing our desire to explore and master. At the same time, the breathtaking beauty of our natural world captivates us. These downhill sports provide us with a medium to escape mental stresses, improve physical well-being and, quite possibly, reduce our risks of various cancers (providing, of course, that we limit our skin's exposure to direct sunlight).

The Exercise Renaissance

Although exercise training techniques have come a long way, there is still much to be achieved before we can truly believe that we are benefiting our 'health' in a more holistic sense. When it comes to putting an exercise program into practice, it helps to understand what the options are, because the approach I use is radically different to that used by the majority of the industry. I am not alone in this, and I do not want to be because I would like everybody to get the most out of their investments and their body. But with so few exercise professionals having a platform such as this to promote their ideas to the world, I am rather proud to be one of the first, and hope that this book makes me more friends than enemies.

Modern exercise training, as we recognize it in health clubs today, came from the strong men of the latter part of the 19th century. The purpose of exercise then was to develop the muscles, which culminated in public displays of strength and muscle size. From those pioneering days, resistance training began evolving into modern weightlifting, power-lifting and body-building sports and competitions.

Prior to the 1950s, nearly all resistance training involved only dumbbells and barbells. Then, various companies set about manufacturing machines for use by body-builders. The logic was that body-builders could use the machines to train specific muscle groups. These resistance machines also acted as a way of training all the muscles, and became an extra string to the body-builder's bow.

The vast majority of trainers still use exercises and programs based on body-building techniques from decades ago. Someone may go into a health club with the goal of improving various aspects of personal fitness, such as becoming better at sport, losing fat, gaining muscle, improving definition, 'toning up', improving health, relieving stress, or simply for social reasons. But for almost every goal, the typical trainer will provide an exercise program based on body-building exercises and techniques.

The problem is that body-building focuses on muscles, and treating the body as a collection of them, whereas in fact the body should be regarded as a unit. If we were to consider the muscles involved in picking something up from a table, the body-building approach would be to consider first the biceps shortening to bend the elbow, thus initiating movement. The movement-based approach of our modern trainers would be more simplistic, because in fact every muscle in the body is going to be involved to some extent in that movement. The body-building logic would ascertain that the best way to improve ability at picking something up from a table is to do biceps exercises. The movement-based expert would advocate for simply repeating the exact movement, so that the body is trained as a whole to perform a specific task.

Taking this example one step further, if we wanted to become better at jumping or kicking, the movement-based trainer would advocate repeating the same movement, and might consolidate this by promoting some exercises that improve joint actions for specific parts of that movement. But, regardless of how many exercises are actually chosen, they will all be either very similar or exactly the same as the movement that needs to be produced. A body-building approach, however, might be to take the individual muscles and muscle groups involved in the movement, and train them individually. This could mean that the person is advised to perform leg extensions, leg presses and leg curls. The problem with this is that we have no confidence in the idea that training in this way will have any carry-over effect whatsoever. What is also important is that training 'muscles' rather than 'movements' may leave the joints untrained and lacking the strength and stability required to prevent injuries.

A large part of this comes down to the body's nervous system. Most of the movements you do every day happen in a very precise manner. When you pick something up, walk, run, sit down, stand up, twist, turn, stick your arm out, close the car door, step up – it all happens in a certain way. Exercise scientists have analysed the way the body moves. All the muscles in the body are supposed to 'fire' (be activated by nerves) at a certain rate, to a certain degree and in a particular order for every single natural movement. The logic behind 'functional,' 'movement-based' exercise training is to embrace this natural way of moving and build on it. Essentially, it involves choosing or creating exercises based on the body's own natural movement patterns.

This means that the body can become stronger and healthier, and better at performing a specific movement simply by replicating natural movements and adding resistance from the correct direction. If you are using this sort of training, then you are training the body the way that it has developed, and therefore improving joint strength and stability, bone strength, motor control and muscle performance in exactly the way that you want for your goals and for your body.

The danger with the more archaic body-building approach is that this very important aspect of human development and movement is completely disregarded. What is worse is that if you break a movement down into component muscles, and then train them individually, you are teaching the body a different way to activate muscles. This will counter the body's natural movement patterns, and may then have a deleterious effect on the way the body moves and responds to physical stress. Even body-building – the use of resistance training to increase muscle size – can actually be performed using movement-based exercises. If you want to go skiing or snowboarding, then it makes sense to adopt a method of training that embraces these sports, and sets out to better train the body.

Eventually, there will be a fundamental change in the way people design and choose exercises. At the present time, there are only a few trainers who truly embrace this logic, and here you are offered an insight into its practical application in order to improve your performance on the hill.

injuries

A good understanding of downhill injuries is paramount to ensuring that due care is taken to avoid an injury occurring. Such an understanding will not only aid in preparation for skiing or snowboarding, but will also increase awareness on the slopes, and may be of use when choosing outerwear and equipment. Should an injury occur, even when following a thorough preventive program, then it is important to understand the nature of the injury and how to promote recovery and prevent recurrence. Because the advice given here is general, there is the chance that other individual factors may contribute to an injury, as susceptibility to a specific injury can only be assessed on an individual basis.

This section of the book may have particular appeal to those who have already suffered an injury, or who have friends or relatives who have been injured while skiing or riding. The information aims to improve knowledge of the condition and to highlight how it became possible to receive the injury in the first instance.

The overall rate of skiing injuries has halved since initial records in the 1970s. There are a number of reasons for this, including developments in equipment, more attention being paid to fitting the equipment, and general care and safety features on various slopes. In general, the rate of injuries is relatively constant the world over, reflecting improved standards of ski-area management. The biggest reduction in injuries has been to the lower body, which is in relation to the improved safety features of ski boots and release mechanisms. Brakes on skis, which help stop a ski from continuing down the slope following a boot release, have helped to reduce the number of lacerations (cuts) to other downhill enthusiasts.

So, now that I have your attention, it is worth mentioning that there is not *that* much to worry about. Despite the fact that every winter or spring you see someone with a leg cast on, a hand bandaged, or an arm in a sling, on average, there are actually very few injuries. There is always a chance that an injury could happen, however, particularly on the second afternoon on the mountain because the skier or snowboarder was out of shape, tired, depleted of energy stores, dehydrated, and possibly feeling the after-effects of the first big night out. The purpose of the rest of this section is to inform you of all the debilitating things that might just happen the next time you hit the slopes, so that we can then look at ways to help prevent that from happening.

One common method for comparing various injuries is to calculate the mean (average) days between injury (MDBI). This is calculated by dividing the total number of days within a downhill season by the number of injuries recorded. The higher the MDBI, the greater the number of days between injuries and the lower the risk. Lower limb injuries occur at a rate of one every 520 days, while upper limb injuries occur once every 1,140 days, suggesting that you are twice as likely to injure a lower limb than an upper limb.

The overall MDBI for skiing is approximately 315. This means that an individual has a risk of receiving a skiing injury for every 315 days on the mountain. This figure is surprisingly low, and may reflect the fact that many injuries are not recorded, and that treatments are only obtained following return home, if at all. The figure also fails to give an indication of how serious the injuries are. To ensure the longevity of enjoyment on the slopes, it is necessary to take steps to prevent injuries from occurring.

Falls are a common cause of injury, accounting for between 75 and 85 percent of skiing injuries. The majority of injuries caused by falls are sprains, followed by fractures, lacerations and dislocations. Because of the injury risk of falls on both skies and snowboards, people tend to fight incredibly hard to maintain balance when they find themselves out of control. However, this is likely to lead to an increase in speed, difficulty in regaining balance and control, and risk of receiving a serious injury. Hence, many instructors will recommend that an individual attempts to encourage a fall when struggling to maintain or regain balance. The intention is to fall under reasonable control and at a reasonable speed, rather than risk falling shortly afterwards anyway, but in a much less controlled and more dangerous position.

As a skier falls, the head should be tucked in, preferably with the skis close together and parallel, with the arms at the side. The fall should be off to the side rather than over the back of the skis, and care should be taken to release the poles, to prevent an injury from either falling on them or having the straps damage the thumb. An injury is most likely to occur from sprawling the arms and legs and hitting the snow haphazardly. Although a perfect fall for either skiing or snowboarding – when an immediate recovery is not possible – is rarely a possibility, it is far better to bail out early rather than increase the risk of serious injury by falling with no control whatsoever.

Connective Tissue

Connective tissue is the most abundant and varied tissue in the body. It includes bone, cartilage, skin and even blood and components of the immune system. Connective tissue is important for attachments of muscle to bone, bone to bone, and muscle to muscle. Here, we are interested in breaks in the skin (lacerations), breaks in bones (fractures) and damage to the connective surfaces around muscles, bones and joints (strains, sprains and dislocations). Sprains and strains are among the most common connective tissue injuries in all sports.

A sprain is a stretch, partial tear or complete tear of a ligament (ligaments are fibrous bands of connective tissue that bind one bone to another). The purpose of a ligament is to stabilize a joint and prevent excessive movement. Ligaments are relatively inelastic, meaning that a strong force that moves a joint beyond its natural range of movement can lead to damage. Ligaments also generally lack the blood supply of muscles and many other connective tissues, meaning that they can take a long time to heal.

The body is made up of three types of muscle tissue:

1. **Cardiac muscle** is the muscle of the heart.
2. **Smooth muscle** is located in some internal organs, including parts of the digestive system, where it is involved in helping food move along the gut.
3. **Skeletal muscle** is the muscle we see that gives our body shape, that allows us to move our joints and to perform movements and exercise (accepting that the heart obviously plays a vital supporting role as well).

In fact, all three types of muscle work in synergy to allow us to perform movements, to breathe and to live. With regard to injury, we are most interested in skeletal muscle tissue. A strain is an injury to the skeletal muscle tissue caused by over-stretching, over-exertion or a direct trauma. In some cases, areas of skeletal muscle tissue can be completely severed from surrounding muscle fibers or tendons (tendons are the connective tissues that bind muscle to bone).

A dislocation (or luxation) occurs when connective tissues around a joint surface are damaged, allowing the joint surfaces to separate. This can be the result of a pulling or twisting movement to the joint itself, causing the bone surfaces to stretch and then tear the supporting connective tissues completely. A subluxation occurs when the connective tissues are stretched to the point of causing damage, but are not completely torn.

Bones have a number of functions, including production of red blood cells, attachments for muscles, levers for movement and protection of internal organs. A fracture occurs when sufficient force is placed on a bone to cause it to break. There are various types of fractures. Some are caused by a single force that directly strikes the bone from one end or across the bone. Fractures can also be caused by excessive twisting forces on a particular bone, which can be generated during falls. Because some bones are also important for protection, such as the skull and the ribcage, it is clear that significant collision forces to these areas can result in fractures. If such injuries do occur, then it is possible that the associated internal organs will also be affected, so swift medical attention is vital.

Upper Body Injuries

There has been little change in the reported rates of head, shoulder and thumb injuries since the 1970s. Injuries to the upper extremities account for approximately 30–40 percent of all skiing injuries. The four main injuries to Alpine skiers are dislocated shoulders, fractured clavicle (collarbone), fractured humerus (upper arm bone) and AC joint subluxations (the AC joint joins the collarbone to the top of the shoulder joint).

Head Injuries

The types of head injuries seen on the slopes vary from minor bumps and lacerations to far more serious, life-threatening fractures. Most injuries, however, are minor and can be administered to quite simply. Although a range of injuries can occur due to the same cause, such as collision with another object, it is often the speed of impact that predicts severity of injury.

Most winter sport-related deaths involve trauma to the head. These are often due to a high-speed collision with a tree, pylon, rock or other slope user. At lesser speeds, an injury to the same area of the head may lead to a slight concussion, but even this will mean foregoing some time on the slopes. Even minor head injuries can lead to headaches, light-headedness and nausea, and poor concentration. These lesser injuries still need to be taken seriously, and should be assessed by a doctor as soon as possible, and definitely before returning to the slopes or driving. If someone receives a head injury that causes a lack of consciousness, then they need to be taken to a hospital for assessment and observation. Injuries to children should be taken very seriously, and any perceived threshold for when to seek medical advice for an adult should be significantly lowered for children.

Spinal Injuries

Spinal injuries themselves are fortunately rare, but the mechanisms by which they can be initiated are far more common. This means that it is best to be safe if someone has fallen and there is the possibility of a spinal injury.

There are two parts of the spine. The first is the bony apparatus that makes up the vertebral column. The vertebrae, like other bones, act as levers to allow movement to occur. Although the movements of individual segments of the spine are relatively small, when acting together much greater movements and ranges of motion are possible. Because the spine is so mobile as a total unit, any excessive movements, such as twisting or bending, or combinations of movements can lead to strains of the muscles that attach to the vertebrae. This can be very painful, and because the muscles are always being used in normal movement, they can often take a long time to heal as they rarely receive sufficient rest. The purpose of the exercises in this book is essentially to strengthen these muscles and to train them to perform necessary movements to help prevent these types of injuries from occurring. Although an injury to these muscles may be incredibly painful, the problem is essentially no more than a muscle strain.

The other function of the vertebrae is to protect the spinal cord. The spinal cord is the nerve highway to and from the brain, with all the major nerve roads running from it all the way down to the base. The higher up the spinal cord, the greater the importance of the area and the greater the damage. For example, a tear in the spinal cord toward its base may be disabling, but there are lots of possibilities for rehabilitation and protection of quality of life. Higher up toward the brain, however, tears may be permanently disabling, and include total paralysis with less likelihood of rehabilitation. Injuries to the spinal cord can happen when such extreme movements of the spinal column occur that shearing forces directly damage nerves or the spinal cord itself. Severe impacts and other trauma can cause a similar effect.

Any of these injuries, whether to skeletal muscle that attaches to the spinal column or shearing forces to the spinal cord, can be caused by excessive movements of the spine. These excessive forces, most likely involving many different movements and angular forces, may be caused by particularly bad falls, jumps with poor landings or avalanches. Although the likelihood of a spinal cord injury is low, it is essential to avoid moving the casualty unless it is a matter of life and death, and to promptly send someone to get help from the ski patrol.

Shoulder Injuries

The shoulder joint is complex and consists of the upper arm bone (humerus), collarbone (clavicle) and shoulder blade (scapula). The clavicle, joins to the acromium (at the top outside end of the scapula) at one end and the sternum (breastbone) at the other. The muscle attachments for these bones extend across the chest, the back and the arms. There is also other connective tissue, such as tendons, ligaments and cartilage, which can all be damaged through winter sport-related injuries.

Dislocation of the shoulder can occur when the arm is outstretched, and there is sufficient force acting in the opposite direction to that in which the body's momentum is traveling. This could be an upward and/or backward force during a fall. It could also occur when moving too fast or when losing control and grasping a fence, a tree, a planted ski pole, or using another person as an anchor.

Once a dislocation has occurred, there is an 85 percent chance of dislocating the same joint in the future, due to weaknesses in the connective tissue. This supports the reason for strengthening joints through resistance exercise and for adhering to physiotherapy advice for effective rehabilitation. In some cases, when the shoulder joint is repeatedly dislocated, with comparatively minor trauma causing the injury, surgery may be required to stabilize the joint and help prevent further dislocations from occurring.

Dislocations and subluxations can also occur to the ligament that binds the acromium to the clavicle (the AC joint). This dislocation, or subluxation, can result from a direct impact to the outside of the humerus. A dislocation to this joint is very rare, with subluxations being more common, and surgery is required in only a few cases to bring the acromium and clavicle closer together again. It is also possible to fracture the clavicle directly; this is often the result of an impact that radiates upwards from the humerus.

Injuries to the Humerus

Fractures to the upper arm bone can result from a direct blow, such as during a collision, or falling onto an outstretched hand. The fractures can occur either across the shaft of the bone or to the end of the bone next to the shoulder joint.

Skier's Thumb

Skier's thumb is the name for an injury to the joint where the base of the thumb joins the bones of the hand, affecting one of the ligaments that joins the bones together. Injury to this ulnar collateral ligament (UCL) of the thumb is the most common upper limb injury for skiers. An injury to this ligament is second only to a medial collateral ligament (MCL) injury in the knee in terms of frequency of occurrence in skiers. Injury to the UCL tends to occur when a skier falls onto an outstretched hand while still gripping the ski pole. The movement causes the thumb to be pulled outward, leading to injury of the joint.

Many people underestimate the significance of a hand injury because big, whole body movements are still possible, making it easy to neglect proper treatment for a thumb injury. The scale of the problem may become obvious only when movement is sufficiently awkward and it becomes too painful to perform everyday tasks, such as writing or typing, eating, carrying bags, drinking tea, using a television remote control, or dressing. In short, injuries to the thumb are serious, and proper care should be taken to treat the injury if it occurs, in order to maximize opportunities for proper rehabilitation. Failure to do so may result in long-term disability.

Injury to the UCL can be reduced by using the straps as well as holding on to the pole, instead of holding the pole directly. The hand should be placed upwards through the underside of the strap before holding the pole. This increases the likelihood that the hand will release the pole during a fall. The goal is to ensure that the pole is let go of completely during a fall. Ideally, if no straps were used and the pole was released during a fall, then the pole would end up further away and the risk of injury would be reduced. Unfortunately, it is more likely, from a psychological viewpoint at least, that a skier will try to keep the pole as close as possible during a fall, if for no other reason than to save a walk afterward. Of course, if the UCL is damaged, then skiing with a pole in the hand is not a possibility anyway!

When skiing in deep powder, the poles are more important, so using the straps is even more valid. New devices are being developed that involve clipping the poles directly to the glove, or securing the hand to the pole in some other manner. At the moment there are too few users to measure the effectiveness of these tools, and the key thing to remember in any case is simply to ensure that the poles are released during a fall. If you can master not using the straps and still releasing the poles, then you will be even less likely to suffer skier's thumb.

Lower Body Injuries

When most people think of skiing and snowboarding injuries, they tend to think about injuries to the knees and legs. Fractures of the lower leg bones (tibia and fibula) used to be common before binding release mechanisms were improved. Although it is still vitally important to ensure that bindings are fitted correctly. Fractures to the top of the shinbone (tibial plateau) account for approximately 1 percent of all skiing injuries, and tend to occur following a bad landing after a jump, which transmits huge compressive forces to that area of bone.

Some fractures still occur to the shinbones when the body is forced forwards of the ski boots, and it is essential to check all equipment for proper releasing before use. Even so, these fractures can still occur if the skis plough into deep, soft snow, and the body's momentum continues forward as the skis come to a stop.

Cartilage injuries are also quite common in skiers. In particular, the menisci that sit on top of the tibial plateau can be damaged during a harsh twisting movement of the knee, when the knee is bent, and is usually accompanied by other injuries to the area. Injuries to the meniscus itself occur in approximately 5–10 percent of all ski injuries.

The evolution of binding release mechanisms has not, however, accomplished very much in the prevention of knee injuries. Damage to the knee ligaments accounts for about a third of all ski injuries. Such injuries can be slow to rehabilitate, although rehabilitaion is possible with good physiotherapy and appropriate exercise. However, in some cases the injury might be bad enough to prevent the individual from ever being able to ski again.

Knee Injuries

Few people appreciate the complexity of the knee joint until they injure it. The knee is able to bend and straighten, and also has a small amount of rotational movement available when bent. The joint is where the tibia of the lower leg meets the femur of the upper leg, with the patella (kneecap) to the front. The ends of the bones are covered in cartilage, including the thick menisci at the top of the tibia, into which the femur sits. The bones are joined together by a number of ligaments. These include medial collateral and lateral collateral ligaments on the inside and outside of the knee respectively, and anterior and posterior cruciate ligaments coming into the knee and on to the tibia from the femur. Because the role of the ligaments is to stabilize the knee and keep the bones in the correct positions, injury to these ligaments is a common result of a bad landing.

Injuries to the knee will often involve the medial collateral ligament (MCL), anterior cruciate ligament (ACL) or the meniscus, or a combination of the three. A key purpose of this book is to strengthen and develop the connective tissue of the various joints of the body to help prevent injury. If the knee has been injured, then it is even more important to engage in an appropriate exercise program to help guard against recurrence. A physiotherapist should be able to assess any inherent weaknesses, imbalances or susceptibility to injury and can offer advice regarding a specific exercise program.

Any obvious deformity of the knee, accompanied by local tenderness, swelling and the inability to either straighten the leg fully or to bear weight on it, suggests a serious knee injury. There may also be an audible popping sound when the injury occurs. Any of these signs indicate a need for prompt medical attention. Avoidance of the slopes is recommended until the knee has been thoroughly assessed and an accurate evaluation given. Because it is possible to function with various degrees of ligament sprain – even complete tears (or 'ruptures') – it is particularly important to have injuries checked to prevent further damage.

A damaged ligament will limit mobility and joint range of motion. Because most ligaments do not have a good blood supply, they can take significantly longer to heal than some other connective tissue injuries. This may mean that the knee collapses during activity, and extra care should be taken to ensure that the approach to therapy and exercise is kept steady and progressive. Reconstructive surgery may sometimes be required to bring parts of the ruptured ligament back together. Full rehabilitation may sometimes take a year, making it all the more important to ensure that preparation focuses on developing areas that were previously damaged (something many people instinctively want to avoid).

MCL Injuries

Medial collateral ligament (MCL) damage is the most common injury in Alpine skiing. This ligament stabilizes the knee in side-to-side movements. A slow twisting fall, or the prolonged maintenance of the snowplough position where the tibia is twisted outward in relation to the femur, can cause sprains to this ligament. A higher speed twisting movement, such as from 'catching an edge' with one lower leg twisting outwards quickly, can also sprain the MCL.

The snowplough is the technique commonly adopted by beginners, with a wide stance and the legs pointed inward. This position makes it difficult to transmit muscular forces down the legs effectively, and one or both legs can easily be made unstable. Conversely, a parallel stance, with the skis not too close together, is more stable but allows greater speeds to be achieved. While this is clearly a good theoretical basis for avoiding MCL injuries, the greater speeds do increase the likelihood of a more serious injury from a fall. Lying between the snowplough and parallel skiing is the 'stem-turn,' a technique utilized by intermediates before progressing to full parallel skiing. Here, one ski is kept straight and the other is pushed out into a 'half-snowplough' position. The problem with the stem-turn is that it does not permit the same control at speed as parallel skiing does, so can lead to injuries in skiers who are attempting slopes too advanced for their technique.

The key to prevention of MCL injuries is due care and personal responsibility when on the slopes. When choosing runs it is important to ensure that you can be challenged and try new techniques without the risk of being out of control and unable to stop or turn efficiently. Proper preparation and conditioning is paramount to maximizing your enjoyment of the slopes.

ACL Injuries

Prior to the millennium, anterior cruciate ligament (ACL) injuries occurred at a rate of about 2,200 MDBI, and this figure had been static for quite some time. Since then the figure has started to reduce, due to the development of carving skis (*see* below). The rate of knee sprains, particularly sprains to the ACL, is not related to ski bindings. This is largely due to the fact that ski bindings are designed to release due to excess forces at the foot and shin, and they cannot detect direct forces at the knee. Hence, although we have seen a decrease in fractures to the tibia and fibula, the rate of injuries to the knee has changed relatively little.

In most cases, it is the tail of the ski that is involved in causing the ACL injury. In normal movement, the heel acts as a short pivot for the leg over the foot. When wearing skis, however, the 'heel' of the foot is effectively displaced quite some way behind the ankle. This then acts as a 'phantom foot,' and when balance is lost backward, that phantom foot creates a greater distance over which to fall backward. This action leads to an overstretching of the knee, and the ACL is often sprained in the process. Significant shearing forces can also sprain the ACL, such as during a high-speed twisting fall or when 'catching an edge.' Rehabilitation of these injuries can be quite difficult, and in some cases may require surgery to bring the two ends of the ligament closer together (for significant partial or complete ligament ruptures).

ACL injuries are now being reduced through the development of new carving skis, which are shorter overall and have a shorter area behind the ski boot. The reduction in ACL injuries has been observed since carving skis first became popular in the year 2000. It is possible that decreasing the required forces for binding release could prevent *some* ACL injuries, although this may lead to skis being released from relatively minor knocks. This is currently being experimented with in France, where reports suggest a reduction in total ACL injuries (the lower ACL injuries could also just be the effect of more people using the shorter carving skis).

Another mechanism for inducing an ACL injury is directly through the boot. This can occur when a skier loses balance to the rear when attempting a jump. If the legs straighten, then the skier will likely land on the tails of the skis, which then causes the back of the ski boot to push against the back of the calf muscles. This pushes the tibia forward of the femur and sprains or ruptures the ACL. A similar path of force, separating the tibia and femur, can occur when an upright and usually stationary skier is hit in the lower leg from the side or behind by a falling slope user. Other means of causing damage to the ACL include twisting falls or when skiing or riding the moguls.

DOMS

Delayed-onset muscle soreness (DOMS) is the uncomfortable feeling that often occurs when we begin a new exercise program, or push our body more than it is used to. DOMS is an indication that the body has been pushed hard and that the affected muscles require time to recover. The cause of the sore feeling is poorly understood. For some time, many people thought that the soreness was related to lactic acid in the muscles, but this exercise by-product is removed and recycled soon after stopping exercise, with most of it removed within half an hour of completing the session.

It is important to understand that muscle fibers require recovery time and that denying them that time will effect performance. In short, using muscles that have not recovered means the body will under-perform, which may lead to premature fatigue and an increased risk of injury. Limiting muscle soreness is a combination of eating the correct nutrients, and steady building up endurance through an exercise training program, rather than launching in too fast and working significantly harder than the body is used to. The intention is that the progressive nature of the exercise programs in this book will help prepare the muscles for use on the slopes, and so reduce the likelihood, severity and/or duration of DOMS after a day of exercise.

Stretching has also been hypothesized to prevent muscle soreness. The wringing action that stretching has on the muscle fibers may help to remove some toxins and any damaged components of cells, and therefore speed up recovery. It is certainly worth performing a few stretches at the end of a day on the mountain.

Collisions

Collisions on the slopes are a common cause of injury. Some people assume that the mountain is their personal playground, and forget that it is a public thoroughfare with rules and regulations. Collisions may happen when an inexperienced skier or rider loses control. On some slopes, where routes go through areas of woodland, there is an increased risk of colliding with trees or other people on the same tracks.

Collisions with obstacles account for 90 percent of all skiing fatalities. Trees are the most common cause of these fatalities (60 percent). Collisions with other people account for approximately 10 percent of all fatalities. There is debate as to how much the wearing of helmets might protect against fatalities. While helmets may protect against many head injuries, including some lacerations, bruises and fractures, they cannot protect against forces to the base of the skull and neck, which lead to many of the most severe injuries. The best means of protecting against collisions will always be to remain vigilant and aware of other slope users, and never to allow yourself to lose control or to move too fast for your skill level.

Minimizing Risks

Aside from the importance of an appropriate training program, and proper rehabilitation from any injury, there are a number of other important factors for preventing injuries when going to the slopes. The binding of each ski should be checked every day before skiing. The bindings need to be adjusted according to height and weight, as well as for the size of the boot itself. The same applies to snowboards and snowboard bindings. Clothing should obviously be warm, but it should not be too loose, otherwise it could catch on ski lifts, branches, fences or others.

At the start of each day, it is important to go down an easy slope, both to warm up and to get an idea of snow conditions. Always be alert for ice patches, rocks and areas of powder. In particular, try to pay attention to others, and notice if they have difficulty over certain areas where nothing is obviously difficult. Any particularly challenging slopes or jumps that you might have been eyeing up the night before should be attempted earlier on in the day. By the afternoon, fatigue will probably be setting in, so it is important to take it easier so as to avoid the risk of causing an accident.

Even on popular slopes it is important to ski or ride with a partner; someone who can help immediately if there is a problem. When heading off-trail, at least one partner – preferably three or four – is essential. Make sure you both know the route down the mountain and always remember to stop and wait in the event you lose sight of your partner.

Conditioning for Injury Prevention

It is my opinion that the best way to *train* the body to better perform on the slopes is to train the body in *precisely the same way* it needs to be utilized while actually skiing or snowboarding.

If you are skiing then you are going to be leaning forward, squatting, transferring weight from one leg to another and at the same time rotating the torso and pushing down on a pole, and that is *precisely* what you should be doing in training. Even more specifically, the depth of that squat and the power generated will depend upon the your level of ability, the speed at which you are traveling, the steepness of the slope, the depth and hardness of the snow, and the angle of the turn. All of this needs to be not just *replicated* but, wherever possible, *duplicated* in training. It is all very well becoming fitter and better conditioned for lifting weights in a gym, but if the goal is to become fitter and better conditioned for skiing and riding, then most books on training can be thrown out the window.

The philosophy of this program is not simply to make people better and more proficient on the mountain. It is also to strengthen and protect the body against the very injuries referred to in this section. As we have seen, the spine, the shoulder and the knee are all susceptible to serious and debilitating injuries, and while there can be no guarantee of prevention in everyone, any steps taken to reduce the risk of injury will allow for greater enjoyment and confidence on the slopes. Awareness of the mechanisms of injury should also alert you to possibly dangerous positions, which can then be averted, thereby offering a direct means of injury prevention when on the slopes.

Flexibility for Injury Prevention

Appropriate levels of flexibility are required to ensure functional control of the limbs, even when the body is thrown in extended positions. If, for example, a skier has a leg knocked out to one side due to an obstacle, some ice or a bad turn, the greater that skier's flexibility then the further that leg can move away from the body before an injury occurs. Not only that, but there will also be a greater range of movement within which the skier can control that leg and bring it back into a normal position. These things happen at speed, so it is important to train the body to move through appropriate ranges of motion at speed.

Food and Drink

Hydration is important for maintaining proper brain function and coordination. Even 1 percent dehydration can have a negative effect on performance. Because of the amount of clothing worn, and how absorbent it is, it is often difficult to be aware of how much you are sweating. This is also true of exposed skin, as the effects of wind and moving through the dry air often whip sweat away, so it is difficult to know that you are becoming dehydrated. The thirst mechanism is also very inefficient, as by the time you are thirsty you are already dehydrated, and only a small amount of water will quench thirst but will not significantly improve hydration status. Alcohol and caffeine have a diuretic effect, causing fluids to be taken from the body, and increasing the risk of dehydration. Any suggestion that alcohol is just what the doctor ordered for anyone stranded on a mountain is pure myth.

Food is also important, and often overlooked, as people want to maximize their time on the slopes. The body requires energy from carbohydrate and fat stores, and carbohydrate is depleted very easily. Carbohydrate is stored in the liver and muscles, and a small amount is always in the blood to supply the brain and nervous system. *Glucose is the only fuel for the brain!* This means that if there is no glucose, the brain is starved of energy, and there will be a significant effect on coordination, judgement and performance. The carbohydrates stored in the muscles cannot be used by the rest of the body, and what is in the liver is depleted by keeping the brain active during the night. This means that a good breakfast will contain plenty of carbohydrates, and carbohydrate levels should then be topped up during the course of the day. Fats and proteins are also important, and as a fuel they allow for a slow release of energy, meaning that they will be better for keeping the body fuelled during the day.

Stored carbohydrate levels need to be topped up after a day on the slopes to ensure there will not be a day-to-day negative trend in the amount of energy available. An energy deficit can be compensated for by eating anything, not just carbohydrates, as the body will naturally convert what it can and store it as energy. A lack of energy *will* increase the likelihood of injury, and must be guarded against.

Temperature

The temperature on trails can change very quickly, and this makes it difficult to have one set of clothes that will be suitable for the whole day. This is not helped by the fact that mountains can throw up their own weather systems very quickly. Combine this with areas of exposure and areas of shadow, together with changing body temperatures and you have a recipe for dangerous temperature fluctuations in the body.

The answer is to wear layered clothing, so that layers can be added and removed as necessary. It does mean carrying a bag – at least one in a group – but this should be the case anyway for carrying water and some food. Clothing should also include a good hat and something to cover the mouth.

The effects of extreme temperature are difficult to notice. If you feel negatively affected by the temperature in any way, either in the form of shivering or an unusual feel to the skin, then it is time to assess clothing and find a solution. Exposure to the cold can lead to frostbite, which is caused when cells in the extremities of the hands and feet, and the face, become frozen. Frostbite will cause a number of symptoms, including pain and a burning sensation, tingling and numbness. The skin may turn hard and white, peeling off or becoming blistered and then discolored. Sufferers of frostbite should be taken somewhere warm and dry, and any restrictive clothing should be loosened or removed to aid circulation to the area. Medical assistance should be sought early to help prevent permanent damage.

Hypothermia, where the body has become too cold, is the result of being kept too long in a cold environment. Symptoms of hypothermia include goose bumps and shivering, numbness, confusion, difficultly speaking, stumbling and feelings of depression. The further into hypothermia a person drifts, the more pronounced the symptoms. Shivering will become worse, as will coordination and sight. Eventually, if the symptoms remain unchecked, the person may become unconscious and die. The most important thing to remember is that someone suffering from extremes of heat or cold will be unlikely to be as aware of the onset of symptoms as someone watching them closely. Keep an eye on each other and if you see someone sufferig from any of these symptoms be assertive and ensure that he or she is taken to safety as soon as possible.

Someone suffering from hypothermia can be warmed in the initial stages by putting on more clothing and being taken somewhere warm and dry. The further into hypothermia someone goes, the less able the body is to warm itself, and so the body heat of another individual can help to restore some warmth.

Children lack the ability to be aware of their temperature in the same way that adults are. This means that extra care and attention should be paid to supervising children on the slopes. Regular breaks for rehydration are more important, and any complaints regarding the temperature should be taken even more seriously than from an adult.

An ounce of prevention is worth a pound of cure. As well as proper clothing, it is necessary to ensure good hydration, to eat well and to avoid alcohol and certain medications, which may affect the body's ability to maintain its correct temperature, and may also lead to drowsiness. If you have been prescribed medication, then it is advisable to check with your doctor before exercising.

Most important is to get anyone suffering from the effects of cold off the slopes and somewhere warm and dry. If someone is getting overheated then layers come off, fluids go in, and you stop exercising until you feel completely back to normal.

Summary

Accidents on the mountain can lead to injury in just about any part of the body. In this section, particular attention has been paid to the common injuries to the upper and lower body. Avoidance of injury is the key, and this should take place in various stages. Initially, avoidance comes down to proper preparation with conditioning training and an assessment from a physiotherapist. When preparing to go out on the slopes, it is necessary to dress appropriately, and to eat a good breakfast. When on the slopes, breaks should be taken regularly to rehydrate and eat. Alcohol should be avoided and kept to a minimum in the après-ski.

Avoid accidents on the slopes by being aware of what other slope users are doing, and especially if they are having difficulties over particular areas of the slope. Also, beware of the dreaded children's ski schools, where the teacher is leading a snake of children down the slope, with every child hanging on to the poles of the child in front. This is often worse when the slope changes from an advanced slope at the top to a lower intermediates' or beginners' slope at the bottom. Hence, there are advanced skiers coming down the slope at speed, and then a bottleneck occurs as the snake of children cuts off one half of the slope.

If a fall does occur, try to limit damage by letting go of the poles, keeping the arms tucked in to the body, and aim to fall over to one side rather than back. Try to avoid sitting down on the tail of the skis as this can increase the risk of an ACL injury. Avoid straightening the legs or arms, and do not try to break the landing by sticking a hand out toward the slope. Once the fall has happened, come to a complete stop, get the skis perpendicular to the slope (or cross them) and get up. Do not try to get up while still sliding as this may lead to further damage, especially around the knee joint. Injuries can happen during recovery attempts once control has been lost at the beginning of a fall. Falling gracefully early is better than either falling badly later on or regaining balance and spraining the knee.

Do not attempt a jump unless you have been given sound advice by an instructor. Also, ensure that if you are going to start jumping, that you do it earlier in the day after a warm-up, and that you begin on easier jumps rather than the more impressive ones. Check the area of the landing first (provided no-one is preparing for a jump at the time). Check for deep snow or powder, ice and rocks, and whether a turn is needed shortly after landing. When landing while skiing, it is important to land evenly on both skis, with the knees bent and leaning slightly forward.

If injured, it is best to avoid skiing or snowboarding until completely rehabilitated. This is not just to prevent further injury to yourself, but also to protect others who might be involved in an accident with you if you are unable to use your normal level of control and skill.

If going off-trail, then proper preparation will include taking maps, a compass and food and water. Emergency transmitters are also important to have for use if caught in an avalanche. If tired, take a break and wind down. Have something to eat and drink, and if you still feel tired call it a day. Most injuries occur when tired, so it is best not to risk injuring yourself and others, and to take the time to recover instead.

Bibliography

www.healthlink.mcw.edu/article/975515965.html
www.iasm.com/brochure.html
www.olympic.org/
www.orthoinfo.aaos.org/
www.ski-injury.com/alpine.htm
www.ski-injury.com/intro.htm
www.ski-injury.com/knee.htm
www.ski-injury.com/nordic.htm
www.sportsinjurybulletin.com/archive/skiers-injuries.html
www.sportsmedicine.about.com/

the exercise programs

The Background

Exercise, like dieting, is an industry. Exercise itself could be free, without the need for any equipment. However, in order to utilize the various methods of training required for an all-encompassing program, it may be necessary to buy a few specific pieces of equipment. Exercise, fundamentally, should be about health and improving people's way of life. Likewise, information on diets should be about health and healthy eating, even if that is with a particular goal in mind. It seems a shame, therefore, that both industries have become so commercialized. This means that companies will jump on anything that looks profitable, with no particular interest in whether or not it will do any good, or even if it will do any long-term harm.

The exercise equipment featured in this book is used because of its relevance to functional training for downhill sports. Maybe in a few years another piece of equipment will come out that is an improvement on what I have used here, but it might offer only a fractional benefit. Fads and trends will come and go, and my aim for this program was to use equipment that has a real purpose. So feel free not to spend a million dollars on the next trendy machine because it is probably flawed. The basics are best – just good old-fashioned medicine balls and an unstable surface.

You need to do a number of different types of exercise to improve performance and reduce the risk of injury. While resistance training is important for developing the muscles to exert power and also for transitions through various postures and techniques, cardiovascular fitness is required to prevent fatigue (among other things), and flexibility training (stretching) is needed to allow the body to maintain optimal postures. In addition, balance and proprioceptive training is required to improve technique and reduce the risk of falls.

While flexibility and cardiovascular training are quite straightforward ('work a bit harder than you did last time and keep improving'), the balance, proprioception and resistance training components all require a much more detailed approach. For this reason, a number of progressive programs have been designed to take someone – regardless of exercise experience – through all the phases necessary to develop excellent performance potential. Much can be learned on the slopes, but a couple of weeks of practicing is not enough time for the body to make all the adaptations necessary to turn a beginner into a pro. Although proper technique can only really be learned and perfected when actually skiing or snowboarding, the muscles, nervous system, heart and lungs can all be prepared in advance.

The exercises in this book have a number of beneficial side-effects, such as toning and strengthening the muscles, improving bone mineral density (a measure of bone health), improving heart and lung function, and reducing body fat (if maintaining the same diet). The cardiovascular exercises will complement these benefits, as well as help to reduce blood pressure and cholesterol levels, and improve mental alertness. The key is not to do too much, and if you feel tired, regardless of how much sleep you have, then it might be time to reduce the number of days exercising. The resistance training can be performed a couple of days a week, as can the cardiovascular exercises, but this can then be tailored according to the individual (resistance training more than three times a week is not advisable). From a practical point of view, it is often most convenient to perform cardiovascular exercise at the end of the resistance training session.

A specific approach to training is required, as we have seen (*see* 'The Exercise Renaissance', page 11). Training the legs by doing leg presses, for example, will only improve the body's ability to perform leg presses. Much thought, practice and discussion have gone into ensuring that the exercises included in this book are of great practical relevance. Because there are few effective skiing or snowboarding exercises available, most of the exercises in this book are hybrids of relatively common functional exercises, which have been adapted to make them highly specific to this program. This being the case, it is unlikely that anybody will recognize many of the exercises from experience, so close attention needs to be paid to the photographs and instructions.

Throughout the entire resistance training section, there is only one floor-based exercise. This is because that exercise is very useful for training for recovery from falls on the slopes. The majority of the exercises are performed upright, so as to mimic the precise positions and movements of skiing and snowboarding. This makes the exercise programs absolutely superb for improving performance.

Although a lot of information regarding technique can be understood by looking at the photographs of the exercises and the text accompanying them, personal experience will also be a huge benefit. If you ski or ride in a particular way, try to reflect those postures during the exercises that look similar. Watching slalom competitions on television, will also give a useful idea as to how the exercises are supposed to be performed.

The speed at which the exercises are carried out should also be based on experience, if possible. To begin with, all the exercises should be performed in a reasonably slow and steady manner so that the position of the joints can be monitored and corrected accordingly. Over the weeks of each program, that initial speed can be improved upon to bring it more into line with the speeds of movement experienced when skiing or snowboarding. The point of the specific program is not just to teach the muscles to move a certain way, or to make them more efficient at doing so, but it is also to make the muscles move at the speeds that will be required of them when on the slopes. Starting slowly is essential for perfecting technique, and a slow start should always be adopted during the initial warm-up set. Once competent in the movements, then it is time to start working at a faster pace. Control is still most important, but appropriate speed comes in at a close second. The point is not to teach the body to be slow.

Training Cycles

The first time you use this program should, ideally, be nine months prior to the ski and snowboard season. This is a 'perfect world' scenario, which ensures very high competence in all of the areas required to suit the goals of this book. Accepting that few of us live in a perfect world where we can dedicate this much time to any sport, the whole process has been put into three different training cycles:

1. A perfect world cycle, where the program is spread out over nine months

2. An abbreviated course, which fits into about three months of training

3. A cycle intended for the second year of training onward – an example of how someone could train over the course of a year to ensure optimal fitness.

How these cycles actually fit around other responsibilities and training goals is up to you to tailor accordingly.

The training cycles are reasonably self-explanatory. They detail which weeks should include a particular set of programs. As you become more experienced with your own training, you may want to prioritize the areas at which you are weakest, or the programs you find most challenging. Flexibility and cardiovascular exercise can take place continually throughout the year and complement the resistance training programs.

If it is not possible to utilize even the abbreviated program in its entirety, then it is best to begin as directed and work through each exercise. This is far preferable to jumping the gun and beginning further along in the program, or rushing through the earlier phases. If anything, the earlier phases are the most important for developing a solid base, and without that the rest is unlikely to be effective.

One thing that is not included in any part of the progam is skiing or snowboarding on artificial slopes. This is because there are so many factors that may make this impractical. The entire course can be completed effectively at home with no need for travel, although recommendations have been made for those wishing to integrate this training with the equipment available in health clubs. Practising on an artificial slope would be of enormous value, particularly for novices who want to have a good idea of what they will encounter when going away to ski or ride for the first time.

Novice to World Champion

This book and the exercise programs are designed to improve performance on the slopes. That means making the body more resilient to muscle fatigue and injury, improving joint function, and improving the speed at which movements can be initiated and controlled. In all of these factors, it is irrelevant if the individual is a novice or a world champion because the point is not to improve technical skills but to improve the body in every way for skiing, including the ability to develop technical skills on the slopes. This means that everybody needs to begin at the beginning. Everyone can benefit from learning and training the proper and fine movements of the joints. From then on, the exercises become closer and closer to the real thing.

The difference between the novice and the world champion might be that the more advanced athlete wants to train faster, with more resistance, generating more power than a beginner. But the programs themselves are the same, and the difference is purely in the specifics of how the individual adapts the exercises to suit personal goals. If you are a beginner, then take your time going through the movements, and make sure you are happy with what you are doing before moving on. If your skills are more advanced, then you will find many of the exercises quite straightforward. You have to feel that the movements are replicating your movements on the slopes, so as to ensure that you are training yourself properly. For the novice, this will largely be guesswork, but the advanced athlete should actually be able to *feel* the movement of the exercise in the same way that they *feel* the movement when skiing or snowboarding. Once that has been mastered, the next step is to increase speed and power so as to push the body and train it specifically for how you want to perform.

Exercise Terminology

While many clients have developed their own terminology to use during training sessions, the purpose of this section is to introduce the terminology specific to the training program in this book.

- **Repetitions**, usually abbreviated to 'reps', refers to the number of times a particular movement is completed within a **set**. Using squatting as an example (squatting is the movement of squatting down as if to sit on the floor and then standing back up again), the repetition is the number of times that someone squats down and stands up before having a rest. That number then makes up one set. In most cases, the recommendation is to complete two or three sets, which does not include the one or two lighter 'warm-up' sets.

- The **rest** is the amount of time between sets and between exercises.

- **Frequency** refers to the number of days per week that the exercise, or program, is to be performed.

Preferred training program

Day	1	2	3	4	5	6	7	8	9	10	11	12	13	14	15	16	17	18
Training phase																		
Balance and proprioception																		
Muscular strength and endurance																		
Advanced joint strength and stability																		
Advanced muscular power																		
Advanced balance and proprioception																		
Flexibility																		
Cardiovascular																		

Preferred training program Cont.

Day	19	20	21	22	23	24	25	26	27	28	29	30	31	32	33	34	35	36
Training phase																		
Balance and proprioception																		
Muscular strength and endurance																		
Advanced joint strength and stability	▨	▨																
Advanced muscular power			▨	▨	▨	▨	▨	▨	▨	▨								
Advanced balance and proprioception											▨	▨	▨	▨	▨	▨	▨	▨
Flexibility	▨	▨	▨	▨	▨	▨	▨	▨	▨	▨	▨	▨	▨	▨	▨	▨	▨	▨
Cardiovascular											▨	▨	▨	▨	▨	▨	▨	▨

Abbreviated training program

Day	1	2	3	4	5	6	7	8	9	10	11	12	13	14	15	16	17	18
Training phase																		
Balance and proprioception	■	■																
Muscular strength and endurance				■	■	■												
Advanced joint strength and stability								■	■									
Advanced muscular power											■	■	■	■				
Advanced balance and proprioception			■	■	■	■	■	■	■	■	■	■	■	■	■	■	■	■
Flexibility			■	■	■	■	■	■	■	■	■	■	■	■	■	■	■	■
Cardiovascular			■	■	■	■	■	■	■	■	■	■	■	■	■	■	■	■

Continued Training Program

Day	1	2	3	4	5	6	7	8	9	10	11	12	13	14	15	16	17	18
Training phase																		
Balance and proprioception		▓	▓	▓														
Muscular strength and endurance									▓									
Advanced joint strength and stability											▓	▓			▓	▓		
Advanced muscular power																		▓
Advanced balance and proprioception																		
Flexibility											▓	▓	▓	▓	▓	▓	▓	▓
Cardiovascular	▓	▓	▓	▓	▓	▓	▓	▓	▓	▓	▓	▓	▓	▓	▓	▓	▓	▓

Continued Training Program Cont.

Day	19	20	21	22	23	24	25	26	27	28	29	30	31	32	33	34	35	36
Training phase																		
Balance and proprioception																		
Muscular strength and endurance																		
Advanced joint strength and stability															▒	▒	▒	▒
Advanced muscular power	▒	▒	▒	▒														
Advanced balance and proprioception					▒	▒	▒	▒	▒	▒								
Flexibility	▒	▒	▒	▒	▒	▒	▒	▒	▒	▒	▒	▒	▒	▒	▒	▒	▒	▒
Cardiovascular	▒	▒	▒	▒	▒	▒	▒	▒	▒	▒	▒	▒	▒	▒	▒	▒	▒	▒

Continued Training Program Cont.

Day	37	38	39	40	41	42	43	44	45	46	47	48	49	50	51	52
Training phase																
Balance and proprioception																
Muscular strength and endurance																
Advanced joint strength and stability	■	■	■	■									■	■	■	■
Advanced muscular power							■	■								
Advanced balance and proprioception									■	■	■	■				
Flexibility	■	■	■	■	■	■	■	■	■	■	■	■	■	■	■	■
Cardiovascular	■	■	■	■	■	■	■	■	■	■	■	■	■	■	■	■

These programs recommend that resistance exercises are performed twice a week. This means that if a phase has one program, then that program should be repeated twice a week. If a phase has two programs, then they should each be completed once a week. If you feel adventurous and want to exercise three times a week, then alternate the program you repeat twice.

As a worked example:

Exercise:	Squats
Reps:	10
Sets:	3
Rest:	30–60 seconds
Frequency:	1–2 days per week

So, you would warm-up by performing one or two sets of squats, through a reduced range of motion and at a slower pace. You would then perform 10 repetitions of squats, followed by a rest period of 30 to 60 seconds. You would then perform another 10 repetitions to make up the second set, have a rest, and then perform the final set of 10 repetitions, before moving on to the next exercise. More details about warming up and so on are included in the following sections.

It is important not to neglect the rest periods. If you do, the chances are that not enough effort is being put into the individual sets. The rest periods exist to allow energy levels to be replenished within the muscles, thereby making the following set more effective than if commencing it too early. Shorter rest periods confer some cardiovascular benefits, but at least 30 seconds is required to ensure that the muscles are capable of performing the subsequent set effectively. Rest periods of longer than a minute allow the heart rate to drop, and when considering what can be high-intensity activities like skiing and snowboarding, it is better to aim for a shorter rather than longer break between sets.

Exercise Equipment

Various items of exercise equipment are featured throughout the exercise programs. The equipment is recommended because it represents the best tools available for the specific training goals of this program. The medicine balls are used because they are a convenient way of introducing more resistance to an exercise. A dumbbell, or pair of dumbbells, could be used in place of the medicine ball for many of the exercises, but for home training a medicine ball is far more versatile for these sorts of exercises. A 5-liter mineral water bottle could also be used in place of dumbbells and medicine balls, but because of the plastic they are less easy to prevent from slipping, so greater care is needed. If you try this and find yourself concentrating more on not dropping the water bottle on your head than on the exercise, it is time to make the investment!

Cable machines can be used in place of the resistance bands featured in some of the pictures. The bands cannot produce as much resistance as a cable machine in a gym, but if training at home then it is a perfectly good alternative. Another option is to train with someone who can mimic the resistance band by holding on to a towel and creating some manual resistance.

The Swiss ball is featured only once in the whole program, and is used for a floor-based exercise. The use of the Swiss ball allows the body to mimic a similar position to that encountered most often following a fall. That one exercise could be performed without the Swiss ball, by keeping the legs bent at 90 degrees in the hips and 90 degrees in the knees. This makes the movement much more difficult and places extra stress on the back. Stress, in this context, is necessary to cause the body to adapt.

The piece of equipment that looks like half a Swiss ball is called a BOSU, which stands for **BO**th **S**ides **U**p. It is much safer for standing on than a Swiss ball. When skiing, it is necessary to lean into the slope. A similar position can be accomplished by placing one foot near the bottom, and one directly on top, of the BOSU. The BOSU is much more expensive than the Swiss ball due to the technology that goes into making them safe, and they are much more versatile.

The half-foam rolls that are used in this course are also a relatively new addition to the exercise trainer's arsenal. They are used primarily by physiotherapists and exercise therapists, and can be used for a number of exercises, muscle tests, and even for a sort of self-massage. They are quite inexpensive and allow for a wide range of stability exercises to be performed.

The purpose of the Swiss ball, BOSU and foam rolls is to create instability. The goal is to perform exercises competently and effectively on a surface that is less stable than the floor. Although this would not be necessary for general resistance exercises in a gym, it becomes essential when training for an outdoor activity. When skiing or snowboarding, the ground is unpredictable and unstable. We cannot know how deep the snow is, whether it is likely to give way beneath us or if there is an ice patch or some sort of obstacle covered by the snow. Because of this, it is necessary to train the body in preparation.

Running outdoors creates similar stability dilemmas. Ice, mud, waterlogged ground, rocks, sand and snow all create problems that can throw a joint into an unnatural position. Training on an unstable surface therefore has great relevance for performance and injury prevention. The key is not to go overboard by training for stability that is not required. Many exercise instructors and personal trainers recommend performing exercises while seated on a Swiss ball to improve core stability. While this may be of benefit in other training programs, it is my goal to focus on posture-specific training. Hence, all the exercises in this book facilitate training in a ski-specific position or posture.

All the exercise equipment featured in this book is available from:
www.thehealthybodyco.com

The Programs

Warming Up

The warm-up is an essential and often neglected part of any exercise program. The purpose of the warm-up is to increase blood flow to the working muscles and joints, which in turn delivers nutrients for energy and increases the elasticity of the muscles, improving performance and reducing the risk of injury. It is also important to warm-up to get the mind into the idea of doing exercise. The warm-up therefore has a cardiovascular (cardio) component that involves increasing the heart rate and warming the muscles.

This cardiovascular component could be completed on any cardio equipment in a gym, such as a bike or treadmill. Ideally, the cardio machine should in some way replicate, or at least be similar to, the exercises in the main part of the program. The cross-trainers or treadmills would be better than the rowing machines and bikes, if for no other reason than that they require the user to be standing rather than sitting.

If training at home, then it is best to mimic the exercises of the main workout, but starting off very gently and going through a much smaller range of motion. To mimic Split Squats (*see* page 65), begin in the same starting position, but bend the knees only a small amount at first, gradually increasing the range of motion until performing complete Split Squats. To mimic Front Squats (*see* page 72), begin in the same position as for Squats, but again bend the knees and push the hips back only a small amount, and gradually increase the range of motion until squatting normally. The same principle works for Forward Lunges (*see* page 75), which could begin by just stepping forward and then in various directions, gradually bringing in the knee bends until finally lunging normally. This should be repeated for all the exercises in the main program, always beginning with a much-reduced range of motion, and starting slowly and gradually increasing speed until moving at a normal pace.

Ideally, the exercises of the warm-up should be mixed together so that you move from one exercise to the next at one speed and similarly reduced range of motion, and then repeat them in a sort of circuit format, but increasing speed and range of motion each time through. This takes some practice to make fluid but is probably the most efficient way of warming up, with the whole process taking anything from a few minutes upward. Once the body is feeling warm and the joints comfortable with the movements, then the body is ready to move on to the next stage of the exercise program.

The next stage in many exercise programs is a mobility phase. This typically includes some light stretching and moving all the joints through a full range of motion. Stretching itself should really be kept to a minimum, unless instructed to do otherwise by a physiotherapist or similar, as it relaxes the muscles and may actually increase the risk of injury. The exception to this is if a particular muscle is predisposed to injury, in which case a very thorough warm-up is required first, followed by specific stretching of the particular muscle, and then a reintroduction to the mimicking exercises of the warm-up. In most cases this would be at the advice of a physiotherapist or exercise scientist only.

The most important point of a mobility phase is to move the joints through the range of motion that will be demanded of them during the main exercises of the program. This would already have been completed if following the home-based warm-up that avoids the use of cardiovascular equipment, and is based solely on preparing the body for the specific exercises of the program. If using cardiovascular equipment, then the mobility phase of the warm-up can be introduced for each exercise of the main program in turn. For example, when preparing to perform Squats, begin by using no extra resistance and moving slowly through a reduced range of motion. This should then be repeated at the beginning of each exercise, and will accomplish as much as the home-based warm-up.

The total length of the warm-up is dependent upon fitness levels and any other factors, such as health conditions. As a general rule, the fitter an individual, the less gradual and more demanding the warm-up should be. So, if a very fit and healthy person can complete a warm-up in about three minutes, then someone who is less accustomed to exercise or suffers from a particular health condition could spend anything up to 10 or 15 minutes warming up.

Fig 2.1 Torso Twists

Fig 2.2 Hip Flexors (Backward Lunges)

Fig 2.3 Squats with Front Raises

Fig 2.4 Adductors (Side Lunges)

General Points on Technique

For all the exercises in this book, unless stated otherwise, the basic technique principles are the same. The spine should maintain its normal curvature, and should not arch forward or backward or straighten. Although many people recommend a 'straight' back, they usually mean that it should maintain its natural curvature. It took

10 million years to develop a spine as adept as ours for maintaining an upright posture and distributing stress throughout the body. Any deviation from this, including a 'straight' back, will increase stresses across the back and increase the risk of injury.

The hips should be kept level. For many of the exercises this may mean placing the hands on the top of the hips for the warm-up sets, just to check that the hips are doing what they are supposed to. The hips should not drop down on one side, move outward or twist forward or backward. The pelvis should also be kept level to maintain the neutral spine, which means that it should not tilt in either direction. The only exception to the above is for rotational exercises, which will require twisting the hips, but they will be mentioned in turn.

The knees should always move in line with the second toe. In some exercises, the natural movement will allow the knees to pass over the toes, and this is important to balance out stresses on the spine. Some people advise against natural movements of the knee because of the stress that it causes to the joint, but this stress is usually equivalent only to that of walking. Furthermore, teaching the body to move unnaturally will affect the major joints across the whole body, and refer the stress to other joints such as the spine where it will have an even more profound effect.

The natural path of the knee should be over the middle of the foot (typically the second toe), while maintaining a neutral spine and correct hip position. The knees should therefore not track inward or outward, and a conscious effort may need to be made to correct this. Doing so will ultimately improve function and reduce stresses on the knee, which is obviously of great importance for sports such as skiing and snowboarding, where the natural movements require the knee to absorb and distribute various forces.

In the initial stages of the course, it may be necessary to spend longer on some of the early programs to ensure that movements can be managed correctly. It is better to perform an exercise through a limited range of motion with good technique than to persevere with poor technique through a full range. A shorter range of motion can be developed over time, and you should progress to the next program only when confident that all is correct.

In a standing posture, the feet can either be parallel, or one foot can be a few inches in front of the other (which reduces stress on the spine, but the hips should remain facing forward). Unless otherwise stated, in static postures the knees and elbows should be slightly bent to allow muscles to be more involved in the distribution of stress. When moving a particular joint, it should be straightened completely (although not beyond a straight line if you happen to have excessive range of motion in a particular joint). Moreover, all the postures and positions should be tailored to replicate the postures and positions utilized when on the slopes. This should not, however, detract from the general safety points of maintaining a neutral spine with slightly bent knees and elbows, and so on, unless specifically instructed to do so for a particular exercise.

With single leg movements, such as Single Leg Squats, the non-squatting leg can either be raised slightly to the front of the body, or else raised behind the body. Usually, the movement would involve raising the knee to the front, but because in skiing the leg doing the work is typically forward of the leg that is not (transiently, at least), it makes sense that in most of the exercises it is more specific to raise the leg to the back of the body.

General Pointers on the Program

When beginning any exercise, it is important to perform one or two sets as warm-ups. This involves moving at a slower and steadier pace, and becoming confident with the technique and movement before making the exercise more demanding and dynamic. Warm-up sets are not included in the set count for each exercise program, but one or two sets of 10 to 15 repetitions should be sufficient in each case.

Rest periods (given in seconds) refer to the maximum amount of time desirable between sets. Due to the dynamics of skiing and snowboarding, I recommend taking short breaks between sets. The next set can commence as soon as you are comfortable to continue, and preferably well within the rest periods allocated, this will improve as your training advances. Where numbers of sets and repetitions are given for exercises such as Single Leg Squats and Lunges, the numbers always refer to each leg, rather than an absolute total for both together.

The trend of the course is that each training phase is more demanding than the phase before, with more concentration and mental focus required on the later programs to ensure proper technique. It is likely that these later training phases will also train the aerobic system (heart and lungs) more, as well as more of the muscles of the body to a greater extent. Therefore, all the way through the course it is necessary to perform the warm-ups and cool-downs as directed, and to personalize them so that they fit your individual needs. Fitness instructors who teach classes spend a lot of time practicing in front of mirrors at home and in the studio, and even then they can only produce a general program that is not suited to everybody in the class. So it is unlikely that each program will be perfect for you, but that will change over time with growing confidence, proficiency and some experimentation.

Balance and Proprioception

Basic Movement Skills: Weeks 1–4

- Single Leg Squats
- Split Squats
- Split Squats with Rotation (weeks 2–4 only).

When beginning an exercise program for the first time, it is necessary to ensure that the joints are moving properly and that everything is in correct alignment. The reason for this is that although the main benefits of an exercise program may come from big progressive exercises, there is little point starting off with a demanding program only to become injured after a few months.

Our joints move most effectively and with minimal stress in a particular way. In early life, most people develop joints that move properly. However, certain factors can change the way a particular joint moves, such as wearing certain clothes, sports injuries, knocks from falls, or always carrying bags on one side. This may not produce noticeable changes at the time, but following repetitive movements such as running or resistance exercise – or even normal daily activities – sufficient wear and tear on a joint can cause pain or injury.

In reality people may exercise relatively injury- and pain-free for months or even years, despite having poor joint mechanics. Because of this people may be causing damage to themselves without realizing it. The damage may manifest itself as pain in the affected joint or another area of the body, and possibly increase the progression of degenerative conditions such as arthritis.

Proprioception refers to the body's ability to know where a particular body part is in space and time. It is the reason why you can move your arms or legs around with your eyes closed and still know where they are and what they are doing. On a finer scale, proprioception is how the brain and nervous system know when a limb is being moved and approaching a position where it is likely to get injured. If you stand on one foot with your eyes closed, then it is proprioception that helps to make the small corrections necessary to prevent you falling over (although there is also the interaction of other balance systems). So proprioception is vital for fast-moving, downhill activities such as skiing and snowboarding, where the body needs to be trained in the various postures, and to make fast alterations and corrections when moving over a changing surface.

The purpose of this preliminary program in basic movement skills is to spend a few weeks training the body to move the way that it is supposed to. Once this has been accomplished, you will have reduced the risk of joint problems, and improved the body's ability to cope with the more demanding aspects of the various exercise programs. This basic program can also be repeated if you start to experience joint pain in the future. The program is unlikely to correct a joint problem completely, especially as this is a generalized, rather than individual, approach. The program should, however, improve the way the joints work, and is better than simply beginning a more advanced routine without first teaching yourself the correct alignments of the joints.

Proprioception and Balance, Weeks 1–4

Exercise	Sets	Repetitions	Rest (secs)	Weeks
Single Leg Squats	3	10	90	1–4
Split Squats	3	10	90	1–4
Split Squats with Rotation	3	10	90	2–4

Single Leg Squats
(Legs, Butt, Calves)

This exercise has all the benefits of the standard squat. Performing the exercise on each leg independently is excellent for correcting any lower body imbalances. The Single Leg Squat can be performed with one foot raised slightly in front of the other, or else with one foot resting behind the body on a step or chair. Ensure that the knee travels forward in line with the front of the foot, and does not move inward or outward. The pelvis should also be kept level and not allowed to dip down on either side.

Fig 2.5 Single Leg Squats

Split Squats
(Front of Thighs, Butt, Calves)

The Split Squat starts halfway through the lunge exercise. Begin by taking a large step forward, as in the lunge, and then bend the front knee while dropping the back knee down to the floor. Return to the beginning by straightening the legs but keeping the feet in place. Ensure that the back remains upright throughout the exercise. Perform the exercise on one side for as many repetitions as necessary, then change and repeat the exercise using the other leg.

Fig 2.6a Split Squats

Fig 2.6b Split Squats, with medicine ball

Split Squats with Rotation
(Legs, Calves, Torso)

This exercise is a combination of the Split Squat and rotation exercises. As the front leg bends, rotate the body so that the opposite shoulder turns toward the front knee. As the leg straightens back to the start position, bring the body back to facing forward.

Fig 2.7a Split Squats with Rotation

Fig 2.7b Split Squats with Rotation, with medicine ball

Muscular Strength and Endurance

Secondary Movement Skills: Weeks 5–12

Program 1
- Single Leg Squats
- Front Squats
- Box Squats
- Russian Twists
- Cable Two Arm Front Raise

Program 2
- Split Squats
- Forward Lunges
- Side Lunges
- Backward Lunges
- Multidirectional Lunges
- Split Squats with Rotation (weeks 9–10 only)
- Lunges with Rotation (weeks 11–12 only)

Secondary movement skills are the first progression from the basic program. By this stage the joints should be moving better than they were when you first started exercising. The attention paid to joint movements should be continued throughout the programs, even more so as the programs become more demanding.

The purpose of this part of the training is to develop muscular strength and endurance through a range of related exercises. As each program develops, the movements become more similar to those employed on the hill. Each time, the basic movement is made more demanding, and for the health of the joints and efficiency of the muscles, it is important to master each aspect of the program before continuing to the next stage. Ideally, you should spend approximately eight weeks on these programs to ensure that the movements have been mastered, and that the resistance used and the speed at which the exercises are performed are improved.

The goal of the training course is to integrate muscular power with the body's ability to keep the joints in a safe position to prevent injury, and for the muscles to work effectively to maintain technique. Before developing power, it is first necessary to train the body in strength and endurance work. The exercises remain the same for both outcomes, but the way in which they are performed changes. The muscles of the body will change and adapt according to the specific stresses placed on them. Because of this, all the exercises replicate specific movements to some degree, with the complexity increasing through the course of the program.

Muscular endurance refers to the ability of the muscles to contract repeatedly for prolonged periods of time. When skiing down a slope, it is muscular endurance that allows the body to squat down and then push through each leg independently to allow for turns. The body is either holding a squat position, or is rising to prepare to push down through the inside edge of one foot and make a turn. At the same time, the torso twists towards the uphill leg/ski, the pole is planted in the snow, and the pressure through the downhill ski allows the turn to take place. The various muscles of the body are going through these phases throughout the downhill sections of the slope, with the energy required being reduced for flatter sections, as the body holds a more static and upright posture. Even then, small corrections will constantly be made according to direction and changes in terrain.

In this part of the program you must aim to perform each exercise at a similar speed to that you expect to move through when going down the slope. This is not power work, which will be rather fast, but more the steady pace you would adopt when going down a pleasant beginner's or intermediate slope.

Muscular power refers to the combination of strength and speed. But before progressing to that level of training, it is first necessary to train the muscles for strength. Muscular strength will also be useful when moving through more demanding sections of some courses, albeit still at a steady pace.

There are two programs in this phase of the course. Both are equally important and should be included in training each week. The first program includes squatting exercises to improve the body's ability to get into and rise out from tuck positions, and also to prepare for turns. There is also a rotational movement for the upper body, called Russian Twists, which improves the body's ability to twist in a good posture, and will help to protect the back from injury. The movement also replicates the motion of the upper body during a turn, as the torso twists to face into the slope.

The final exercise on the first program is a Two Arm Front Raise, using either a cable machine in a gym or resistance bands secured at a low level. The relevance of the exercise is to improve the body's ability to raise the arms out to the front of the body, which is important in preparation for planting poles during turns or for increasing speed.

The second program includes predominantly lunge-type exercises. These movements are important when walking with the skis, and also when pushing through one ski during turns. The various types of lunges also improve the body's ability to recover from skis going astray, and are intended not just to improve and correct technique but also to prevent injuries. The second program also introduces more advanced rotational movements. This is again to develop the skills required for turning, and to improve the muscular strength and endurance required to do so. This should then improve efficiency on the slopes and reduce the risk of fatigue and injury.

Muscular Strength and Endurance, Weeks 5–12

Program 1

Exercise	Sets	Reps	Rest (secs)	Weeks
(Endurance Phase)				
Single Leg Squats	3	15	30	5–8
Front Squats	2–3	15	30	5–8
Box Squats	2–3	15	30	5–8
Russian Twists	2–3	15	30	5–8
Cable Two Arm Front Raise	2–3	15	30	5–8
(Strength Phase)				
Single Leg Squats	3	10	90	9–12
Front Squats	2–3	10	90	9–12
Box Squats	2–3	10	90	9–12
Russian Twists	2–3	10	90	9–12
Cable Two Arm Front Raise	2–3	10	90	9–12

Muscular Strength and Endurance, Weeks 5–12

Program 2

Exercise	Sets	Reps	Rest (secs)	Weeks
(Endurance Phase)				
Split Squats	2–3	15	30	5–8
Lunges	2–3	15	30	5–8
Side Lunges	2–3	15	30	5–8
Backward Lunges	2–3	15	30	5–8
Multidirectional Lunges	2–3	15	30	5–8
Split Squats with Rotation	2–3	15	30	5–8
Lunges with Rotation	2–3	15	30	5–8
(Strength Phase)				
Split Squats	2–3	10	90	9–12
Forward Lunges	2–3	10	90	9–12
Side Lunges	2–3	10	90	9–12
Backward Lunges	2–3	10	90	9–12
Multidirectional Lunges	2–3	10	90	9–12
Split Squats with Rotation	2–3	10	90	9–12
Lunges with Rotation	2–3	10	90	9–12

Program 1

Single Leg Squats
This exercise is described in the previous section (*see* page 64).

Front Squats
The Front Squat is the same as a standard back squat, but with either the arms or a medicine ball held out in front of the body, or else a barbell or dumbbells positioned on the front of the shoulders. This position allows for a more upright posture during the movement, and is an excellent exercise for strengthening the muscles that stabilize the hips. If using a barbell, the arms should be crossed over, with the elbows kept slightly above shoulder height, so that the weight is supported by the shoulders rather than arms.

Fig 2.8 Front Squats

Box Squats
Box Squats are a standard back squat but with a much wider stance. The feet should be placed at greater than shoulder width apart, sufficient to elicit a slight stretch on the inner thighs during the movement. This trains the body to work when in a stretched position. As with Front Squats, this movement is excellent for strengthening the muscles that stabilize the pelvis.

Fig 2.9 Box Squats

Russian Twists

This movement can be completed with either a cable machine or a resistance band secured at mid-chest height. The stance should be wider than shoulder width, with the body at right angles to the cable or band. From there, twist toward the band or cable and move away from the band or cable so that you can feel the resistance. Then, keeping the arms stiff, twist the body away from the cable or band until you are facing the opposite direction. The movement should begin through quite a limited range of motion, with the hips facing forward throughout, and the body weight distributed evenly on both feet. As you become more comfortable with the movement, allow the body weight to transfer from the foot nearest the cable or band to finish on the opposite foot when facing the other way. Hip and leg movement should be quite natural, permitting a greater range of motion, and utilizing a steady tempo throughout the movement. This tempo can be developed over time. Howerver, it is most important to be comfortable with the movement first, to ensure that the body is stable enough for the greater demands of a slightly faster and fuller movement.

Fig 2.10 Russian Twists

Cable Two Arm Front Raise

Stand forward of the cable machine or site where the exercise bands are secured, so that the arms are extended slightly behind the body. With the arms slightly bent, raise them upward in line with the shoulders. The movement should go as high as is comfortable, hold, and then return to the start position.

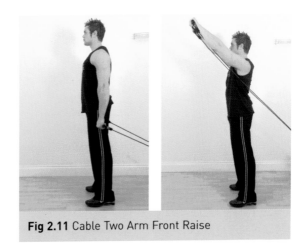

Fig 2.11 Cable Two Arm Front Raise

Program 2

Split Squats

This exercise is described in the previous section (*see* page 65).

Forward Lunges

A lunge is just an extended step in a particular direction, usually followed by stepping back to the start position. Lunges can be performed in any direction, but we begin with a standard Forward Lunge. Take an exaggerated step forward, planting the foot down and bending both knees (without allowing the back knee to touch the floor or the front knee to move excessively over the front foot). This is simply an exaggeration of a natural movement, and many people will do this when picking something up from the floor or while walking. If the knee does travel beyond the middle of the foot, then you might need to take a bigger stride or bend the back knee more (both knees should be close to 90 degrees). Once you have completed this first phase of the movement, then push back off of the front foot to get back into the start position, and then repeat on the other leg.

Fig 2.12 Forward Lunges

Side Lunges

The concept for this movement is the same as for the Forward Lunge. This time the movement is directly out to the side of the body and back, keeping both feet pointing forward, and only bending the leg that moves out to the side (this allows for a slight stretch on the inside of the other leg). Alternate which foot moves out to the side, and which stays in place.

Fig 2.13 Side Lunges

Backward Lunges

This version of the lunge requires a little more practice to get right as the step is behind the body, so you cannot see where you are planting your foot. As the foot moves back, the balls of the foot touch the ground and then both knees bend, and then return to the start position and repeat on the other side. You can alternate between pushing off from both legs, just the back leg and just the front leg.

Fig 2.14 Backward Lunges

Multidirectional Lunges

Multidirectional Lunges can be completed in a number of ways. You can either imagine a clock face, or else just come up with random patterns, but the idea is that you move in any direction. Utilize forward, backward, sideway, diagonal and crossover lunges, and work until you feel you have worked your legs from every angle. As

Fig 2.15 Multidirectional Lunges

long as the knee does not move excessively over the foot, the hips remain relatively stable, the back remains mostly neutral, and you do not feel that you are going to hurt yourself, then you are doing a good job.

Split Squats with Rotation (weeks 5–6 only)
This exercise is described in the previous section (*see* page 66).

Lunges with Rotation (weeks 7–12 only)
This exercise is a standard Forward Lunge, but involves twisting toward the leg that moves forward. This is simply a more dynamic version of the Split Squat with Rotation, utilizing more speed and power. Try to keep the hips level. Twist comfortably, beginning slowly and increasing speed to a more natural pace when ready. If using a medicine ball, be sure that you are controlling the movement, and do not use momentum at this stage as you are unlikely to have the stability to control the movement effectively.

Fig 2.16 Lunges with Rotation

Advanced Joint Strength and Stability

Tertiary Movement Skills: Weeks 13–20

Program 1
- Alternate Single Leg Squats with Tuck
- Front Squats with Behind the Head Reach
- Alternate Single Leg Squats with Internal Rotation
- Hip Adduction with Single Leg Squats (band at 45 degrees behind outside leg)
- Pull-downs with Squats
- Single Arm Pull-downs with Single Leg Squats
- Swiss Ball Pelvic Twists (Knee Rocks)

Program 2
- Step-ups
- Reverse Step-ups
- Side Step-ups
- Lunges with Rotation
- Multidirectional Lunges with Rotation
- Wood Chops (Single Arm) with Squats
- Cable Two Arm Front Raise with Squats
- Cable Two Arm Front Raise with Lunges

As with the previous phase, this third phase of developing movement skills also comprises two programs. Both programs are a development of the two in the previous phase, with movements requiring much greater control, coordination and concentration in order to perform the exercises correctly. Again, these exercises are much closer to the actual movements of skiing and snowboarding than the ones in the previous two programs.

This phase of the program introduces a quite specialized movement in the form of a Tuck Squat. Throughout the programs so far, the technique used in squatting has been precisely that required for proper movement. It is the same squat that you did when you first learned to stand up, and the same squat that many people do if they sit on the floor more than they sit in chairs. That normal squatting movement is usually distorted as an effect of muscular imbalances or injuries, or through being taught the wrong way to squat in exercise classes.

Professional jockeys are taught to adopt a 'Martini glass posture' when racing. This means that there is a straight line from the ankles to the knees, which is perpendicular to the ground. There is then a 45-degree line from the knees to the hips, and an invisible 45-degree line from the knees to the shoulders. This is not by any means a sound posture to adopt unless it is required, as is the case for jockeys.

In skiing, the tuck position requires a slightly lopsided Martini glass. Ideally, the knees would be positioned slightly forward of the toes, but this position is not possible due to the restricted movement within the ski boots. Although the hips have to be positioned behind the knees, the body weight is kept forward to aid in control and balance. The back also tends to be rounded, although this should be minimized as much as possible, depending upon how much flexibility there is in the back of the legs (hamstrings). Because the torso is perpendicular to the lower legs, it is necessary to tilt the head back in order to see what is ahead down the slope. Over a prolonged period, this will lead to neck discomfort and pain, so you should try to tilt the head as little as possible.

The dilemma here is that the tuck position is not by any means a good posture to maintain for any length of time. The position is included in this phase, but more as a transitional movement while going through Single Leg Squats. Many normal squatting movements have been included to ensure that you will not learn to use the Tuck Squat in place of a normal Squat, and so that you will have the ability to perform all the required movements when you put them to use on the slopes.

The second exercise is the Front Squat with Behind the Head Reach. The purpose of this exercise is to help teach the body to come into a forward position when the torso is extending backward. This movement is useful for improving balance and helps prevent against falling.

The Single Leg Squats with Rotation are another progression of the original Split Squats with Rotation. This exercise will improve the body's efficiency and accuracy for turns. The Hip Adduction with Single Leg Squats is to help improve control on the slopes. This may also prove useful for control over patches of ice, when it is necessary to change weight distribution. The introduction of the skiing specific Pull-down exercises is to train the muscles required for planting the ski poles during turns, or for producing more forward propulsion off the poles.

The Swiss Ball Pelvic Twists (or 'Knee Rocks,' as my chief scientific adviser John Hardy suggested) were included following a flash of inspiration. Swiss Balls are often used in many exercise programs. This exercise has been tailored to suit the needs of a skiier who has fallen over. Should you fall over, then it is necessary to get the skis pointing across the slope, if you try to get up while the skis are pointing down the slope then you tend to fall over again quite abruptly. Manoeuvring the skis often also includes twisting the hips so that the skis are pointing in the opposite direction (across the slope rather than off the side of it). The movement required is very similar to this exercise using the Swiss Ball, with the height of the ball being similar to that gained from the back of the skis. This exercise may therefore save much effort from being expended when compared to encountering this position for the first time on the slopes. It is bad enough to fall over, but even worse to not be able to easily get up again afterward.

The second program begins with different versions of Step-ups. These have good practical relevance for moving around the side of the slopes, for side-stepping, for getting into a good start position, and for stepping up the slope. The Step-ups and Reverse Step-ups in particular are also good for promoting correct knee and hip movements.

The Lunges with Rotation are also useful for turning. The Wood Chops are a progression from the Russian Twists, and again are closer to the actual muscle involvement in various twisting manoeuvres employed on the slopes. The two variations of the Two Arm Cable Raises are in preparation for turns and propulsion. The squat and lunge movements make this original exercise more appropriate to how the movement is actually used on the mountain.

Advanced Joint Strength and Stability: Weeks 13–20

Program 1

Exercise	Sets	Reps	Rest (secs)
Alternate Single Leg Squats with Tuck	2	8	60
Front Squats with Behind the Head Reach	2	8	60
Alternate Single Leg Squats with Internal Rotation	2	8	60
Hip Adduction with Single Leg Squats	2	8	60
Pull-downs with Squats	2	8	60
Single Arm Pull-downs with Single Leg Squats	2	8	60
Swiss Ball Pelvic Twists (Knee Rocks)	2	8	60

Advanced Joint Strength and Stability: Weeks 13–20

Program 2

Exercise	Sets	Reps	Rest (secs)
Step-ups	2	8	60
Reverse Step-ups	2	8	60
Side Step-ups	2	8	60
Lunges with Rotation	2	8	60
Multidirectional Lunges with Rotation	2	8	60
Single Arm Wood Chops	2	8	60
Cable Two Arm Front Raise with Squats	2	8	60
Cable Two Arm Front Raise with Lunges	2	8	60

Program 1

Alternate Single Leg Squats with Tuck
This is a standard Single Leg Squat but involves alternating the legs from one side to the other. At the bottom of the squat position, the back/torso should be rounded forward into a 'tuck' position. This allows the body to replicate similar leg movements required for turning and varying ground conditions, such as ice and bumps.

Fig 2.17 Alternate Single Leg Squats with Tuck

Front Squats with Behind the Head Reach

This is a medicine ball movement, starting with the ball held out in front during the downward phase of the squat, and then reaching the ball up above and slightly behind the head on the upward phase. Actual range of motion is dependent upon shoulder and core strength. This exercise should be performed slowly at first, with both range of motion and speed increased gradually as the body becomes stronger and more stable with the movement. The head should remain in line with the upper body during the movement (so if the arms go a

Fig 2.18 Front Squats with Behind the Head Reach

reasonable distance behind the body, the head and neck should also be leaning back slightly, rather than straining to stay looking forward).

Alternate Single Leg Squats with Internal Rotation

As with the first exercise in this program, this also involves a standard Single Leg Squat, which then alternates between sides on each repetition. The difference is that this time the body should be twisted, so that the second foot is placed down at right angles to the first, as if stepping around two sides of a square. The next repetition then twists back to the start position. The twist comes from the hips, with the squat pushing down straight through the hip, knee and ankle (there is no twisting once the foot has been placed). This is a similar movement to that required for turns on the slope.

Fig 2.19 Alternate Single Leg Squats with Internal Rotation

Hip Adduction with Single Leg Squats
(band at 45 degrees behind outside leg)

This unusual movement requires an exercise band or cable with ankle attachment to complete effectively. The band/cable should be attached to one ankle so that there is a line of 45 degrees out behind the leg toward the band attachment/cable machine. The legs should be at a similar width apart, as for Box Squats (*see* page 72). The leg with the band/cable then moves to be right next to the other leg. Once in this position, perform a single leg squat (the free leg is therefore raised during the squat and planted again before the other leg moves back to the start position). This exercise is to help train the body to work when resisting backward forces (typically momentum, although a small obstacle could have the same result on the slope).

Fig 2.20 Hip Adduction with Single Leg Squats

Pull-downs with Squats

This exercise should be performed facing a cable machine, or with a band secured in the middle above head height. The arms should be pulled down to the sides of the body and slightly back. The arms should start off bent, straighten during the movement until they are completely straight, then return to the start position. You should descend into the squat position as the arms come down so that the arms are back and straight when at the bottom of the squat.

Fig 2.21 Pull-downs with Squats

Single Arm Pull-downs with Single Leg Squats

This movement is similar to the above but uses a Single Leg Squat while performing a Single Arm Pull-down with the opposite side. This one may be a feat of coordination, so you might want to get one side right before changing to the other. The goal, however, is to be able to alternate from one leg to the other, while at the same time alternating between opposite arms.

Fig 2.22 Single Arm Pull-downs with Single Leg Squats

Swiss Ball Pelvic Twists (Knee Rocks)

Begin by lying on your back with your calves and ankles on top of the ball. The arms should be out to the side of the body and resting on the floor for stability. The movement is then a slight rock of the hips, allowing the feet to roll the ball from one side to the other. Gradually increase the range of motion, but keep the back relatively flat on the floor, with the head down, and always

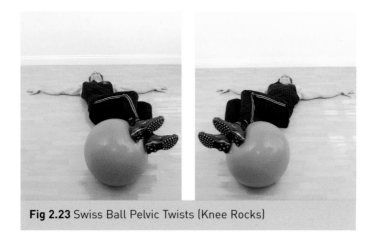

Fig 2.23 Swiss Ball Pelvic Twists (Knee Rocks)

perform the movement in a steady manner. This is purely to improve recovery following falls, so in real life you might be lucky to test the effectiveness of this exercise once or twice at the most, perhaps more if you are a beginner or just into testing yourself.

Program 2

Step-ups
Begin by facing a step, then raise one foot and place it in the middle of the step so that neither the front nor back of the foot is hanging off. Bring the other foot up alongside the first, and then step back in the same order. On the next step-up, alternate which side leads so as to keep everything even. The head position should be forward, helping to maintain the neutral spine, but glance down to check that the knee is moving forward of the middle of the foot rather than in or out. At the same time, the hips should be level rather than tilted downward or twisting forward or backward. If this does occur, slow the movement down and concentrate on keeping everything in good alignment.

Fig 2.24 Step-ups

Reverse Step-ups

As the name suggests, this is basically the opposite of a standard Step-up but allows for much greater care in maintaining correct alignment. Begin at the top of the step, with one foot hanging off the back. Concentrate on the supporting leg, maintaining level hips and ensuring the knee travels directly forward over the middle of the foot. Slowly bend the supporting knee and allow the other foot to descend toward the floor, but bring it up to the start position rather than allowing it to rest on the floor.

Fig 2.25 Reverse Step-ups

Side Step-ups

This mimics the action of side steps up a ski slope. This is an integral part of a beginner's skiing program and important for anyone wanting to position themselves a little higher up the slope or else to retrieve wayward poles. Standing side-on to the step, raise the leg nearest to it and plant the foot flat down in the center of the step. Raise the other leg and bring it alongside the first before stepping down onto the other side of the step. Make sure that the whole foot comes to rest on the step, and that the foot is placed in the center of the step rather than precariously off to one side.

Fig 2.26 Side Step-ups

Lunges with Rotation

This exercise is a standard Forward Lunge, but involves twisting toward the leg that moves forward. This is simply a more dynamic version of the Split Squat with Rotation (*see* page 66), but utilizes more speed and power. Try to keep the hips level. Twist comfortably, beginning slowly and increasing speed to a more natural pace when ready. If using a medicine ball, be sure that you are controlling the movement, and do not use momentum at this stage as you are unlikely to have the stability yet to effectively control the movement.

Fig 2.27 Lunges with Rotation

Multidirectional Lunges with Rotation

This is a progression of standard Lunges with Rotation (*see* above). As you work through a set of Multidirectional Lunges, twist the torso in the direction of the leading leg. There may be some movements for which this feels unnatural, such as crossover or backward lunges, but work out for yourself in which direction the twist feels best for each direction of lunge, or vary between both sides. Start off slowly and deliberately. As you get used to combining the two movements, gradually increase to a more natural pace as you become more confident and comfortable.

Fig 2.28 Multidirectional Lunges with Rotation

Single Arm Wood Chops

This movement is a progression of the Russian Twists (*see* page 73). The cable or band should be set at above shoulder height. Stand sideways on to the cable/band and hold on to it by reaching across with the opposite hand. Twist the body (as for Russian Twists) but allow the arm to finish in the opposite position to where it started (opposite side of the body and lower than the hips). The arm should be kept stiff all the way through the movement. Integrate a squat so that you bend your knees as the arm comes across and down, and then stand up as the arm returns to the start position. The hips should be kept relatively stable, with the knees moving normally and therefore resisting any excessive twisting movements associated with what the torso is doing (some movement is natural, but the twisting movement should be lead from the torso rather than all from the hips).

Fig 2.29 Single Arm Wood Chops

Cable Two Arm Front Raise with Squats

This exercise is a development of the Cable Two Arm Front Raise used in an earlier program (*see* page 74). This time, begin in the bottom position of a squat with the arms out behind the body to grasp the cable/band. The body should be positioned to be facing away from the cable/band. As you come up out of the squat, raise the arms to complete the front raise, and then return to the start position. This exercise can be performed well with a medicine ball in a similar fashion, although the resistance will be through a slightly limited range of motion.

Fig 2.30 Cable Two Arm Front Raise with Squats

Cable Two Arm Front Raise with Lunges

This movement is similar to the exercise above, but this time you perform the front raise while doing a Forward Lunge. Again, cables and bands are good and allow for a better range of motion, but a medicine ball is certainly adequate. Ensure that you do not lean back

Fig 2.31 Cable Two Arm Front Raise with Lunges

excessively as the arms pass shoulder level, as this may compromise the lower back. This should not occur if the movement is performed slowly and comfortably.

Muscular Power

Advanced Power Skills: Weeks 21–28

- Forward Lunges
- Power Lunges
- Power Split Squats
- Power Lunges with Rotation
- Power Split Squats with Rotation
- Jumping Squats
- Jumping Front Squats (with Medicine Ball)
- Jumping Front Squats with Rotation (90 degrees)

Performing proficiently, safely and efficiently on the slopes involves a number of factors. Balance and proprioception are key to preventing falls and injuries. Muscular endurance is key to preventing muscular fatigue. Muscular power, however, is what ensures muscles initiate sufficient forces to turn fast, to jump and to work in conjunction with balance and proprioception in order to prevent injuries at even the fastest speeds. Muscular power is necessary on all slopes because the body nearly always needs to integrate its strength with speed in order to move and react as required. Power is also required, in differing amounts, when skiing or riding in the steeper or softer off-trail slopes.

The exercises in this phase may not seem as technical as the ones in the previous phases. This is because there are fewer exercises and they are progressions of otherwise quite basic movements. However, the amount of concentration required – in ensuring that the hips remain level, the knees are moving in line with the second toe and that the back retains its neutral curvature during the jumping exercises – is far greater than that required in previous phases. While it is possible to forget about all that and just get on with the exercises, you could undo a lot of work put in so far to ensure correct movement and joint alignment.

The development of power at this stage, particularly in the form of jumping movements, is essential for advanced downhill techniques. Having that power available, however, is just as necessary for preventing injuries on the gentler slopes. There will always be fleeting moments when the skis are pointing in the wrong direction, when some evasive action has left you out of space, or when another user of the slope has knocked you or you have gone over some ice or a concealed obstacle. When that happens, it is the ability of the muscles to react accordingly, and at speed, that prevents a fall or an accident. The impact of these exercises will also strengthen the joints to help prevent injuries caused by repetitive impacts or joint movements on the slopes.

Advanced Power Skills: Weeks 21–28

Exercise	Sets	Reps	Rest (secs)
Forward Lunges	1–2	6	60
Power Lunges	1–2	6	60
Power Split Squats	1–2	6	60
Power Lunges with Rotation	1–2	6	60
Power Split Squats with Rotation	1–2	6	60
Jumping Squats	1–2	6	60
Jumping Front Squats (with Medicine Ball)	1–2	6	60
Jumping Front Squats with Rotation (90 Degrees)	1–2	6	60

Lunges
This exercise is described in a previous section (*see* 'Forward Lunges,' page 75).

Power Lunges
This movement is the same as for standard Forward Lunges (*see* page 75), but a more forceful push-off is required from the front foot in order to generate more power through the hip and leg. The aim is to complete a full movement but to return to the start position as quickly as possible.

Fig 2.32 Power Lunges

Power Split Squats
This movement is similar to standard Split Squats (*see* page 65). This time, however, you should generate sufficient force through both legs on the way up so that you can alternate the front leg in the air, and then perform a Power Split Squat on the other side, and so on. This is a continuous and very fast exercise where you jump at the top of the movement, switch leg positions and keep alternating the movement from one side to the other.

Fig 2.33 Power Split Squats

Power Lunges with Rotation

This movement is the same as the standard Lunges with Rotation (*see* page 78), but again demands the production of as much power as possible through the front leg, thereby completing the full movement with rotation much faster than with the standard movement.

Fig 2.34 Power Lunges with Rotation

Power Split Squats with Rotation

By this stage in the course you should have developed the speed, strength and stability to perform this exercise safely and effectively. The key is still to get the movement right before developing speed and power. Perform a Power Split Squat (*see* above) and rotate as with the standard rotation exercises. Be aware of the position of the spine and hips, and try to avoid allowing the hips to drop down or twist forward excessively. Practice a few repetitions of Power Split Squats before introducing the rotation. The rotation should be toward the leg that moves forward. This is very dynamic movement because the forward leg switches quickly between each repetition.

Fig 2.35 Power Split Squats with Rotation

Jumping Squats

This movement is a Front Squat (*see* page 72) but with acceleration on the upward phase. The acceleration should be sufficient to allow for a jump straight upward. When the feet touch the ground, be sure to absorb the energy of the landing by bending the hips and knees sufficiently. In fact, you should allow that bending to be the first part of the downward phase of the next repetition. Again, this is a very dynamic exercise, and if you start getting tired it is better to rest rather than risk allowing technique to deteriorate.

Jumping Front Squats (with Medicine Ball)

This movement is similar to Jumping Squats (*see* above), but this time you must hold a medicine ball in front of your chest. Vary the distance from the chest as a progression of the exercise, but be aware that the further the ball is from the chest, the greater the stress put on the lower back. If you do want to hold the ball a significant distance away from the chest, it is advisable to bring it in for the landing phase of the movement.

Fig 2.36 Jumping Front Squats (with Medicine Ball)

Jumping Front Squats with Rotation (90 Degrees)

This movement is the same as the Jumping Front Squats (*see* above) but involves holding the ball close to the chest throughout. Jump so that you twist and land at 90 degrees to where you started, and then jump back. You should naturally try to jump off from the outside leg a little more than the inside leg in order to make the rotation work.

Fig 2.37 Jumping Front Squats with Rotation (90 degrees)

Advanced Balance and Proprioception

Advanced Movement Skills: Weeks 29–36

Program 1
- Single Leg Hops
- Lateral Hops to Single Leg Squats
- Twisting Hops to Single Leg Squats
- BOSU Squats (Flat Side Up)

- BOSU Squats (Round Side Up and Off-center)
- BOSU Squats (Flat Side Up and Off-center)
- Jumping BOSU Squats (Flat Side Up)
- Jumping BOSU Squats (Round Side Up and Off-center)
- Jumping BOSU Squats (Flat Side Up and Off-center)

Program 2
- Front Squats
- Half-foam Roll Squats (1 Foot on, 1 Foot on Floor, Varying Angles)
- 2 x Half-foam Roll Squats (Both Feet in Varying Angles)
- Half-foam Roll Split Squats (Varying Angles)
- Single Leg Half-foam Roll Squats (Maintain Position)
- Wood Chops (Single Arm) with Single Leg Squats
- Alternate Single Leg Squats with Tuck on BOSU (Flat Side Up)
- Alternate Single Leg Squats with Tuck on BOSU (Round Side Up)

This final program is the culmination of all the skills developed thus far. Balance and proprioception are now developed further and you should be integrating the improved joint strength and muscular endurance with the power developed in the latest phase of the course. These exercises are the most demanding of all the programs, and once completed with competence, it is reasonable to suppose that overall risk of injury will have been reduced, and that general ability itself will have been improved. These exercises should be sufficient to test the most seasoned professional, and in doing so will ensure that everyone, from absolute beginners to advanced athletes, will be better prepared for the slopes.

Staying upright is all about how the muscles work to maintain balance and how the body is able to make corrections according to proprioception. When physically on the slopes, you are entirely reliant on your balance and proprioception to know how to correct yourself and how to prevent a fall or to make a turn. Good balance and proprioception, when static on the ground, is of little relevance when moving or when on an unstable or unpredictable surface. This is when muscular power is integrated. This is not just about the big squatting-type movements that have been practiced thus far. It is also about the small movements around all the joints of the body that bring everything back into correct alignment. This principle underlies the importance of such a thorough and comprehensive set of programs.

The use of various movements on the BOSU and foam rolls at this stage is to ensure that the body can perform all the downhill movements and can react accordingly when thrown into an unusual position. So the point of this part of the course is to develop balance and proprioception further, as well as to develop joint strength and muscular power, by moving the joints through various relevant positions. Keeping this in mind, the point of each exercise should be clear.

Because there are so many different positions that might be encountered on the mountain, it is advisable to move the foam rolls around to test the body in as many different positions as possible. The speed, sets and repetitions, and rest periods should all be varied, so as to develop all aspects of muscle function. This might include some high-repetition work for endurance, lower repetitions for strength, and lower repetitions and higher speed for power. Always begin by improving competence at endurance work before progressing to the more demanding work required of strength and power exercises.

Finally, the exercises in these two programs are more advanced than those encountered by many accomplished exercise professionals. The reason for this is to ensure that the body is properly trained to react when necessary to the conditions of skiing or snowboarding sessions. Because the program is so advanced, it is essential that you have prepared for it by completing all the other programs up to this point in their entirety. You should then begin the movements of these two programs in a steady and controlled manner before increasing speed to progress to a more natural pace.

Advanced Movement Skills: Weeks 29–36

Program 1

Exercise	Sets	Reps	Rest (secs)
Single Leg Hops	2–3	6	45
Lateral Hops to Single Leg Squats	2–3	6	45
Twisting Hops to Single Leg Squats	2–3	6	45
BOSU Squats (Flat Side Up)	2–3	6	45
BOSU Squats (Round Side Up and Off-center)	2–3	6	45
BOSU Squats (Flat Side Up and Off-center)	2–3	6	45
Jumping BOSU Squats (Flat Side Up)	2–3	6	45
Jumping BOSU Squats (Round Side Up and Off-center)	2–3	6	45
Jumping BOSU Squats (Flat Side Up and Off-center)	2–3	6	45

Advanced Movement Skills: Weeks 29–36

Program 2

Exercise	Sets	Reps	Rest
Front Squats	2–3	6	45
Half-foam Roll Squats (1 Foot on, 1 Foot on Floor, Varying Angles)	2–3	6	45
2 x Half-foam Roll Squats (Both Feet in Varying Angles)	2–3	6	45
Half-foam Roll Split Squats (Varying Angles)	2–3	6	45
Single Leg Half-foam Roll Squats (Maintain Position)	2–3	6	45
Wood Chops (Single Arm) with Single Leg Squats	2–3	6	45
Alternate Single Leg Squats with Tuck on BOSU (Flat Side Up)	2–3	6	45
Alternate Single Leg Squats with Tuck on BOSU (Round Side Up)	2–3	6	45

Program 1

Single Leg Hops
A hop is the progression of a Single Leg Squat (*see* page 64). Begin by performing the downward phase of a Single Leg Squat, generating sufficient force to allow the foot to leave the ground. As with Jumping Squats (*see* page 100), it is important to absorb the landing by bending at the hips and knees, and to then use this position as the beginning of the next repetition.

Fig 2.38 Single Leg Hops

Lateral Hops to Single Leg Squats

A Lateral Hop is a standard hop but out to the side and then back to the start position. The addition of the Single Leg Squat is to add a control element to the movement. Hop out to the side, then as you absorb the landing, perform a standard Single Leg Squat (*see* page 64), and then hop back to the start position.

Fig 2.39 Lateral Hops to Single Leg Squats

Twisting Hops to Single Leg Squats

This movement is similar to the previous exercise, but when you jump the body should twist so that the foot lands planted at 90 degrees to where it started. Perform the Single Leg Squat (*see* page 64) and then hop back to the start position. Because the movement is quite difficult to master, it may be best to perform the exercise on one side and then alternate, rather than alternate for each repetition.

Fig 2.40 Twisting Hops to Single Leg Squats

BOSU Squats (Flat Side Up)

This is a progression of the Front Squat (*see* page 72) but uses the BOSU to make the movement less stable, which requires the body to stabilize in order to perform the exercise correctly. A common mistake is to use stabilization exercises before the body is ready for them, in which case you may only be training imbalances. For this reason, it is important to perform the exercises slowly at first, with the feet wide on the flat surface of the BOSU, and maintaining a level surface.

Fig 2.41 BOSU Squats (Flat Side Up)

BOSU Squats (Round Side Up and Off-center)

This exercise is similar to squatting on the flat surface, but again incorporates an unstable surface. Place one foot just off the center of the BOSU, and the other close to the edge. You should be able to lean the body across the BOSU, with the outside of the upper foot and inside of the lower foot pressing into the BOSU. This squatting position is very similar to that required for cutting into the sides of the slope when parallel skiing. The knees should still travel forward, although the hips have to push toward the center of the BOSU to maintain a stable position

Fig 2.42 BOSU Squats (Round Side Up and Off-center)

BOSU Squats (Flat Side Up and Off-center)
This exercise replicates the above but with a less stable surface. By using the flat side, the tendency is for the BOSU to pivot over the center, which needs to be controlled during the movement. This added balance requirement is sufficient to elicit improvement in balance similar to that required when moving fast over an unpredictable surface. Start by performing the squats slowly, and getting used to how the BOSU tends to move when squatting on it, before progressing to a more natural pace.

Jumping BOSU Squats (Flat Side Up)
Although the word 'jumping' is used, it is much more of a 'lift' of momentum, rather than an actual jump with the whole body leaving the BOSU. Begin by just transferring the body weight onto the balls of the feet as the heels rise at the top of the movement. If the feet leave the BOSU completely, it should be a relatively slow movement

Fig 2.43 BOSU Squats (Flat Side Up and Off-center)

and you should travel only an inch or so above the BOSU. Make sure to concentrate particularly on ensuring a safe landing. The movement is very appropriate for jumping and landing when skiing, but there are risks both in skiing and training, and this should only be attempted if you are likely to utilize ski jumps when on the slopes. The landing on the BOSU should replicate a proper landing, with a good bend in the hips and knees, a slightly forward body position, with the hands slightly out to the front.

Fig 2.44 Jumping BOSU Squats (Flat Side Up)

Jumping BOSU Squats (Round Side Up and Off-center)

This movement is the progression of the BOSU squats with the round side up and off-center. The movement should be practiced for the first few repetitions without the jump to ensure correct foot and body position, you can then gradually increase the speed, again only allowing the feet to travel an inch or so off the surface of the BOSU.

Fig 2.45 Jumping BOSU Squats (Round Side Up and Off-center)

Jumping BOSU Squats (Flat Side Up and Off-center)

This movement is the progression of the BOSU squats with the flat side up and off-center. This time the movement involves lifting the body up, without taking the feet off the BOSU, and simply transfering body weight from one foot to the other. This means that the body will desend into a squat, then as you come up the momentum of the movement takes your weight away from your feet, and then you press down through one side and go back down into a squat. During the next repetition the body weight is transferred to the opposite leg and so on. The BOSU will tilt from one side to the other, replicating the forces and movements through the lower limbs that are associated with certain turns. The movement is particularly good for training the muscles that support the ankles when jumping and turning, but the initial training has to be very controlled and deliberate.

Fig 2.46 Jumping BOSU Squats (Flat Side Up and Off-center)

Program 2

Front Squats

This exercise is described in a previous section (*see* 'Front Squats,' page 72).

Half-foam Roll Squats
(1 Foot on, 1 Foot on Floor, Varying Angles)
The half-foam roll is an excellent tool for developing stability across a number of joints in the body. As with the BOSU, this is quite challenging, and it is important to work through the movements slowly and deliberately, only progressing to a more natural pace when controlled and confident enough to do so. This exercise is basically like a Front Squat but with a wide stance, and one foot placed on the flat side of the half-foam roll. Once you can squat

Fig 2.47 Half-foam Roll Squats

comfortably, having stabalized the foam roll, perform the squats with the foam roll tilted slightly inward or outward. It is important that the movements are controlled throughout, with both knees traveling forwards over the center of the foot and the normal backward motion of the hips.

2 x Half-foam Roll Squats (Both Feet in Varying Angles)

This is the same as the previous exercise, but with both feet on half-foam rolls. Once competent at performing the exercise with the flat sides of the foam roll staying in position all the way through, the movement can be progressed to allow the foam rolls to tilt. Aim to perform the squat with the foam rolls held in the tilted position throughout. The foam rolls should be tilted in the same direction and at the same angle, either both to the left or both to the right.

Fig 2.48 2 x Half-foam Roll Squats (Both Feet in Varying Angles)

Half-foam Roll Split Squats (Varying Angles)

This movement is more demanding than the parallel squats, as the narrower stance decreases stability. Training for this position may help avert a fall. Place the foam rolls on the floor with the flat sides facing up in an appropriate position for split squats. The majority of the repetitions should be performed with the flat sides up and stabilized all the way through. A few repetitions should be practiced with the tops of the foam rolls tilted to one side or the other. The exercise should be performed slowly at first, especially with special consideration paid to the greater stabilization requirements of this movement. You can then progress to move at a natural up and down tempo.

Fig 2.49 Half-foam Roll Split Squats (Varying Angles)

Single Leg Half-foam Roll Squats (Maintain Position)

This exercise will be a real challenge but may be useful in training for turns, and for those nightmarish moments when you find yourself off balance. Begin by performing a squat with one foot on the flat side of the half-foam roll and one foot on the floor, with the legs close to each other. Progress to having the foot that was on the floor raised and pointing downward, so that you can balance yourself, when necessary, using the toes of that foot. Finally, perform the exercise entirely with the one foot that is on the foam roll, keeping the foam roll in the same position throughout.

Fig 2.50 Single Leg Half-foam Roll Squats (Maintain Position)

Single Arm Wood Chops with Single Leg Squats

This movement is a progression of the first Single Arm Wood Chops (*see* page 93). The only variation is the inclusion of a Single Leg Squat. You can vary whether it is the leg on the same side as the exercising arm or the opposite leg. Both movements are useful and should be experimented with.

Alternate Single Leg Squats with Tuck on BOSU (Flat Side Up)

This movement is a slightly more dynamic progression of the Single Leg Squats on the half-foam roll. Perform a Single Leg Squat with one foot slightly off center on the BOSU, and then

Fig 2.51 Wood Chops (Single Arm) with Single Leg Squats

alternate to a Single Leg Squat on the other leg. The feet should be close enough to the center of the BOSU so that they touch when you alternate the squatting leg. In the bottom position of the Single Leg Squat, the body should be in a tuck position, with the torso rounded forward, before alternating legs.

Fig 2.52 Alternate Single Leg Squats with Tuck on BOSU (Flat Side Up)

Alternate Single Leg Squats with Tuck on BOSU (Round Side Up)
This movement is similar to the previous exercise, but performed on
the round side of the BOSU instead of the flat side. The movement is
performed with one foot close to the center of the BOSU, and the
other held out behind the body. The foot on the BOSU should be kept
in a relatively neutral position, by pressing into the side of the BOSU,
through the inside of the foot. The improper way to perform this
exercise would be to allow the foot to turn inward so that the whole
foot is pressing into the BOSU, and the ankle is leaning away from the
BOSU. This should be avoided. The non-squatting leg should be
allowed to drift backward during the movement to avoid the top of the
BOSU, and as with the previous movement, the tuck should be
performed on every repetition.

Fig 2.53 Alternate Single Leg Squats with Tuck on BOSU
(Round Side Up)

Maintenance/Recovery Program

- Front Squats (page 72)
- Forward Lunges (page 75)
- Step-ups (page 89)
- Side Step-ups (page 90)
- Russian Twists (page 73)
- Single Arm Wood Chops (page 93)

This program acts as a break in the normal progression of the various phases. It can be used as required, with speed if you feel that you need to develop power, or just as a basic phase if you need to recover from the main program. If you feel that your movement skills are fine, but you need to get back into the rhythm of general exercise before going through the more advanced exercises, then this could work well as a starting point.

Maintenance/Recovery Program

Exercise	Sets	Reps	Rest (secs)
Front Squats	2–3	8	90
Lunges	2–3	8	90
Step-ups	2–3	8	90
Side Step-ups	2–3	8	90
Russian Twists	2–3	8	90
Wood Chops	2–3	8	90

Please refer to the photographs and explanations of these exercises in the earlier programs.

Cooling Down

The purpose of the cool-down is to prepare the body to stop exercising. During the course of any of the programs, your heart rate should have increased quite considerably, and it is not safe to simply stop exercising at the end of the last set. Instead, the heart rate needs to be gradually reduced so that it approaches a resting level (although actually achieving a resting level is highly unlikely). Failing to do this could lead to blood pooling in the legs, as the leg exercises require preferred blood flow, and the sudden stopping of exercise means that the blood is left in the legs for a short period of time. This can lead to faintness or dizziness, and if it happens then the remedy is to move the legs around to encourage the veins to shunt the blood back toward the heart.

The way the main body of the exercise program is constructed is to begin with the most demanding exercises (perhaps following a couple of smaller exercises to ensure proper technique) and to finish on significantly less demanding exercises. A graph of the exerciser's heart rate would show a gradual increase through the warm-up and into the main body of the exercise session, and then after the last demanding exercise the heart rate would reduce toward the end of the main body of exercises. The cool-down should be a continuation of this to ensure it is safe to stop exercising. In some cases, the last exercise may be so easy that there is no need to perform any other specific 'cool-down' exercises.

When a deliberate cool-down is required, this can be completed on a piece of cardio equipment, and this time any cardio equipment that involves the legs should be sufficient (a specific exercise is not really required as at this point the goal is to get the body prepared for doing very little, rather than in preparation for exercises). If exercising at home, then a reversal of the warm-up is probably the most straightforward means of cooling down. Otherwise, walking around the home, running up and down some stairs, or anything else that comes to mind that begins with an elevated heart rate should suffice. The goal is to reduce the workload over time, so that after a few minutes the body is completely ready to finish exercise.

Stretching

Stretching is a rather complicated issue, and often either carried out ineffectively or disregarded altogether. There are many benefits to proper stretching, but it is important to understand why it is important, and its relevance to this program.

When a muscle is stretched, it returns to its normal length once the stretch is finished because it is elastic. This is an important point if the goal of stretching is to increase a muscle's length over the long term. Stretching has also been associated with reducing muscle soreness following exercise. When a muscle is trained, it is possible that it may become tight in the days following the exercise session. This can alter the position of the associated joint, and eventually contribute to postural problems. Stretching can therefore be used as a means to help ensure that the joints are in their correct position, and that posture does not suffer over the long term.

If a muscle has become shorter than it is supposed to be, such as through the effects of exercise training, poor posture, injury, or fashion (such as wearing high heels), then it will be necessary to lengthen that muscle to ensure that it can work properly. For this program, it is useful if the muscles at the back of the upper legs (hamstrings) are longer than would be required for normal activities of daily living. When bent forwards in a tuck position, the longer the hamstrings then the better the spine can be held in a more neutral position.

So, aside from general stretches associated with the exercise program, it may also be necessary to stretch a particular muscle if there is a length discrepancy or insufficient range of motion, or specifically because it may be of benefit to some of the postures adopted on the slopes. Assessing a length discrepancy or range of motion is something that could be done by a physiotherapist or appropriately qualified exercise professional. Self-testing is particularly difficult. Any queries on this issue should be discussed with a physiotherapist or exercise professional.

The length of time that a stretch should be held depends on the intention of stretching. If stretching is just to compensate for the workout, then the stretches can be held for about 30 seconds. If the intention is to increase muscle length more permanently, then the stretches should be held for up to a few minutes each. As the feel of the stretch eases off, gently push the stretch a little further. Stretching in this manner should be repeated three times a week. Some guidelines for stretching individual muscles and parts of the body follow.

For a more detailed explanation of the anatomy and physiology of stretching, please see three related articles I have written for: www.ptonthenet.com

Chest Stretch

Stand with one hand pressing against a wall, with the arm extended out to the side. Slowly twist the body away from the arm until you feel a stretch in the shoulder.

Fig 2.54 Chest Stretch

Fig 2.55 Abdominals Stretch

Abdominals Stretch

Stand with one foot in front of the other and reach the arms back above and behind the body. If the pelvis is kept in the same position, or tilted downward at the front, then the abdominals should stretch as the chest moves up.

Fig 2.56 Spinal Erectors Stretch

Spinal Erectors Stretch

Begin by getting into a tuck position. Then wrap the arms around the underneath of the legs, just above the bent knees, and (keeping the lower body and arms fixed) push the back up toward the ceiling so that you stretch all the muscles that run down either side of the spine. Adjusting the angle of the hips, and how the spine is bent, can affect which areas of the spinal erectors are stretched. Experiment until you find the positions that elicit the best stretch.

Hip Flexors Stretch

Begin in a Split Squat position (*see* page 65) and as you bend forward on the front leg, extend the opposite arm up and across the body. If the pelvis is tilted downward and the leg is stretched back, then the arm acts as a lever to pull the torso up and away from the hip, developing a stretch in the hip.

Fig 2.57 Hip Flexors Stretch

Quadriceps (Front of Thigh) Stretch

A standard stretch for the front of the thighs is to bend the knee so that the heel is close to the buttocks. The ankle can be supported by the arm on the same side, and the foot pulled further towards the buttocks, thereby increasing the stretch. The knees should be level at the beginning of the movement, and a progression to target a particular muscle in the quadriceps (as well as the hip flexors) can be achieved by allowing the knee on the stretched side to move slightly rearward. The body should remain upright throughout.

Fig 2.58 Quadriceps (Front of Thigh) Stretch

Fig 2.59 Adductors Stretch

Adductors Stretch

This exercise is similar to the Sideways Lunge. Begin by stepping out to the side, keeping the other foot pointing forward and that leg straight. The other leg (that moved out to the side) should be bent with the foot pointing out to the side, and the hands resting on that knee.

Fig 2.60 Hamstrings Stretch

Hamstrings Stretch

Begin by taking a step forward with one leg. Keep that leg straight and bend the other, pushing the hips back while keeping a neutral spine, until the knees are level with each other. The hands should be rested on the bent (back) leg. The stretch in the back of the straight leg can be accentuated by placing the front foot further forward and sitting back more with the hips.

Fig 2.61 Glutes Stretch

Glutes Stretch

This stretch can be performed by standing upright on one leg and grasping the other around the knee and pulling it into the body. Different areas of the glute muscles can then be stretched by moving the knee slightly across the body, or changing the angle of the upper leg. The stretch can also be performed by resting the foot on a support and bending the other knee until a stretch is felt.

Gastrocnemius Stretch

The gastrocnemius is one of two muscles that make up the calves. To stretch this muscle you can perform a movement similar to a backward lunge. Step backward while keeping the front (supporting) knee bent. Straighten the back leg and push the heel into the floor. Rest the hands on the front leg or push against a wall. The stretch can be accentuated by placing the back foot further out behind the body.

Fig 2.62 Gastrocnemius Stretch

Soleus Stretch

The soleus is the other muscle that makes up the calves. This can be stretched in a similar position to the stretch for the gastrocnemius but by bending the back knee to initiate the stretch.

Alternatively, use a block to brace the front foot against, and bend the front knee and lean forwards so that a stretch is initiated in the calf of the front leg.

Fig 2.63 Soleus Stretch

Cardiovascular Training

Cardiovascular fitness refers to how well your body works to get blood to where it is needed. It causes the heart to become stronger and the smallest blood vessels to increase greater delivery of blood to exercising areas. The greater your cardiovascular fitness, the more efficiently and comfortably you will be able to perform cardiovascular exercise, such as running, cycling, skiing and snowboarding. Cardiovascular exercise is essentially any exercise that aims to increase heart rate for a prolonged period. Although resistance training with weights increases heart rate, the regular rest periods mean it is not regarded as cardiovascular training in the same way as running or cycling.

Cardiovascular exercise also brings benefits when not exercising. Resting heart rate and blood pressure will eventually be reduced, metabolism will be increased, and the body will prioritize fat stores to be used for energy in greater ratios than carbohydrates.

Cardio exercise also helps to relieve stress and improves mental well-being. Cholesterol levels will also be improved following a good cardio program.

Cardiovascular fitness will improve endurance when performing any exercise that causes heavy breathing and increases heart rate. If spending a day skiing or riding, then the body is not only producing muscular effort and power for short periods of time, but is also expending greater amounts of energy throughout all the time spent on the slopes. This means that the better your cardiovascular fitness, the more energy you will have and the less tired you will become. This will have benefits in terms of overall enjoyment of skiing, and will also help to offset the fatigue associated with lapses in concentration and accidents.

Because we favour specific cardiovasclar exercises, then aside from the warm-up exercises at the beginning of the main program, it is quite difficult to find a truly specific cardiovascular exercise to replicate either skiing or snowboarding. One solution could be to spend months by the slopes gradually increasing the workload by practicing and training. However, for those of us who live in warmer climates this is not possible, and although using artificial slopes is useful, it still will not challenge the body as much as an actual mountainside.

If exercising at home, the best compromise is to spend a couple of sessions a week performing a prolonged warm-up over 20–30 minutes. This creates what is essentially a personal aerobics class. If exercising in a gym, then some cross-trainers are very similar to skiing movements, although they are far from perfect. The next best is the treadmill, which at least permits exercise in an upright posture. Steppers, cycles and rowing machines are less specific and only good for the general benefits of cardiovascular exercise.

Following a progressive and thorough warm-up, the main cardiovascular exercise can last as long as you have available. As long as the session is slightly more difficult than the one that went before it, then benefits will be derived. The session should conclude with a thorough and gradual cool-down over a few minutes, or longer as required. It is necessary for the body to recover before performing cardio exercise again, but two to three sessions per week of at least 20 minutes will be adequate to begin improving cardio fitness and general health. Cardiovascular exercise predominantly utilizes different muscle fibers to those used during heavy resistance work, so cardiovascular and resistance sessions can take place on consecutive days, or even on the same day. The trick is to start off gently, and exercise when you feel that the body is ready to do so.

3

nutrition

Some people would have us believe that we can eat what we want so long as we exercise sufficiently. Others regard exercise as something artificial, and believe that the key to a healthy mind and body is proper nutrition. Few and far between are the people who regard exercise and nutrition as equals. Exercise performance cannot be maintained or developed without a sufficient intake of all the required nutrients. Eating properly is an essential component in maintaining a healthy body.

Having a good diet is not the preserve of the ultra-health-conscious and the dieter. Physical appearance, in terms of body weight, gives little indication of physical health. This is even more the case for people who exercise, for whom more nutrients are required for overall energy levels, for muscle repair and recovery following exercise, and for maintaining the health of the body's cells and organs.

There are a few general dietary rules that most of us know but fail to apply effectively. There is such variety between individuals that it is not practical to dictate or advocate a particular dietary strategy for everyone. Instead, we have to try to find the foods that work best for us, and ensure we get all the nutrients we need.

There are two categories of nutrients:

1. The **macronutrients** are the carbohydrates, fats and proteins
2. The **micronutrients** are the vitamins and minerals

Today's diet fads tend to promote one type of macronutrient and criticize another. The arguments often contain a heavy bias that fails to take into account both sides of the story. In addition, because we are all so different, what might prove beneficial to some might be disastrous to others.

The best thing we can do is adopt a whole-food approach to nutrition. Whole foods are free from mechanical and chemical processing. Processed foods are generally higher in calories, salt and sugar, and have been broken down and heated up to the point where there is little real nutritional benefit to them. They might provide energy, but the body needs more than just energy. Our vitamins and minerals should come from good quality fruits and vegetables, eaten throughout the day. This means leaf and root vegetables, and an intake of varied fruits.

Carbohydrates can be found in rice, potatoes, fruits and vegetables. Proteins can be found in meats, fish, dairy products and eggs. Fats tend to be found in protein-rich foods in sufficient quantities. There are various different carbohydrates, proteins and fats, and there are none that should be avoided entirely. If there is a health problem related to diet, such as high blood pressure or cholesterol, then some foods may need to be avoided, but this is such a specific area that it is not possible to devote more space to it here. Instead, a dietician should investigate any dietary health problems.

In order to supply sufficient energy for exercise sessions and recovery afterward, it is important to obtain enough carbohydrates from the diet. Proteins are also important for recovery. Fats are important for supplying the body with certain vitamins, and stored fat is preferentially used as energy. In short, we should eat plenty of everything and neglect nothing. Rather than giving specific quantities and ratios, which cannot be done here with any kind of accuracy for individuals, it is better simply to advise that people eat plenty of all the various foods that can be included in a whole-food diet.

While it is true that some people are healthier with a diet that prioritizes a particular macronutrient, this sort of personal dietary analysis should be sought through a dietician. In addition, it is important that people who want to lose weight prioritize reducing total calories rather than assuming that one particular type of macronutrient is to blame. The most accurate and yet basic advice, therefore, is to avoid processed foods in favor of whole foods, and to ensure a good variety of different foods so that everything the body needs can be obtained freely from the diet.

When exercising, it is best to eat carbohydrates before, and then a mix of carbohydrates and proteins soon after. The quantities and timing of these meals depends upon the individual, and there is a lot of trial and error to find out what works best. Fluid intake is also important. Even 1 percent dehydration will have a negative effect on performance, so it is essential to make sure that water or an isotonic sports drink is available during exercise sessions. Our thirst response is actually quite ineffective. We only feel thirsty when we are already dehydrated, and then we can stop feeling thirsty by having a solitary, almost insignificant, mouthful of water. During exercise, the body can need approximately 250ml of fluid every 15 minutes.

On the Slopes

When away at a winter resort it is likely that there will be some significant changes in the diet. This will most likely be due to the combination of food availability, and the fact that for most people going to a winter resort is a holiday, and when we are on holiday we like to treat ourselves to the sorts of food we would not eat much of otherwise. Because spending most of the day on the mountain requires a lot of energy, it is important to eat plenty of food, including more than we would expect when not exercising as much. So we therefore have permission to eat more, but it is still important to aim to eat a variety of whole foods, including fresh fruit and vegetables, to ensure that we have covered all our nutritional bases. The increased volume of exercise means that we have an increased requirement not just for energy, but for all the nutrients the body needs.

Having a good dinner will help to ensure that the body recovers effectively for the following day. The increased number of accidents following injury-free first days on the mountain is often regarded as being related to fatigue. Proper nutrition will help reduce the chances of becoming fatigued on the slopes, and this approach will complement the need for proper exercise training.

Because energy, specifically carbohydrate, is reduced overnight, it is important to have a big breakfast in the morning. During the day it is also important to stop every few hours to top up on food. This could be integrated into a hot chocolate break in a chalet. Hot chocolate contains more energy than tea or coffee, before the addition of sugar, and the relative lack of caffeine is also preferential in the early part of the day. Because caffeine has a diuretic effect, taking some in during a break from exercise can increase dehydration. Sufficient intake of fluids is important to ensure hydration, so opportunities should be taken as often as possible, as dehydration can lead to fatigue and can even affect coordination.

Après-ski

Much as skiing holidays should prioritize skiing, there seems to have been an increase in the attitude that après-ski is what the holiday is all about. Certainly the social aspects of après-ski, and the opportunity to stock up on food and aid the body to recover, are good things. Alcohol, however, really should be taken only in moderation, if at all. The main reason for this is the safety of yourself and other skiers. Over the last few years we have come to accept that driving the morning after we have had a few drinks can still affect our coordination and reactions. This is therefore the same for skiing ability.

That is not to say that we should abstain from having a drink, but rather that we should be aware of how much we are drinking, and probably have a few fruit juices during the evening as well. Alcohol can deplete the body of some vitamins and minerals, so it is even more important to make sure we are eating plenty of good foods in the evening and for breakfast. Because alcohol is a diuretic, it also increases water loss, which can lead to dehydration. So, in summary, if we decide to have a drink, then we need to be aware of how much, and we need to take in plenty of other fluids and good foods to ensure that our skiing performance does not suffer as a result.

The Final Word

Unlike taking up running, cycling or fishing, skiing and snowboarding are activities that place huge demands on the body through their sheer intensity. It is not the case that runners do not work hard, but a runner would be unlikely to do nothing for 50 weeks of the year, and then run for five or so hours a day, every day for two weeks. Yet this is precisely what many people do when they decide to take up winter sports. More fortunate are those who can ski or snowboard for most of the year, or the seasoned professionals who head off to the slopes and habitually condition themselves whenever possible. But most people are nowhere near this stage. Because of this, most offer themselves up to a huge risk of injury, or at least exhaust themselves to the point of not enjoying themselves as much as they could.

The best way to ensure that you make the most of your precious time away is to train yourself and to prepare accordingly. Proper preparation requires a multifaceted approach, encompassing physical conditioning, awareness of the mechanisms of injury, a good knowledge of the importance of proper nutrition, and a good daily plan for attacking the slopes.

The rewards of this commitment to hard work center on improving the body's fitness for skiing. Accomplishing this will leave you better able to enjoy the rigors of skiing and snowboarding, while promoting your ability to improve technical skills for an even greater physical and mental challenge on the slopes.

Notes

Notes

Notes

Notes

Notes

Notes

Pray to your Father in secret

Jean Lafrance

translated by
B. Green and R. Jollett

Éditions Paulines

Originally published as
Prie ton Père dans le secret
by Jean Lafrance, Paris, France.

Phototypesetting: *Les Éditions Paulines*

Cover: *Antoine Pépin*

Imprimatur: Msgr. Jean-Marie Fortier,
Archbishop of Sherbrooke
January 25, 1986

ISBN 2-89039-982-6

Dépôt légal — 1er trimestre 1987
Bibliothèque nationale du Québec
National Library of Canada

© 1987 Éditions Paulines
250, boul. St-François nord
Sherbrooke, Qc, J1E 2B9 (CANADA)

Contents

Preface

This is a series of short readings of equal length meant, first of all, as an aid to prayer. Very often they are presented as reflections on the Gospels, to introduce prayer to those who have shared in a "prayer experience." Sometimes, after a retreat, people have asked for a "souvenir text," something which would help them to renew in their everyday prayer what they have found in this short ten-day experience. This book was written to meet this need.

Let me tell you something about it; the people for whom I wrote it and the way in which it can be used to help us pray.

This is not a series of meditations written at random, using various themes to encourage prayer. First of all, it is concerned with a well directed prayer-experience — and when we talk of experience we mean growth and direction of a specific nature. This is not an abstract, subjective structure; the spiritual experience joins the Christian experience, which is the objective experience of salvation through the chosen people, the prophets, Jesus Christ and finally the Church. We can see it as a progressive revelation of the love of God Who calls man to enter into deep communion with Him, until the day when He fulfills it in Christ. Such an experience is given to us in the Bible, and the Church invites us to relive it today in the liturgy and in our daily lives.

We have followed the path of God's revelation which

7

calls man to live with Him on friendly terms. The union of God and man is so intimate, so firm, so complete that from now on, to talk of God without at the same time talking of man is to leave something out, and to talk of man without talking of God is again to leave something out. We cannot read the Word of God like a curious tourist or like someone looking for pictures and ideas. We are involved, challenged by the Word of God which reaches out to the depths of man.

This brief sketch is divided into four parts which try to set out by successive approaches the stages of the economy of salvation. First of all, we put ourselves before God Who comes out of silence and speaks to man, to tell him of His wish to join with him in an alliance of love. It is in this dialogue that God reveals Himself as the Entirely Other, the near and also as the Creator. This revelation of God as thrice holy, God Friend and God Host plunges man into adoration and love, calling him to live before God, with God and in God. This contemplation of the God of dialogue is the first stage in the story of salvation.

But this salvation is made completely and fully evident when the Word of God becomes flesh and comes to live among men. Men are thus placed before Jesus Christ and called upon to recognize Him as the revelation of the love of God. At the heart of faith there is a well defined choice for or against Christ, the Word of God. It is on this level of welcome or denial of Christ that the deep feelings of the heart are revealed.

In the loving look of Christ at us, we feel our sin and our need for salvation. If we refuse to be penetrated by this look, we are like the wilfully blind who refuse to see in Jesus the revelation of the Father's love.

Standing before Christ, there is no alternative except to follow Him or to run from Him. But to follow Jesus Christ is to go with Him into the mystery of the glorious Cross and the Kingdom of the Beatitudes. It is only on these terms that we can become His disciples. So we have to empty ourselves, to enter into the poverty of Jesus, without illusions, accepting the play of His love. When

8

we have reached this second stage, we are invited to enter with Jesus into the way of salvation.

Jesus carries out this salvation in the paschal mystery made present today in the sacraments, especially in Baptism and the Holy Eucharist. In a third stage called the "carrying-out" of salvation, we are asked to contemplate Jesus giving up His life to the Father in the glorious Passion and giving His Body to men in the Eucharist. Our life following Jesus having thus become part of His death-resurrection, takes on a new dimension; it becomes life for the Father in Christ. Jesus teaches us to give ourselves completely, without reservation, keeping nothing back. The paschal mystery brings us directly into the mystery of the Trinity, making us adopted sons of God.

Finally, in a fourth and last stage, we put ourselves in the place of man, to come close to the mystery of this dialogue with God. God speaks to man to express His love; He expects a loving response from man, expressed in prayer and the unconditional gift of his life. Simply, we have gone back to the essential laws of training in prayer which permit man to relate to God on every level of his person. Much more than a method, this is an anthropological essay on prayer. We do not learn to pray attending lectures and seminars on prayer, but in practicing it in the reality of everyday life.

It is the whole man who is committed to the relationship with God. Prayer then raises the problem of the Christian experience. Certain expressions used in this book must not be wrongly interpreted. We often speak of prayer of the heart, tasting the Word or of experiencing the working of God in us. Also the Exercises leave a large place for the movement of the Holy Spirit in man's heart, what St. Ignatius called "consolations" or "dryness": these are seen as so many signs of spiritual understanding. These have nothing to do with emotions or impressions which are experienced passively, but the act by which the person lays hold upon God. This is why, before the last section, we have tried to assess briefly the Christian experience. The fine book of J. Mouroux should be reread on this subject as well as that of K. Rahner on the ex-

9

perience of grace. It was these studies, describing the essence of the Christian experience, which prompted us to write this note.

These pages are primarily for those who have lived a continuous experience of prayer and who feel the need to deepen their understanding of it and to find again their reasons for living according to the Gospel. It is clear that our experience of salvation unfolds in the same rhythm as our personal life. During a retreat it is lived in a concentrated and synthetic way, but it must also be above all the very thread of our lives. It is to allow this steady assimilation, and pondering on the Word of God, that we have put together these short readings. It can only be done little by little, time being a very important factor in spiritual experience.

This is why these texts must be prayed, rather than read. They should not be approached as accounts of prayer, to furnish the mind with fresh ideas to discuss later. Let me repeat, it is not by describing prayer that we learn to pray, but by practicing it in our daily work. For this reason we have deliberately chosen the vocative rather than the usual style, so that the reader feels he is personally called by Another in a real dialogue. These themes should be taken up in continuous prayer, appreciating them fully, rather than finishing them at any cost. You should not go on to the next text unless you have completely absorbed the first reading into your prayer life.

Although these notes are frequently used in a retreat of 8-10 days, they can also serve as a guide for anyone who wishes to work out alone an experience of prayer, in a personal retreat. However, let me point out that nothing can replace a real experience under the guidance of someone who has used the discipline of these Exercises and who is certain of the path and can bear witness to prayer. Once this experience has been made with a trained director, it can easily be done again alone, and that is why these notes may serve as a guide for a prayer experience alone.

One last question should be considered — how should these texts be used for prayer? First of all, there should be a certain gradual growth pattern, going deeper into the experience, penetrating into all the stages, not trying to do everything from the start. This is, in effect, the same as in the path of baptismal initiation which sets man as sinner in front of God the Holy One, where man allows himself to be enlightened by the Word of Christ and is finally united with Him in the mysteries of salvation.

Above all, I cannot emphasize sufficiently that those who take part in a retreat must offer an uncompromising fidelity to prayer. Success is not required, but you must put yourself resolutely into complete interior silence and be faithful to the hour set apart for contemplative prayer. Apart from these moments of explicit prayer, it is good to live simply in the presence of God, pondering freely over the themes used. Special care should be taken not to have too many readings, but to select a few fairly short ones from the Bible or any other book which is relevant to the stage being lived through. A single truth absorbed in a serene atmosphere and calm concentration opens all other truths to us, without our knowing it.

We have prepared a schedule at the end of the book for the benefit of those who might use these notes for a private retreat. We have spread this experience over ten days, leaving it up to the individual to shorten or lengthen it. The most important thing is to cover the whole process even though certain notes with overlapping themes could be set aside and taken up later.

We think it is good to set aside four periods of prayer each day; the ideal would be to spend one hour each time but care must be taken to avoid fatigue, living rather in a relaxed atmosphere which lets each one find his own rhythm.

Usually, as we grow in prayer, it becomes easier for us. If it is impossible to pray, we must look for the reasons which are not necessarily due to bad will, but sometimes to faulty human conditions apart from prayer. Here it is a good idea to find an experienced spiritual director in order to examine your prayer life and with his help discern the weak areas.

Two outlines are provided for each prayer period; the

first gives advice on prayer and the other sets out a theme, drawn from Scripture. Evidently this text is simply an aid, but the essential is to refer to the Word of God itself. There is a link between the first and second outlines since the way of praying must be adapted to the subject chosen; we do not meditate on the Passion in the same way that we meditate on the Sermon on the Mount and the Beatitudes.

All this advice about prayer might seem complicated and tedious to anyone looking at it from the outside, but it should be tried before being dismissed as useless. It is only by doing something that you discover how helpful it can be. In the beginning, you have to analyze any action so that you do it well; later you do it easily. Like any skill, prayer demands that you do it patiently even making use of setbacks. But having said this, these notes have only one aim: to introduce us to prayer and to help us to develop it. We must not ask too much of them. All human techniques are only a crutch in training us in prayer; only the Holy Spirit is the true master of prayer. Once we can walk alone, we must give up the crutch. The Holy Spirit is able to make us poor human beings into people of prayer. It is when we have finished with these pages that we begin our real search for a life in the presence of God.

I

The God of Dialogue

1. Do not come forward to look at God as at some strange sight, but take off your sandals before Him.

If you want to know God, you should walk in the steps of the men of prayer in the Bible, those to whom God revealed Himself. Think today of the picture of the burning bush and Moses (Ex 3:1-6), take off your sandals to see God and He will reveal Himself to you as a consuming fire.

First of all, when we see Moses going deep into the desert, it is always in some "beyond" that he will reach the mountain of God. But there again, Moses must change his ideas and be converted. He goes forward to examine this strange sight, to see why the bush is not consumed. Moses is curious, he is attracted by the sensational and he wants to examine the question of God. "Yahweh saw him go forward to see better" (Ex 3:4).

Moses tries to understand the "why" of God from the outside, using rational means. But you cannot reach God as a curious onlooker since He does not let Himself be enclosed on human terms. He is always above and beyond your ideas, unyielding to your grasp. God is not a problem to be resolved, but a mystery to discover. A personality cannot be grasped in a psychological study; it will escape when you want to hold or explain

13

it. God is the Unknown, the Unexplainable. "A thing once explained ceases to interest us," wrote Nietzsche, "so God will always interest us!"

This is why Yahweh takes the initiative in the meeting when He calls Moses by his name. The only attitude before God is to say to Him: "Here I am." This is an act of humility, of poverty, of assent, of being at God's disposal. Yahweh asked Moses to take off his sandals, which implies that he gives up his security, his protection, his idea of God. Yahweh is the thrice-Holy One Who reveals Himself in a dialogue of freedom and adoration.

To know God is to recognize that He is there, unyielding to your ideas, that He will reveal Himself when He wishes and to whomsoever He wishes. In prayer, reject any image of God. You are in the order of faith, not that of clear sight. St. Paul says: "The mystery of God surpasses all knowledge." You grasp the essential of God, "as in a mirror, indistinctly" adds St. Paul (1 Cor 13:12).

Do not try to approach God to inventory Him. Stop treating Him as an object, call upon Him as a free person. The first step to this end is to humble yourself, to take off your sandals. The decisive moment when the real encounter with God begins is not the movement you make towards Him, but the movement of withdrawal, of humility where you see yourself as unimportant before Him. God is not a conquered country, but a holy land where you must tread, barefoot.

When you realize that you have no ideas on the matter, then God reveals Himself. Again you will not be able to express the experience in clear and precise terms. Yahweh reveals Himself to you, as to Moses, like fire, something which cannot be grasped nor held in the hands. He gives Himself as a consuming fire. Fire is a strange and fascinating thing. It lights up and changes everything it touches. When St. John of the Cross wished to call to mind the greatest heights of union with God, he compared it to a log being burned away by fire.

In prayer keep yourself poor and empty before the burning, glowing bush. Say nothing, but offer to this consuming fire the emptiness of your very self. God is the one who wants to consume you. You form one being with Him and you will share His divine nature. He transforms into Himself those who humbly offer themselves to His transforming grace. By your union with Him, He is strong enough to light up the world with the fire of His love.

2. Be filled with wonder at God Who is speaking to you. He always takes up the dialogue which you have cut short.

Each day you feel Adam's loneliness in the Garden of Eden: "No helpmate suitable for man was found for him" (Gn 2:20). Like him, you are filled with wonder when someone like you looks at you, smiles or says something which pulls you out of the misery of your loneliness. You have been made to meet others, to smile, to see them, to relate to other people, to have a lasting love. As Mary at the Annunciation was overwhelmed with joy, seeing herself as loved by God, so you too know the experience of the fullness of love; suddenly you are alive since you are known and loved by your brother.

When you open your Bible to hear the Word of God, do you feel the same wonder? Or, are you like the prodigal son who is so intent on using the gifts of the Father that he is not grateful to the giver? He does not accept them as a gift nor as a sign of the deeper giving that the Father wishes to make of Himself to His son.

You can rise early in the morning or even in the night to pray; God is already before you in your prayer and it is He who begs you to accept Him in the proposal of love He makes to you. To open the book of the Word is to unseal a loveletter addressed to you personally. You should be astonished before this disturbing love of God which searches for man, watching for his slightest response.

You are not the one who goes seeking Him, but He is the One Who keeps knocking at the door of your heart

(Rv 3:20), hoping you will open it to Him and share the joy of His friendship.

God does not need you; He is above all, He is the Entirely-Other; He is joy in Himself, happiness, love, truth and holiness and He wants to call you, to enter into a dialogue of love so that He can impart to you all that He is. He is hungrier for you than you are for Him. When He speaks, it is not empty words, just the opposite: He utters a word which expresses His deepest being. When God speaks to you, the most important thing is not just what He says, but the very fact that He is talking to you. When someone speaks to you, it is always wonderful since you see in it the gift of a person who expresses freely, who communicates, who gives himself. As with Abraham, God shares with you His desire to create a new alliance with you. His word tells again and again of the infinite love that He has for you. He only speaks to say "I love you."

You will never finish your contemplation of this love. Some days it will seem unbelievable folly to you. Do not be discouraged, whatever your sin, your forgetfulness, your lack of faith — it is always God Who takes the first steps and picks up the dialogue that you have broken off: "While he was still a long way off, his father saw him and was moved with pity. He ran to the boy, clasped him in his arms and kissed him tenderly" (Lk 15:20).

To pray is to stay in the embrace of a father moved with compassion at the sight of our wretchedness. Furthermore, in the depths of your poverty you find that God has never stopped wanting you. True contemplative prayer is born from this wonder before the love of the Trinity.

When you have felt a hint of the love that God has for you — for you can never grasp it completely — you will emerge a little from your meanness, your heart will burn with the very fire of the burning bush: "Oh, someone like myself would run a league to escape this love if he felt it prowling around him" (G. Greene).

3. The sign that you have begun to know God is your desire to know Him better.

Do you want to know whether you are on the way to knowing God? Ask the great men of prayer in the Bible and be willing to relive their long experience. Moses contemplated the unknowable God of the burning bush; he allowed himself to be won over by God and became one of His true, His intimate friends. "Yahweh used to speak to Moses face to face, as a man to his friend" (Ex 33:11).

Moses had come to such a deep knowledge of God Who revealed His name to him, Who revealed the substance of His innermost being. He is Yahweh's friend. However, Moses asks for a still greater knowledge of God. Reread in silence the prayer of Moses (Ex 33:12-23) and make your own the threefold prayer he made to God: "Show me Your ways, show me Your grace, I beg You, show me Your glory!"

The sign that you have begun to know God is not the fine ideas that you have about Him, still less the pleasure your prayer gives you, but rather your ardent desire to know Him better. You would not desire God if you did not know Him. If you did not have God in you, you would not be able to feel His absence. It is in the ache of desire that God's presence is disclosed. It is presence in absence.

God is mystery. He discloses Himself to you gradually. The further you go in the knowledge of God, the more you see that the mystery is still there and deepens and you will want to know even more of Him: "If there is truly desire, if the object of one's desire is truly light, the desire for the light produces the light" (S. Weil).

Do you want to know the quality of your prayer-life? Start by asking yourself what are your hopes, your desires. Saint Paul says: "Those who live according to the Spirit desire spiritual things" (Rm 8:5). The more you are taken over by the Spirit, the more your desires will be in tune with the Spirit. Yet these desires must be real and have at least some fulfilment. So ask yourself

17

this question: "Do I thirst for God? Do my heart and my body cry out to Him?" True knowledge of God cannot be expressed. God is indescribable. "Lord, make me desire You." The intensity of your desire for God is a mark of the quality of your love. Do you yearn to pray?

God responded to Moses' request by admitting him gradually into His mystery, but to do this Moses had to endure a fundamental death. "You cannot see my face, He said, for man cannot see Me and live" (Ex 33:20). At present you know God as in a mirror, later you will know Him as you are known, face to face, when you have accepted death. You cannot imagine what you will see tomorrow.

For the moment, accept that you must stand in the cleft of the rock, immersed in deep shadow, hidden in the hand of God. Then like Moses, you will see Yahweh from behind, that is in the signs of His presence. God is passing by. He cries out His name: "Yahweh, Yahweh, God of tenderness and mercy, slow to anger, rich in kindness and faithfulness" (Ex 34:6). Each time God shows Himself to you, He reveals Himself as complete mercy.

Then, see Moses' reaction when God has gone by. He falls to his knees, lies prostrate on the ground, humbles himself completely. The result of love is adoration, self-abasement. Moses' prayer of intercession follows: "If I have indeed won your favour, Lord, let my Lord come with us" (Ex 34:9). You will recognize the truth of your prayer in the humility found in your whole life and your care to serve your brothers and intercede for them. As with Moses, you can only intercede and be a mediator to the extent of your closeness with God. May the Holy Spirit deepen in you a soul of desire.

4. Go to the experience of Elijah on Mount Horeb with a disciple's heart. You will share his intimacy with God.

In contemplation, be careful not to leave in the shadow some aspects of the mystery of God which seem inconsistent to you. Thus, the sense of His holiness must blend with the knowledge of His intimacy. You have already seen the closeness which existed between Moses and Yahweh; in going with Elijah to Mount Horeb, you will share in his intimacy with God.

These men, such as Abraham, Moses and Elijah are not characters out of the past; they are our fathers in faith, saints of the Old Testament. You can pray to them to act on your behalf as spiritual fathers. So Abraham will obtain for you the grace to root your life in faith in the Word of God. Go to the deep life of Elijah as a disciple. He is the father of those contemplatives who live in endless search of God. He can pass on to you a share of that inner fire for God which consumed him: "I am filled with jealous zeal for Yahweh Sabaoth" (1 K 19:14).

Fit this experience into the general setting of the theophanies. In this very spot God revealed His name to Moses, that is His inner being. He gave him the Law and the Covenant.

In terrifying, with thunder and lightning, He made apparent His holiness. But you must go beyond these violent manifestations to find His spiritual presence in gentleness and intimacy.

Elijah is the one stands before God to serve Him (1 K 17:1). He worked untiringly for His kingdom. He is an apostolic heart filled with enthusiasm for the house of God. But Elijah prefers to say, "God, before Whose face I stand." You too burn for the mission, but God does not need your services — the only service He expects from you is your attentiveness and your presence. He wants you to stand before Him. "This is a man who loves his brothers and prays much for the people and for the holy city — Jeremiah the prophet of God" (2 M 15:14).

19

God takes pleasure in being with you (Pr 8:31) — He expects you to live with Him. To pray is to lose time freely before Him. It is a grace to be happy with Him and to recognize His presence.

Before He revealed Himself to Elijah, God had him pass through the desert, alone, weary, discouraged, owning nothing. Elijah knew the feeling of failure which is so often in your heart, both as a human and as an apostle — "I am no better than my brothers." St. James draws this parallel: "Elijah was a man who suffered the same wretchedness as we do" (Jm 5:17).

At the end of this long, painful desert road, Elijah found the love of a God Who was close to him. Turn your tired face to that intangible breath of wind which expresses as much as any symbol can, the spirituality and sweetness of God.

Elijah was given, in a vivid meeting, an additional revelation of God's being. He is not only the Most High, the Almighty, but the God present in that intimacy which belongs to the Spirit. Prayer should let you taste emotionally the presence of God. "Is His Word sweet to the taste, more than honey in the mouth?" Your eyes and your human heart should see and taste how good God is: "Your decrees... are the joy of my heart" (Ps 119:111).

Only the fullness of this revelation in the Gospel would tell how far this intimacy goes; in the Holy Trinity, it is the close communion of the Three Divine Persons who greet and give to one another mutually. In the degree that you listen and keep the word of Jesus, you live in this movement of communion and the Trinity is present in you. Throw light upon this theophany with the help of St. John's teaching (16:23 and 15:1-17).

You can say like Jacob: "Yahweh is in this place and I never knew it" (Gn 28:16). In your prayer always go down deeper into this indwelling God. He does not pull you away from the real world, but makes you ever more present to it. When you come back among your brothers, you will see this mystery in their hearts and you will walk in the presence of the Lord in the land of the living.

5. You exist and you live by the look of love that God gives you.

You know how modern atheisms reject a God who would stop you from living as a free man. On this, Merleau-Ponty wrote: "Consciousness dies on contact with the Absolute." In a way they are right; if God were truly the Other, you would have a real need to struggle to free yourself. But God does not fit into the category *other* any more than into the category *same*.

For God, creating you does not mean putting you into existence in an impersonal way. He is not for you some *other*. In the same way, you cannot think of your relationship to Him in terms of identity, you are not the *same* as God. To say that you are created by Him is to say at the same time that "God is not you", but also "neither is He some *other*."

This apparent contradiction baffles expression in concepts, but you can see it in your religious consciousness. This is why you should find in your prayer the link of creation which unites you to God. At the root of all prayer, there is this awareness of the loving look of God which creates you ceaselessly. Many prayers fade away because they do not begin with this reality. Your whole spiritual and prayer life is based on this bond of creation. This is why at the start of a retreat, after contemplating the Entirely Other God, you must contemplate God's creative presence. Psalm 139 said slowly can set you before God Who keeps making and remaking you.

Become aware of your life, of your body and of your mind; it is God Who has made you live and think. He did not create you as a thing or an inanimate being by an impersonal act of will. This is not how God creates a person for this would be meaningless and atheists would be right to refuse a God who would restrict their freedom. He creates you by an act which foresees and is the foundation of your dignity, that is, by a call. God then is not another subject on the same level as you, but He is the true source of your being, closer and more present to you than you are yourself.

"God sees, that is, He turns His face towards man and thereby gives man his own countenance. I am myself by the fact that He sees me. The soul lives by the loving look God casts on it. Here we have an infinite depth, a blessed mystery. God is He Who sees with love. Things are what they are by His looking upon them; I am myself by His looking upon me" (R. Guardini).

This creative presence of God who enfolds you is thus a loving, universal presence (Ps 139:13-22). God in creating you calls you and stands before you as a *You*. If you exist, it is because you are one of God's works of love.

To pray is simply to become aware of this existential dialogue between God and yourself, between God and all men. Your being has in its depths an ability to communicate. To say *You* to God in prayer is to recognize that He is the source that has made you a free person. Reread verses 19-22 of Psalm 139 and you will understand that the ungodly man is he who does not let himself be created and acted upon by this presence. You are ungodly when you aim at self-fulfilment apart from God or when you refuse to accept yourself from God or to respond to His creative call. You still remain a free person but you are in contradiction to your own being, and to continue this refusal would be damnation.

God has made you free only to beg for your consent to His creative love. To pray is to accept and want to be known by God. Do not imitate Adam in the Garden of Eden who did himself to escape from the creative look of God. Accept the name He has given you when He calls you. In prayer, be glad to be the work of God's look, go deep within this creative flow and offer God all that you have and all that you are, in a movement of praise and thanksgiving.

6. In His look at you, the face of God is revealed and from this is born the relation of friendship where two beings look directly at each other.

Have you noticed how often the psalms give human attitudes to God? He leans towards man, He sees, He searches, He knows, He listens, He understands, He is near, He greets and He has pity. Yet God is not human and no creature can have any idea of His glory. He is simply the God you know in meeting Him.

However, God has plans and designs; He wants to enter into communion with you. God's being is ultimately Love and Love's wish is to share. He uses metaphors to express that love. He compares Himself to a mother rocking her child and pressing it against her cheek. This God-Mother love shines throughout the whole Bible: "The love God feels for us is *rahamim* in Hebrew, the plural of maternal breast, hence a motherly love, multiplied to the infinite" (E. Charpentier). He also compares Himself to a father, a husband, a friend. In a word, the heart of God overflows with tenderness for you, and the different loves you can know on earth (marital, maternal, paternal or friendship) are but a pale reflection of this total love which is the heart of God.

It is because you read this love in God that you see in Him the face of a mother, a friend, a spouse. God is someone Who turns His face to you and Who at the same time gives you your own face. He looks at you directly, He opens Himself and shows Himself to you. You know that the look on a man's face is a door to the depths of his heart. When your friends move you by their way of looking at you, you know that they understand and love you.

So God is He Who sees but His look is love, expressing the infinite tenderness of His heart. He sees you with all your potential and invites you to measure up to it. He sees the evil in you and knows its extent, He sees your sin and judges it. His judgment reaches to the bottom of your heart and nothing can stand against Him. But you know that His glance is merciful and forgiving and that He saves you. The glance of God does not disclose your own mystery but He holds and shelters you. To be seen by Him is not to be judged or abandoned but, on the contrary, it is to be protected in the safest of shelters... His love never ceases to create you while arousing in you desires for resurrection.

To pray is to walk in the sight of God and to desire that He see you in the most secret depths of your being. True prayer begins the day you discover this loving look, but to do that, God has to open your eyes. You cannot see the face of God unless you allow yourself to be enlightened by the light of His eyes.

To see the face of God is to know that you have been pierced by His gaze, in which alone you can contemplate the light: "By your light, we see the light" (Ps 35:10). The brightness of His face will enlighten you and will make the world glow.

In prayer beg God to disclose Himself to you — "Lord let your face shine on us and we shall be safe" (Ps 80:3). Then you will know the amazing experience that to want to see God, is to be seen by Him Who knows the depths of man and the abyss. At this moment, a relation of friendship will be born where you will look directly at God: "Your watchmen raise their voices, they shout for joy together. For they see Yahweh face to face as He returns to Zion" (Is 52:8).

Once this relationship is established, words become useless since you understand everything in the look of God. You put yourself in front of Him, in your poverty, your shortcomings and your sinfulness, but also with your yearning to understand His intent and to be in harmony with His will. In His sight there is always the possibility of renewal. All is possible with God, but everything is in danger when you do not accept this.

"Christian contemplation is Trinitarian, the fire of two gazes consuming each other out of love" (M.-D. Molinié, O.P.). In the heart of the Trinity, the Persons contemplate each other, in mutual greeting and loving surrender.

When Jesus lived on earth, you often heard Him

glancing with praise and admiration at His Father. At your baptism, Christ gave light to your eyes, enabling you to take part in His loving look. To pray is to take part in this mutual look which unfolds in loving communion.

7. When God loves you, He changes you in the deepest part of your being.

Have you had a true friend? You are unhappy and you need someone to call you by name. You need to meet someone so that you become truly yourself. The day you receive the joy of a real affection, you will be changed, transformed in your very depths. When a creature of flesh and blood comes into your life, your life is transformed and takes on new meaning. You have met someone who has spoken to you and needs a response and it changes your whole life. You still have your questions, your problems, but you look at them in a new way — as a man might say to a girl: "Loving doesn't do anything, but it changes everything."

The same thing happens when God meets you and speaks to you as a friend. The love of God is so strong, so powerful that it can give you back your innocence of heart. Remember the prophet Hosea and his wife who was a prostitute. St. Augustine spoke of the way God's love renews the purity in the soul. God does not love you because you are kind; He loves you so that you may become kind. You can change, you have changed because God Himself has met you, has talked to you, because His very love has changed you.

The love of God for you is not an empty word, it is a word which carries out what it tells you. It is effective, practical. Just as meeting another person can change you, so the meeting with the God of Jesus Christ can change you in the depths of your being. Between the Three in One God and yourself, the union is so complete, so real, so ultimate that from now on it is impossible to talk of Him without talking of yourself.

Between you and Me, says God, there is a bond which nothing can destroy. I am your God, you are my son. We shall hold in common; I, — My eternity, My life and My holiness; and you, — your daily life, your earthly existence and your poverty. Your life will be united with Mine and we shall never be separated for I am your God and I shall never withdraw my alliance. In a way our destiny is linked together. He is the God of Abraham, Isaac and Jacob just as He is the God of each of our names, letting us know by that that He links our lives to His life.

Between us there is a sharing of being in which is rooted a sharing of love and insight. It is above all in Jesus Christ that this sharing is achieved perfectly. Go down into the depths of your heart and there you will see in its springs the flow of the life of the Trinity which floods all your being. Let this divine life overflow and carry you to the bosom of the Father, moved by the Spirit of Christ.

Your prayer roots itself deeply because you are so sure of your alliance with God. It is not a vertical climb which will make you reach out for God in a hopeless straining after Him. It is a clear, simple realisation, rewarding but sometimes painful, that God has freely chosen you and wants to link His destiny with yours: "If Yahweh set His heart on you and chose you, it was not because you outnumbered the peoples, it was for love of you" (Dt 7:7-8).

Prayer is that special moment when you contemplate the love of the Father drawing you to the life of a son. Free the son of God who lies captive deep within you and allow him to flourish. You will no longer need to search for words or ideas to express your prayer. To live as a son of God will be enough and your very being will be a prayer.

8. In the night you cry out so that God will call you by your name.

Have you ever left the place where you are known and loved to live in a foreign country where you do not count for anyone? Perhaps in this impersonal crowd, someone comes along who *recognizes* you and calls you by name and suddenly you feel reborn. From the moment when real friendship is born between two people, there is always a *before* and an *after* and from this we can say: "Since I have known you, I am no longer the same." J. de Bourbon Busset has one of his characters say: "Before knowing you I was a nobody who thought he was somebody. Today I am somebody who knows himself to be a nobody."

So, when you open your Bible you see men who are content or dissatisfied, holy or sinful — all made happy by their meeting with God, because their lives have taken on a new meaning. Those who have met God can sing with Jean Ferrat: "What would I be without you, who came to meet me?" Whoever you are, you are brother to these men in their experience. Were you the greatest sinner, the most unbalanced man, the poorest — all these situations mean a chance for God to meet you.

In prayer our desire is to be captivated by God: "Every man cries out to be called by his name" (S. Weil). You suffer without knowing why and like Elijah you wish to die as you are so unhappy with things. Be truthful when you pray, don't pretend everything is fine, but set out before God the mountains of your suffering, bitterness, pride and impurity. If you pray in truth and with faith, God will move these mountains into the sea. Pray long and hard that He will change this bitterness into sweetness.

At the heart of this austere peace, you will find that God loves you. Nothing escapes Him, He sees you in secret and He loves you. Cling to the words of Isaiah: "I have called you by your name, you are mine... Because you are precious in my eyes, because you are honored

and I love you... Do not be afraid for I am with you"
(Is 43:1-5).

You count in God's sight, you are the apple of His
eye, He loves you. Take time to spell out each word,
write them out to have them before you as a reminder.
You like to keep the letters and photos of those you
love, in the same way keep the words of God close to you.
God has given you a new name as He did to Abraham.
Your name is important! When you call someone by his
given name, you have begun to build a personal relationship with him.

When you have a special name for someone, it is a
sign that you have become someone special for him, that
you have emerged from the anonymous crowd which
smothers us. Friends use nicknames, secret names,
names which only they can truly use.

God has a special name for you, a name that He alone
knows and He reveals it to you at one and the same time
as your vocation takes shape. A Carmelite nun wrote to
me recently how meeting an authentic man of prayer had
revealed her own name to her: "In the ten years that I
have known Dom L.S. he has given me a secret word of
the Lord." And this word commits you, for it expresses
what you do or what your destiny will be. When God calls
you by your name, He knows you to your very depths.

For your name is indeed a call. When a child calls
a woman "Mother" it is a sign that she is truly his
mother. When God named his friend "Abraham" it was
so that he might be "father of nations." The name God
gives you is unique and it is a call to a unique mission.
Have you found your real name? You are the only one
who can love God in this particular way.

To pray is above all this — to know, to believe that
you have a name from God, which is a call to a special
friendship in which you may lose yourself and which
gives meaning to your life. But — and this is out of the
ordinary — because you accept this friendship with God,
God Himself has a new name. From now on His name
in the Bible will be the God of Abraham, the God of Isaac,
the God of Jesus Christ. You will know Him in prayer

and you will call on Him as the God of your own name. He is truly YOUR GOD. He cannot show more clearly that He is a God known in the meeting: "God is not ashamed to be called their God" (Heb 11:16). It is through the way you meet God that others around you will have the chance to find or not find the true face of God. When you are held by God and in turn you call your brothers by name, it is God Who meets them through you.

9. Now suddenly you have become Someone.

These words of Paul Claudel on his conversion could also apply to Christian prayer. Often you wonder what you should say or do in prayer and you put to work all your resources, but this does not express your whole self. Prayer is above all an experience of your very self and of being present. When you meet a friend you are naturally interested in what he says and thinks and does, but your real pleasure is in being with him. The closer you are to him, the more useless, even awkward, words become. Any friendship which has not known this silence is incomplete and unsatisfying. Lacordaire said: "Happy are those friends who love each other enough to be silent together."

Ultimately friendship is the long experience of two people who mutually "tame" each other. They want to get away from the anonymity of life to become unique to each other. "If you tame me, we shall need each other. To me, you will be the only one in the world — I shall be the only one in the world for you" *(Little Prince)*. You suddenly discover that the other has become someone for you and that his presence lifts you up beyond words.

The parable of friendship might help you understand something of the mystery of prayer. Until you have been captivated by the face of God, prayer remains something outside of you, imposed from outside, but it is not that face to face where God has become Someone for you. The path of prayer opens for you on the day when you really experience the presence of God. I can describe the mapping of this experience, but at the end of the description, you will still be on the threshold of the mystery. You can only be admitted by grace, without any merit on your part.

You cannot reduce the presence of God to a "being-there" in a face to face brought about by curiosity, necessity or compulsion, but rather a communion — a going out of yourself towards the Other. It is a sharing, a Passover, a merging of two "I's" into a "We", which is at the same time both gift and welcome.

The presence of God means a sort of death to yourself in that feeling that drives you to want to take over the people who surround you. When you allow God to come in, it is to make an opening in yourself, to open a window on God Whose look is His most meaningful expression. And you know that in God, to look is to love (St. John of the Cross).

In prayer let yourself be captivated by this presence, for He "chose you to be holy and blameless in his sight, to be full of love" (Ep 1:4). Whether you know it or not, this life in the presence of God is real, belonging to the order of faith. It is living for each other, a mutual "face to face" in love. Words become fewer; what need to recall to God what He knows already, since He sees deep down in you and loves you... Prayer is living intensely in this presence, not to think about nor to imagine it. When the Lord thinks fit, He will give you the experience beyond words; all that you will then be able to say or write will seem weak and absurd.

Every dialogue with God assumes that in the background there is the basis of "presence". Once you have fully settled down in this face to face in which you look straight at God, then you can touch on any note in prayer; when it is in tune with this main and basic theme, you are really praying. You can see this being present to God in three lights which take you ever more deeply into the reality. To be present to God is to be before Him, with Him and in Him. You know that in God there is no outside, no inside but a single being, always active; it is from man's point of view that this action can be seen from many angles. Never forget that if you talk to God, it is because He wishes to talk to you. This triple attitude in man matches the three faces of God in the Bible: the God of dialogue is the Holy One, the Friend and the Host.

10. You are before God.

When you have felt the presence of God, the words of the Psalms begin to speak straight to your heart, especially one small word which comes in each verse: "You". If we had to sum up the attitude of the men of prayer in the Bible, we could say that each stood before God, but this God was not an object, an impersonal being. He became a "You".

On a human level you have to stand near a man or a woman to take part in a dialogue. It is dangerous to want to put yourself too quickly into the other's position. It means that, to speak to someone else, you must be yourself. Your presence requires the presence of the other. Before taking part in a dialogue, there has to be a coming together, a face to face situation. The other person transforms you, he *alters* you in the etymological sense.

This is also the first condition for entering into a relationship with God. In the case of Moses, Elijah and Isaiah, each man stood always before God (Ex 33:18-23; Is 6). The one who prays must stand before God, in His presence. Underlying the placing of one's self before God is the belief that God knows the heart of man. "Before I formed you in the womb, I knew you" (Jr 1:5). To know God or to be known by Him, is to enter into a relationship with Him, to be brought close to Him, to feel His presence, to endure His action, and share His life. "But You, Yahweh, You know me, You see me, You examine my heart, it is with You." This says two things at the same time: You stand at a distance. There is an abyss between you and God because of His transcendence. In the Bible you will find nothing resembling pantheism. God is always "Other", distinct from His creature. In pantheism, there is a mixture, a fusion but no real dialogue since the people are not self governing and free.

You are nonetheless near. Despite the difference, you are sure that there is no distance. God is near you and sees you. God's otherness and indwelling are both observed. God is heedful of your complaint, He listens, He understands, He is near, He welcomes you and grants you a hearing. "Truthfully, Yahweh, have I not done my best to serve You... You know I have" (Jr 15:11).

"For Yahweh has heard the sound of my weeping. For Yahweh has heard my petition. Yahweh will accept my prayer" (Ps 6:9).

God is not only a listener, taking care of your requests. He answers you and takes part in a dialogue. "I am here, I call You, You answer me, O God" (Ps 17:6). "You know my heart, You come to me at night" (Ps 17:3).

In fact, God turns His face towards you and in doing that, saves you.

In the Bible those who had the greatest awareness of the nearness of God are also those who had the greatest awareness of the distance and transcendence of God.

Often it is when you do not begin with a sense of the presence of the Holy God that your prayer declines into a monologue. You have to spend enough time in recollection so that you come to prayer in interior peace. Before praying, take a calm walk, breathe deeply and put all your concerns in the hands of the Lord. Take care in the beginning to put yourself fully in the presence of God. If you spend ten minutes becoming aware of this presence, you will not have wasted your time. After that, let the Holy Spirit "take over"; He will initiate your dialogue with the Father.

Bear this well in mind: you are before Him, you are close, you are seen, you are heard, you are loved. "I keep Yahweh always before me, Lord, you are there! (Ps 16:8). When you come to pray, do not continue with old habits, but enter resolutely into the sight of God and go into His dwelling: "My heart clings close to You, Your right hand supports me" (Ps 63:8).

11. You are with God.

In this position of one who is before God, who is understood and considered, there is the beginning of "partnership". This is the second aspect of the dialogue and the second movement, the will to be with this God before Whom you stand. You are with Him, you want to serve Him. It is here that the Jerusalem Bible speaking of Elijah has translated "to stand" in a different way. Instead of saying "the living God before Whom I stand" it says "the living God Whom I serve." Take the measure and strength of this little word "with" — it does not mean just nearness or togetherness, but a friendship in the fullest sense of the word.

Being with God means three things.

— You are in agreement with Him. "He who is not with Me, is against Me", said Christ. This raises the question of your real acceptance of the will of God in your life, your way of thinking and acting. Are you happy with the life God has given you today? Do not play a double game, contradicting in your life what your lips proclaim.

"You are always on their lips, yet so far from their hearts. You know me, Yahweh, you see me. You probe my heart, it is in your hands" (Jr 12:2-3). So the first result for you: "I do Your will, I want to do Your will."

You are united to Him. This is the language of love. Your human heart needs to be excited by the love of Christ: "I delight in nothing else on earth. My flesh and my heart are pining with love. My heart's rock, my own, God for ever" (Ps 73:25-26).

You desire never to be separated from Jesus, you long to be with Him face to face forever: "I long to die to be with You... we shall be with Him forever" (Saint Paul). Your prayer cannot do this without the known and aroused love of God. It is the gift of a warm and loving prayer. Hence the second result for you: "I love You, I want to love You."

— You work with Him. Go back to the text of Mark 3:14 and you will understand how Christ insists that His apostles are His friends and companions: "He appointed twelve to be with Him (Jerusalem Bible translates: 'to be His companions'), to send them out to preach the Good News". This friendship for Jesus is not a vague feeling which comes from your poor heart, but a friendship which comes from Jesus Himself. It is the same love with which Christ loves the Father and men and which He pours into your heart. He Himself said a few hours before His death: "You are my friends, if you do what I command you."

"I shall not call you servants any more, because a servant does not know his master's business; I call you friends because I have made known to you everything I have learned from my Father" (Jn 15:14-15).

An apostle is a man on friendly terms with God, a man who is turned towards Him and meets Him in all His presences.

Reread the dialogue between the Little Prince and the fox and see if you know how to spend time in prayer, letting yourself be sociable with Christ. It is in this time spent freely for Him that He shares the secrets of the Father. Let Him say these words to you: "You are no longer a servant, you are my friend." And you know that for Jesus friendship is not an empty word. He Himself said that He gave His life for His friends. Open your hands to welcome the friendship of Christ.

— A third result is that you work with Christ, you want to work with Him. In prayer develop this attitude of dialogue with God. Call upon Him in a union of will, of friendship and of work. "My joy lies in being close to God" (Ps 73:28).

The Holy Spirit will give you this awareness and this desire to be united with the person of Jesus and His work.

12. You are in God.

To live with someone united in friendship, it is the beginning of closeness. The Old Testament has indeed told us that God lived among His people, even hinting of the presence of the Spirit in the heart of man (Ez 36), but Jesus alone will tell us how far this friendship of God for man extends. God truly makes your heart His dwelling-place.

In Jesus the life of God has been, so to speak, humanised in a being of flesh and blood; that is why He possesses this life in fullness and can communicate it to you by the power of his Spirit. Clinging to Christ in baptism and faith, you become the *dwelling* of God and you are part of the loving relationships which flow between the Persons of the Holy Trinity. Prayer is the awareness of this divine life in you and the desire to be at one with God, despite the immense distance which separates you from Him.

In prayer you consciously exercise this filial relationship. You are His son and you know this since the Spirit intercedes in you. Thus, in the act in which you say to God "Father", you see yourself as son of God. Someone — Who is the very Spirit of God — stands guarantee for you, bears witness for you, convinces you that you are a son of God. You have the obscure but very real experience of this prodigious filial relationship with the Father.

"The proof that you are a son is that God has sent the Spirit of His Son into your heart; the Spirit that cries Abba, Father" (Gal 4:6). In prayer this obscure experience will become more and more clear to your human awareness.

You are right at the heart of that intimacy with God which is part of the experience of the believer as Paul described it in Chapter 8 of his letter to the Romans. You might wonder if such an experience might abolish the distance separating you from the most Holy God. No, Paul was careful in verse 15 to use an expression well known in Roman law, "son by adoption." You are a son by adoption which marks you off from Christ Who was the Son in a real sense, by nature. But a son by adoption is nonetheless a real son. You are a child of God and the

Holy Spirit makes you sure of that. You are in Christ, you are in God, you are in the Trinity.

When you pray, believe in this permanent presence in you of the Holy Trinity — even if you do not feel any actual sound, God lives in you and He calls you to live in Him. You will never pray well if you do not know how to stay for a long time facing this mystery of the Holy Trinity. Let yourself be taken in this movement of love which carried Jesus to the heart of His Father. It is why Christ asks you insistently to live in Him: "May they all be one. Father, may they be one in us, as You are in me and I am in You" (Jn 17:31).

Enter deep into God, into the family of the Trinity through the Incarnate Word. By drawing near to God, you develop your faith through unceasing communion with the divine life. Sustain yourself with the Eucharist to be one with the Trinity: "He who eats my flesh and drinks my blood lives in me and I live in him" (Jn 6:56). By receiving Jesus in communion, you live the very life of the Father and the Spirit. Here you are in the last stage of prayer, the ultimate attitude of the dialogue with God.

Prayer is being present, a partnership, a closeness with the God of Jesus Christ, in the action of the Spirit.

To pray is to be before God, united to Him, to let your whole being abide in Him; your body, mind, heart and will — either in your daily life, your concerns, your work or in the time given especially to prayer. One never works without the other.

13. God shows Himself to you as the Holy One, the Friend and the Host.

If you can stand before God, with Him and in Him, it is because He wanted to show Himself to you as the Holy One, the Friend and the Host. These three names of God as He revealed Himself correspond to your seeing three "Alls" of the God of the Bible. Here are some ideas to help you contemplate this mystery.

God is the One apart, the Entirely Other; He shows Himself as the Holy One. He is the Entirely Other by His infinite, mysterious power. Before Him you are dust and ashes (Gn 18:27) for all is nothingness except Him (Is 40:25 and 45:5). When He shows Himself to you, He shows Himself in the transcendence of His being, that is in His glory which is the radiant force of His presence and His life (Ex 3:6; Is 6:1-5; Ez 1:28). You can only fall face down on the ground and adore Him. He is also the Entirely Other in His infinite moral purity which makes you feel your innate impurity (Is 6:5). If the men of prayer in the Bible knew they were before God, witnesses of His glory, it is because His holiness was revealed to them. This is the first objective indication of dialogue with God. To adore God is to feel His greatness and at the same time to recognize your own wretchedness.

But God never reveals His unapproachable greatness without at the same time revealing His love which is why He is the friend of man. God is He who loves (Ho 11:13) and He is also the One who loves you. "You are my friends" said Jesus. It is a confidence told from mouth to mouth, a revelation. On the human face of Jesus you discover friendship (Tt 3:4) and the tenderness God has for you. The proof that He is your friend is that He shares the secrets of the Father with you as one does with friends.

Today still, just as in the time of the prophets, God says to you: "I am with you." The risen Christ will stay with his own until the end of time. He knows you by your name for He loves you and gave Himself up for you. The revelation of the intimacy of the thrice Holy God in Jesus Christ is the second objective indication of this dialogue. Between you and God there is a relationship of friendship. Between the Holy One and you, Jesus is your friend. If you can be with Him, it is because He wanted to be with you. Emmanuel: God with us. Ask Saint John, "the disciple Jesus loved" (Jn 13:23), to let you feel the friendship of Christ.

Above all, He will teach you to live in God while living in constant communion with the personality of Jesus. In

Jesus, — the permanent dwelling of God at the heart of the world — God has set up His tent among us. By the gift of his Spirit, Jesus is the one who makes you live in God. If you eat His body, if you live as He did and keep His word, the Holy Trinity will take up its home in you. God becomes your guest, as He was for Abraham by the oak of Mamre: "If anyone loves me, he will keep my word and my Father will love him, and We shall come to him, and make our home with him" (Jn 14:23).

The deepest part of the mystery of the dialogue of prayer is the presence of God in you. If you can be in God, it is because He wanted to be in you. The relationship of the indwelling of the Divine Persons in you is the third objective indication of your dialogue with God. There is no more beautiful definition of the intimacy that can be established between God and you in prayer than that found in the Book of Revelation: "Look, I am standing at the door, knocking. If one of you hears me calling and opens the door, I will come in to share his meal side by side with him" (Rv 3:20).

Father de Beaurecueil tells of this sixteen-year-old Afghan boy who said to him one day: "You come and eat at my house, then I shall come and eat at your house, then we shall be friends."

14. It is not you who begs God to come to you, but it is He who asks you to open your heart and your hands to welcome His Son, Jesus.

You have a climber's mentality and every day you set off to storm God, to overcome Him by sheer force. Or you might ask God to come to you, reminding Him politely that He seems to have forgotten. Such a prayer and such an attitude make no sense nor should they exist in a Christian. You cannot try to seduce God by your offerings and your prayers.

Long ago God came towards you and seduced you. He first loved you to the extent that he gave His Son Jesus Christ to save you. You no longer need to look for

Him since He has filled the gap that separated you from Him. God needs no persuading, He has long since come right into the midst of His own people, but the tragic thing is that you have not accepted Him: "He came to His own domain and His own people did not accept Him" (Jn 1:11). To pray is simply to allow God to look for you and find you.

Basically, all the teaching about God is to remind you of this presence, this coming of the Son into the world. The world is not a desert where God is absent but it conceals the hidden presence of Christ. Think a little about Lent which might seem a sad and dull time because you stress your efforts to do penance, whereas it is above all a time of grace and salvation. Throughout this time God offers the presence of His Son, Who died and rose again. You do not have to perform feats of valour to reach Him for He is there, within your reach, and He offers Himself freely in the bread of the Word and the Eucharist.

What is asked of you is a prolonged contemplation of the love of God which is always coming to meet you. St. Theresa of Lisieux spoke of this faith in the love of God: "How much more does Your love long to enkindle souls since Your mercy rises to the heavens... O my Jesus, may I be that happy victim, consume Your holocaust in the fire of Your divine love!"

You will discover this love, not by your own efforts, but in silent, intense prayer. God will tear away the veil and will show you the treasures of love contained in the heart of His Son. This awareness of God's love is a mysterious grace, impossible to put into words and in human concepts, but if one day you experience it, you will understand why St. Dominic and St. Francis wept whole nights saying, "Love is not loved!"

If you receive the grace of this discovery, you will realize how hard and impervious is your heart. Your great sin is knowingly to refuse to allow yourself to be loved by God. Christ never stops knocking at the door of your heart so that you will open it and share the meal of friendship with Him. May the Holy Spirit break your heart of stone and through this opening He will clear a way for love's invasion.

In prayer you do not ask God to change His mind and to come all the way to you to love you, but on the contrary you dig deep into your stony heart, so that you may change your own attitude and finally accept the love of God.

Lent is the ideal time for this coming of God into your life. Give yourself up to inner silence to hear God's voice better. He becomes present in Jesus and calls you to share in the intimacy of the Trinity. Do not imitate the blind Pharisees who did not see the coming of the Father in Jesus.

To be converted is to agree to open your heart to the infinite love of God and that is to open wide your hands to receive the Eucharistic bread. Then, you will see what signs of penitence will help you best to welcome Christ. But the essential thing is to be, throughout every day and night, in a state of watching and listening so that you do not miss this rendez-vous with love.

15. "It is proper to God's goodness to make, but it is proper to human nature to be made" (Saint Irenaeus).

I shall translate these words of Irenaeus in another way: "You must let yourself be loved, let yourself be acted upon by God." All your human and spiritual difficulties come from the fact that you want to build yourself up and achieve self-fulfilment by yourself. You believe that holiness is a tower to build by sheer strength and the same for prayer, fraternal life and the unifying of your life. You do not pray, but the Spirit prays in you and a genuine community is not a human achievement but the work of the Trinitarian love.

True prayer and the other graces are the gifts which come from on high. You must receive them, welcome them and give them a soil where they can grow and flourish. The tiny seed of divine life deposited in you at baptism contains its own germ-cell dynamics of growth. This is the meaning of the parable of the mustard seed and the yeast in the dough. Reread often in Mark 4:26-29 the parable of the seed that grows by itself. "While he sleeps and when he is awake, day and night, the seed is sprouting and grows without his knowledge." The peasant knows that the lapse of time separating sowing from harvest is an element of growth, part of the work. The same is true of a mother; she gives life to the child, but afterwards she must observe the stages of growth and of human maturing.

Stop rushing around; the fulfilment of your life is not a natural effect or a proud conquest by your will but a gift of grace. All your troubles stem from the clash between your short, limited personal views and the broad spacious aims of God. You want self-fulfilment according to a plan you dreamed of in your little self-improvement workshop, and God has a far better design of love for you. Give up your aims of wanting to make something of yourself and let God act, even if you don't understand His plan. It would never occur to you to judge a play at the end of the first act... At the end of your life, you will be amazed at God's plan of love for you.

To begin with, be sure that God loves you since He has let you share His very life which must grow throughout your own life. So you must reckon with time — do not wish to be today what you will be tomorrow, with time and the grace of God. He builds up the inner man in you, He breaks down and destroys the mountains of sin. Do not impose your ideas, your plans, your desires on Him — His are far better.

He only expects one thing from you: let yourself go, but be careful — to let oneself drift with God does not mean just to let oneself live — time will only bear fruit in you if you decide to love God completely in good will. Without active abandonment to God, your spiritual being will break up into a multitude of whims. God does not work with a magic wand which would excuse us from a burdensome faithfulness.

But from the time that you give yourself up to God without reserve, without conditions, letting Him act as He deems best and preferring nothing but His will, then you will find joy and peace. Every happening is a gift from the hand of God and it will shape your interior being according to the will of the Father. "When you have done your best" wrote Teilhard de Chardin "then all that happens is good, this is the last word in human wisdom and holiness." When you have abandoned yourself to God, every event whether good or bad, transforms you from within and brings you closer to God.

Your very sin and your weaknesses, provided they are known, regretted and forgiven, can push you forward. Your action and your daily efforts in a humdrum repetition can become part of the current of interior life flowing in you. This inner perfection created by God alone grows little by little and He works in you inasmuch as you let yourself be shaped to His image. To understand this work of God, you need the perspective of faith and long and intense prayer.

II

The Way of Salvation

16.   The love of God for you takes flesh in Jesus Christ.

God was not satisfied just to say He loves you; one day in time He became man, someone like yourself with flesh and blood and consciousness. You don't need a college education to understand what a human being is. Feeling yourself alive, able to love and cry is enough. A man was born, lived and died and he was God: Jesus of Nazareth, son of Mary, son of God. If you have known the thrice Holy God, you cannot help being amazed, astounded, dumbfounded before the mystery of Jesus.

He is wholly God, without reservation, without difference; He is wholly man, without reservation and without difference in His humanity: "Not only a man is born in Bethlehem, works in Nazareth, speaks to the crowds of Palestine, cries out in fear at Gethsemane and dies in Jerusalem; God is born, works, speaks, cries out and dies" (J.P. Deconchy). Jesus embodies the link between God and man and man and God and for this, His very existence was enough, he needed to do nothing more. It is truly the love of God for you that took flesh in Jesus Christ. Receive the Incarnate Word in your heart and examine tirelessly the mystery of His personality. Often ask Him to plunge you into the heart of God and into the heart of man. When you contact Jesus Christ in faith, you discover your true dimension as a human being who has become the house of God.

Something has changed radically in the heart of the world since Christ pitched His tent among us. Mankind has entered into God and God has penetrated all earthly reality to the very heart of the universe. In Jesus Christ the presence of God shines out to the centre of the world and above all to the heart of man. We can no longer speak of God without speaking of man, nor talk of man without naming God which led Saint Jerome to say: "No man is born without Christ."

You will find your complete human fulfilment only by penetrating deeper each day into the mystery of that perfect human being which is Christ and through Him into the Mystery of the Trinity. In Jesus you meet not only the Father, but you are one with your brothers in their yearnings for God.

Too often you set prayer and life against each other, service of God and service of your brothers, contemplation and action. The day when you know the depths of the mystery of Christ, there will be no more opposition. Since God has met man in Christ, there is nothing profane or unhallowed (etymologically *pro — fanum*, before the temple, outside the temple), since God has come out of His temple, His "heavenly dwelling," to live in the midst of His creation. He is right here, present and alive in these daily chores that you perform more or less successfully. By living completely in your daily routine and your relationships with others, you reunite yourself with Christ and through Him, with the Father.

It is now, in your daily life, in your daily work, in the love of your brother that you must meet Jesus. Kneel in prayer before the Father, continually begging Him to understand that "Christ lives in your heart through faith" (Ep 3:17). Believe in His presence within you, says the Rule of Taizé, even if you do not feel any perceptible reaction. Use every resource at your disposal to send this prayer to the Father, for the Spirit of Jesus must live in you. Then, a little at a time, the Holy Spirit will give you light and strength to "grasp the breadth and the length, the height and the depth... you will know the love of Christ which is beyond all knowledge'' (Ep 3:18-19).

The awareness of the presence of Christ must be deeply rooted in you. It is the only aim and object of prayer. If you spend your whole prayer time asking for this grace, you would adopt the outlook of God about yourself. Know that what you ask for so persistently, corresponds to the Father's will. He waits for you to open your pleading hands so that He may set His Son there.

17. **You may know your faults, but that does not mean you have a sense of sin, for that comes in a revelation from God. Pray first of all before examining your conscience.**

You understand now that true knowledge is a revelation. It does not come from an intellectual process but in humble prostration of your very self before the Holy God. As K. Rahner says: "If your theology is no longer a theology on your knees, in the sense that it must be the theology of one who prays..., it will degenerate into a dilettantism for belated bourgeois.''

The same is true for the knowledge of your sinfulness. You may know the sins you have committed — failings in observing a rule or an established order, but that does not mean you have a sense of sin. The recognition of your sins stirs up in you a remorseful conscience and a guilty feeling, but not true repentance.

To have a real sense of your sinfulness, you have to have a relationship with God. Whereas prayer is a presence before God, sin seems like an absence, a refusal to accept yourself from God, an obstacle to His love. You can only know your sinfulness if God reveals it to you, just as true knowledge of God is the work of grace.

So here you see an outline of a first spiritual law: when you want to discover your sinfulness, self examination is less important than intense prayer. "Lord, may I know Thee and may I know myself'' (St. Augustine).

What you ask the Lord for is not just an exact list of your sins as you might make an account of your breaking traffic regulations — that is the work of your reason —, but you ask Him for the supernatural knowledge of a hidden reality. You know that to confess your sin is not to tell it to a priest so that he knows it, but to acknowledge it to God, who has first acknowledged you in expressing His love to you.

You ask God to let you know fully how far you are from Him. Sin is not in itself an objective reality; it is not the violation of a law which brings about a want of grace, but man before God in an attitude of disagreement, refusal. The sinner is he who turns his back on God and who refuses to accept his being from Him. By this very fact, he is no longer present to himself, which is why sin causes a disintegration of human nature. The sinner, like the prodigal son, goes away from the Father into a faraway country, selfishly enjoying the gifts received without connecting them to the giver. Instead of using his benefits to enter into communion with Him, he uses them for his own profit. The sinner is one who has lost his way and is far from God, in exile. He is outside the truth since for him, to be true, means to be in communion with the Father.

The tragedy of the sinner is that he does not suffer from this, he is even unaware of it — on the contrary, he feels a certain happiness. It is only on the day that his eyes are opened to the love of the Father that the prodigal son discovers the depth of his misery. Sin has not only separated him from his Father, but it has cut himself off from himself and the community of his brothers. Sin makes a crack in you and in the human family and this brings suffering and death. As Gabriel Marcel says: "We are in a broken world."

In standing before God, you really are like a blind man. Like the Psalmist you recognize that you have gone far away from Him, breaking off a loving relationship. "Having sinned against none other than you, having done what you regard as wrong" (Ps 51:6). Going deeper still you admit, not only your actions, but a state of sinfulness: "You know I was born guilty, a sinner from the moment of conception" (Ps 51:7). You do not however know your real sin which is not necessarily the sin of weakness which you denounce and bewail, but the sin deep down which you love and call by a smooth name: "Wash out my hidden faults" (Ps 19:13).

In the light of His love, God will open your blind eyes and pierce you with the painful revelation of your sinfulness. This rending apart is much deeper and more painful than all your scruples and guilt feelings... Pray as long as you must to obtain this revelation; you will recognize it by the austere peace it creates in you. A sense of sinfulness is always painful, but then it comes together with confidence in the merciful love of God Who forgives us. May you receive this knowledge of sinfulness that has made the great saints weep.

18. In Christ's loving look at you, you receive both the revelation of His heart and that of your sinfulness.

Since you are not left to yourself in the intense prayer, it is helpful to consider the revelation of sin in the Bible. Reread quietly, a little at a time, the prayer of the exiles (Ba, ch. 1:15-3:8; Ps 25 and 51; the story of the fall, Gn, ch. 3; Rm, ch. 1-7; Jr, ch. 2-11; Is, ch. 1-12; Ho, ch. 1-3). You will place yourself in this story of sinfulness and you will understand that this comes from higher up and further back than you, and that Satan is its author. After the fall of Adam, humanity has been engulfed in sin which makes you know your deep wretchedness.

But, at the same time, you discover an uplifting fact. God never reveals man's sin just to make him feel his weakness and wretchedness, but at once shows him the Savior. You see your sin in the very act of being forgiven. Reread Rm 5:12-20, and you will see that St. Paul never speaks of Adam without speaking of Christ the Savior at the same time. "But the gift itself considerably outweighed the fall. If it is certain that through one man's fall so many died, it is even more certain that divine grace, coming through the one man, Jesus Christ, came to so many as an abundant free gift" (Rm 5:15).

When your sin is forgiven, at the same time you find out its malice and spite. When your friend forgives you your hateful behavior, don't you see at the same moment, both his love and your ingratitude? Don't strain, don't rush, stop looking at the sin in you, but look instead at the eyes of God and you will know how much He loves you in your wretchedness.

St. John Chrysostom says on this matter: "God discloses your evil to you only when you already have your Redeemer and have been healed by Him." Wait patiently for the revelation of yourself which God wants to give you today; you cannot bear everything now. "If you knew your sins you would lose heart. You will know them as you expiate them and you will be told: 'See the sins that you are forgiven... Fear not, your conversion is my concern. I love you more ardently than you loved your filthiness'" (Blaise Pascal). This is why you must own up to this sin, for this is the sin God wants to forgive you — the other sins are only the results of this.

In the Gospel there is a vivid illustration of this second spiritual law concerning sin. It is found when Peter meets Jesus during His Passion. Peter believes he knows and loves Jesus, but he is not aware of his threefold denial and he is still concerned with it as a fault: "The Lord turned and looked straight at Peter and Peter remembered what the Lord had said to him: 'Before the cock crows today, you will have disowned Me three times' and he went outside and wept bitterly" (Lk 22: 61-62).

In this look, Peter received the revelation both of Christ's love for him and that of his sin. He discovered his real sin which was to refuse to see a particular aspect of Jesus (the injured face of the Suffering Servant). This is the sin that God wanted him to weep over. There are others which are the result of this fundamental sin, but at that moment, it was this sin that God wanted to forgive. Peter could not be fully aware of his sin when he had not seen the face of infinite love which he was hurting.

This is why the discovery of your sin does not come from introspection, but from the contemplation of Christ on the cross. In the bruised face of Jesus, you see the infinite love that God has for you, the sinner. You know your need of Christ and His forgiveness. You cannot discover this face without discovering at the same time what you are rejecting in your heart. This is your real sin. But discovering your sin is less important than discovering Christ — then you are close to the blessing of tears.

19. You do not believe in Satan's work — it is not surprising that you are so far from God. The closer you are to God, then the greater is your understanding of the mystery of evil.

Who today dares to speak of Satan — unless he doesn't mind appearing out of date? Yet, without him, how can we understand to what depths parts of old Europe sank not too long ago? You do not have to go far to find today real oppression, torture and cruelty practised by some in the name of order. What a priest who escaped from one of Hitler's concentration camps wrote thirty years ago, could still be written today: "I have come back from hell."

There is not just this physical violence but the results of our consumer society. How can we explain the crudity of certain books and shows without seeing a real will to degrade people? A well known film critic Henri Agel spoke recently of "a world in dissolution." We could add to the list by wondering what further elaborate techniques or publicity will be invented to plunge the world yet further into the shadows.

Some days we need to reread Bernanos who in *The Sun of Satan* makes one of the priests say: "My child, evil just like good, is loved for itself and served for itself."

Truly, in the world there is a mystery of evil and Jesus himself revealed its author, "inventor mali," the inventor of evil, Satan. He has been spoken of in such simple minded imagery that no one believes in his reality any more. Yet he is there, cowering in the shadows. His greatest cleverness, his greatest lie — for he is the "father of lies" (Jn 8:44) — is to persuade you that he does not exist. He is the adversary lying in wait for your lust, the evil one who never tires of the same deceitful, lying song that he hummed to the first man.

As with Bernanos' characters, the presence of Satan in someone cannot be exposed unless that person comes before the mystery of grace. In the Gospel, the possessed cannot endure the presence of the Son of God. Jesus and Satan are essentially opposed in character. The same holds in the case of a person surrounded by truth, love and purity. Satan cannot bear his presence and would kill him if he could, to avoid this confrontation.

Bear this in mind: the more you are given over to the thrice Holy God, the more you will be aware of the presence of sin and evil, both in you and in the world. It will not appear certainly in extraordinary events, but an increased perception of the mystery of evil. A true man of God arouses not only grace, but an unleashing of the forces of evil.

The presence of Christ drives out the presence of Satan, for they are totally opposed to each other. You will understand why Jesus called Satan the liar and the father of lies. Jesus does not live for Himself, He lives for the Father and does His will (Jn 8:44). His centre of gravity is the Father, that is why He is the Truth since He lives in harmony with the Father.

In the opposite case, the devil and the sons of darkness do not want to acknowledge their relationship to God. They shut themselves in on themselves and on their gifts, to become their own centre. There is no truth in them because there is no reference to, no relationship with the Father. In effect Satan denies God and men; if he could, he would kill them; that is why Jesus accuses him of murder: "He was a murderer from the start, he was never grounded in the truth; there is no truth in him at all, when he lies he is drawing on his own store, because he is a liar and the father of lies" (Jn 8:44).

Now you understand why Satan fights relentlessly against Christ and the sons of light. Jesus is totally "eucharist" since He is given up to the Father. Satan is "absence of eucharist" because he is closed in on himself. Thus you discover what is the sign of the presence of Satan in the world, what characterizes sin. It is neither weakness, nor ignorance, but an attitude of shutting one's self off from God in order to achieve self-fulfilment by yourself. Clouzot said of the time before his conversion: "I think the real sin I committed when I was fifteen or sixteen years old was wanting to be myself by myself." Satan can disguise himself as an angel of light and point out some good he finds in you as the sole purpose of your existence, as he did to Jesus when he tempted Him in the desert. On the contrary, prayer opens you more and more to love and sets you against the mystery of evil.

20. "My sacrifice is a contrite spirit; you will not spurn a contrite and broken heart" (Ps 51:19).

You will be truly converted when, like Peter, you experience tears of contrition, your heart is literally crushed, that is, broken in pieces by the revelation of God's love. You can be tortured by the desire to follow Christ more closely or oppressed by the need to be free of your sin, but this does not mean you have a sense of sinfulness. All this can increase your repentance, but contrition is truly something else: the fruit of a wonderful gift from God which purifies you by the blood of Christ in the sacrament of penance.

Then you must have a broken, crushed heart as David did after his sin. This is something different from being aware of your sin or having the desire to love Christ which are no more than feelings coming from your own heart. Contrition is "the painful revelation (usually coming from the sight of Christ on the Cross) of the Infinite Love that God has for us and the nameless cruelty of our indifference towards Him" (Fr. Molinié).

You yourself cannot obtain this blessing of tears; it would be a strained and artificial feeling. To be authentic, you ask the Lord to draw "tears of contrition from your heart of stone." You can say this prayer all your life and it will always be true. True contrition is the work of grace, therefore of prayer; it springs from the discovery of "Someone": God, present and calling you. Such a meeting will upset your life and give new meaning to your existence. Christian clearsightedness is the result of knowing the living God. The unrepentant man is blind: having known neither the Father nor the Son, he does not recognize his sinfulness. The penitent is one who sees, he has recognized the coming and the call of God in Jesus Christ; his eyes have been opened.

The more you know God, the more you will know yourself to be a sinner, but a sinner who has been forgiven. It is the sorrowful prodigal son and not the elder son who really knows the Father. In this, you discover the link between your baptism and repentance which, as St. Augustine says, is a daily baptism, that is the sign in which each day you show your baptismal faith. To show the link between conversion and your painful awareness of your sinfulness, St. Augustine defines repentance as baptism by tears, referring to baptism of water and the Spirit.

You will understand how this feeling of sinfulness will encourage and invigorate you, whereas the feeling of guilt will depress and discourage you, leading perhaps to arrogance. You are a sinner, which means you need Jesus Christ, but you need not be discouraged, for you know in Whom you have placed your trust. In Him you can do all He asks and your sin is a means of grace. Without Him your life has no meaning.

You must actually undergo an "initiation" in order to receive an understanding and a sense of sin; you cannot yourself instigate such an upheaval. In prayer, free yourself from childish and sterile fears of sin which are caricatures of true contrition. Your real sin is to have a heart of stone (Ez 36:26) and you are not grieved by it. You remain unfeeling towards God's infinite kindness because of the shell around your heart, developed during years of hardening. Deep down, you do not truly accept that you must build your Christian life on a free gift of God.

If you do see your heart of stone and your unconscious refusal to allow yourself to be loved by God, then you are threatened by an invasion of love. You know how the love of Christ is hurt by your indifference as any ardent love is hurt by the thoughtlessness of the person loved. But for you to have a heart crushed by tears of repentance, the Holy Spirit must intervene and wake you from your deep sleep. In the sacrament of penance, the actual coming of the Spirit will burst open the shell around your heart of stone, freeing the inner presence of the Spirit Who can pray to the Father.

21. Let yourself meet Christ — this is the greatest grace.

In Jesus you know the fullness of God and you deepen your own true humanity. You must go to Him then as the foundation and source of your life. At every age, you must rediscover Christ as a living person Who will unify and give meaning to your desires and a direction to your life. Life becomes unliveable when we do not look for the living Christ with all our strength. Like Paul you can say: "For me to live is Christ." Is Jesus the reason of your own life? Do you thirst to see Him, to speak to Him, to be united to Him, in a word to meet Him face to face? So long as you have a small part in your life which has not been set afire by Jesus, you are not living by the Gospel.

So you must meet Him and keep visiting Him each hour of the day, so that you become one being with Him. Jesus is not an historical character nor an event out of the past. By His Resurrection, He has become a living mystery which you can experience spiritually. Do not try to meet Him in some interstellar space. He is near you, in you, since He lives in your heart by faith.

You can personally experience Jesus, alive and present in you. Even if I describe Him visually, make comments on the Gospel, talk of His psychology, if you have not met Him in an intimate and living touch, then my words are only "sounding brass." There are too many apostles who speak of Jesus Christ without living and experiencing Him inwardly. Do not stay aloof from the events described in the Gospels — it is always Jesus and His mystery who stand in the centre of the story.

Don't think you will meet Christ unless you give long periods to contemplating Him in silent prayer. Let Him be the only object of your attention and your heart. Aim your camera at Jesus, trying to find the secret of His mystery beyond His face and his words. You are not seeking Him, He wants to show Himself to you. Jesus answered the man born blind who wanted to know the Son of God: "You are looking at Him, He is speaking to you" (Jn 9:37). Do not compete with Him in affection but let Him love you.

Jesus speaks to you in your most hidden feelings; He unveils His glory to you and asks only one question: "Who am I to you?" You cannot answer without the profound action of the Holy Spirit Who works in you to reveal Christ to you. So, reverse the question, saying to Him: "Who are You, Lord?" Looking at you, Christ's face will be shown and it is then that the bond of friendship will be born where two people look directly at each other.

You must come to a knowledge of Jesus without a mediator or proxy. What you ask here in prayer is not the external knowledge gained from the work of your mind or an effort of will, but the coming of Jesus to you. The knowledge that comes from this is that of a being known and loved from within, beyond words or things.

St. John found this personal experience of Jesus. Ask him for this grace while savouring these words: "Something which has existed since the beginning, that we have heard and we have seen with our own eyes; that we have watched and touched with our hands; the Word who is life... we are telling you" (1 Jn 1:3).

In allowing yourself to be met by Jesus you will enjoy His presence and friendship, but He will not hold you for Himself since He is wholly directed towards the Father. This is the paradox of encountering Jesus: the more familiar and intimate we become with Jesus, the more human we are, and we move to the heart of the Father. You have not come to the end of sounding such depths. The meeting with Jesus sends you back to others — "Go to my brothers" to announce the Good News you have found, and which alone is able to satisfy men's hearts.

22. Blessed are you if you have caught the "sickness" of Jesus — you will never be healed but you will have true life.

Contact with most of the unbelievers around you can seriously challenge your faith. Someone will tell you that your faith is the product of an outdated priest-led civilization or the result of a middle class society which invented God to quieten the revolt of the poor. If you ask anything of psychology, the reply will be still more painful. You will find out that your faith is burdened by determinism, begun in infantilism and a need for security, that you have not yet wiped out; or by fear or a need to escape loneliness. Some days you wonder if you have not built your life on an idealistic dream and if you are not wasting your time, praying and living for others. This temptation throbs more painfully since you have put all your strength in Jesus and in His Kingdom.

Do not reject any of these questions — let yourself be open to questions by unbelievers and also by those interpretations which come from within. It is good that you share in your own person this agony that men feel when confronted by their destiny. Like Theresa of Lisieux, you are with sinners and you are going through the long tunnel of darkness. Don't be superior about your knowledge of religion and don't think you have a right to speak of God as if you had seen Him, or of Heaven, as if you had visited it.

Your faith is being purified of all the idols and false goods that you make all your life to protect yourself from the true God. You reach a certain stage where every reason to believe becomes a reason to doubt. Then, in the depth of night, will come this little spark which has lighted the way for years. There is a conviction, deep inside you, a belief you have never abandoned, even if it is fragile and only seems to hand by a thread. You have left everything for this belief, known poverty and loneliness. You want it to give direction to your whole life.

If you dig down deeper, you will find that at one time, the face of Christ was revealed to you, He fascinated you, leaving you no rest, so much so that you have sacrificed everything for Him. Of course, you did not see Him with your bodily eyes. His face is still veiled, but He has left His mark in your heart and many years later you know this, since otherwise your life would have no meaning. Like Paul you can say: "Life to me is Christ" (Ph 1:21). On the wall of her cell, Theresa of Lisieux wrote with a pin: "Jesus is my only love", and you know that she did not have a bright and shining meeting with Christ every day.

This is where you must look for the source of your vocation to prayer, for the mystery of a river is always the mystery of its source. It is strange but true, some people have a passion for prayer. They are driven by desire, by a thirst to pray, to find the face of Christ at any cost. They are not better than others, they are more aware of their sinfulness, but even in the depths of their wretchedness and poverty, they cannot separate themselves from Jesus' face of Glory and from His person. They long to spend endless happy hours, living in the radiance of His presence. Even in their sleep, this irresistible occupation rises in their hearts. Like Charles de Foucauld, they are only happy in a loving dialogue with their beloved brother and Lord, Jesus.

You are blessed if such a grace has come to you. You will never be cured of this longing for Jesus Christ. Bear in mind too that you have a secret which must shine to the ends of the universe. You can be buried at the heart of the world with no way to tell your brothers that the face of Christ is burning you, yet your faith reaches to the ends of the earth. This is nothing for you to be proud of, it is a free gift of God. So, day or night, in suffering, in the wilderness, in the joys of friendship, alone or among your brothers, attentive of absent-minded, you will feel yourself drawn by this mysterious presence of Jesus. The heart of Jesus will have a magnetic appeal for you, nor will you ever be able to forget Christ.

23. Every day of your life you must say: I cling to Jesus, I give myself up to Him.

A friend of mine, after a painful experience in which he had become aware of his inherent poverty, said to me: "My sin makes me still more in love with Jesus Christ." True, he had had to rechoose Christ by dedicating himself to Him again. You are sober while thinking of your sinfulness, but you are not discouraged for you have caught a glimpse in God's forgiveness of the love of Jesus Who gives Himself up to you. St. Theresa of Lisieux said: "Love is only paid with love." This is why you now begin the work of renewing your faith in Christ.

Sometimes you believe it is enough to choose Christ just at the important stages of your life. This is not so, each day you must live the Good News. So, every year at Easter, the Church invites you to renew your faith in Christ. Since He is the purpose and the source of your life, you must "acknowledge" Him each day. This means not just an intellectual act of faith, but directing your whole life so that it conforms to Christ's way of thinking and acting and loving.

Certainly, there are stages in your life where the choice is radical, since it is a choice which deals with the depths of your being and your destiny. This is the case of the choice made in adolescence or between the ages of forty and fifty when you want to add a dimension of love and liberty to your life. This choice, the most profound expression of your personality, always remains possible. Often it provokes or resolves a crisis of growth in your personal history, for it polarizes and unites all your desires around Christ. It gives new meaning to your life and marks you, both in time and in eternity.

Pray intensely and ask for the desire and will to respond to the love of Jesus, giving yourself totally to Him. You want to renew today, with full knowledge and all the strength of your being, the offering made at baptism. You want to aim at yet greater love and, with the grace of God, to serve His Kingdom.

In prayer, you must put yourself resolutely before Jesus Who wills to fulfil you completely. Jesus is alive. He lives in your heart by faith. What does it matter if you do not feel His presence, the essential thing is that He is there.

Reread John 1:35-51, the first meeting of the disciples and Jesus. Let yourself be questioned by Him: "What do you want?" (1:38). Make Andrew and John's answer your own: "Rabbi, where do You live?" Then follow Christ, that is, enter into the profound mystery of knowing Him and stay with Him all day long.

You can spend a day with your best friends, why not spend one day with Christ, living intimately with Him? If you can remain waiting silently for Him, He will let you experience His presence, you will have the "grace" of His presence. Spend the day simply reading the Gospel, allowing the words of Jesus to drop one by one into your heart. In this way His thought and His love will enter into you.

He will be able to reveal the secret of His inner self, He will write his real name on your heart, and above all, He will give Himself to you in a friendship which no human word can express. You will hear Him ask this ultimate question: "My son, give me your heart." May you answer Him with the "yes" of Mary at the Annunciation.

24. Jesus Christ meets you at the crossroads where your life takes shape.

"I bring you good news... a saviour has been born to you; He is Christ the Lord" (Lk 2:10-11). Do you know what is good news? Ask those who lived in the concentration camps and who, one fine morning, saw the Allied troops arrive — they will tell you! Well, the coming of Christ on the earth is positive good news, a statement which unites the deepest values in your life. St. John ends his Gospel pointing out his aims clearly: "These (signs) are recorded so that you may believe that Jesus is the Christ, the Son of God and that, believing this, you may have life through His name" (Jn 20:31). The Gospel is revealed Truth inasmuch as it reaches you at the decisive point where your life takes shape. You can know "the fact" of Jesus Christ, but if He is not your Saviour, you do not have faith.

The first time Jesus spoke to anyone it was to ask: "What do you want?" (Jn 1:38). Announcing the good news, Christ tries to reach you through the values you consider vital and urgent. Paul said he sought man's deepest aspirations *(a-spirare)*, that to which he ultimately aspires, the degree of excellence in your deepest desires. When Jesus met men who were no longer seeking anything, He "disturbed" them in the good sense of the word and started them searching again. See how He reached deeply into the heart of the Samaritan woman, discerning in her a desire for God, which was hidden by sin, and offering her living water.

Paul said: "May the Word of God live in your hearts." In giving you the Gospel, Jesus puts his Word "in" your heart. The heart is really the source of your whole life, beyond your intelligence or the experience of your moral life. Pope Paul VI addressing the representatives of the United Nations spoke the same language: "We shall listen to these profound voices of the world." Jesus seeks not only the aspirations of individuals but He responds to those of entire nations.

You must allow these desires which lie deep in you

to rise to your consciousness. You must also listen to the voices of the modern world and share in its aspirations, the call of the youth for freedom, for sharing, for real experience, for success in the future, for peace, dignity, and justice. Listen to what the other person is saying without rejection. Like him you hope for light, peace, liberty, holiness, good fortune. Jesus brings all these things when He comes to you. To perceive these voices, you must be aware of the invisible activity of the Spirit, in you and in your brothers. Prayer is not a waste of time when you become aware of these aspirations and lay them open to the sight of Jesus the Saviour.

You are hungry for bread and food, but this material hunger expresses a deeper hunger: you want to live happily and escape the agonizing tragedy of death.

You aspire after knowledge and enlightenment, not that which comes from science and technology, which is the work of human intelligence, but understanding of your own life. You want to discover the meaning of your life. True, man has a hunger for justice and for love, but he has a still greater hunger for meaning: "Where have you come from? Where are you going?" Man today hungers more for meaning than for food, he needs reassurance more than power. You run after life without any hope of catching up at the last moment, just as one jumps on the steps of a train which has begun to leave (Ionesco). How many men think of being alive as a misfortune. "Man is a useless passion," said Sartre.

You want to love and be loved. You cannot be satisfied with consumer goods and the rewards of power. You are made to meet people, to smile, exchange looks, to share. You want to escape from loneliness and you need to be known by another to get a feeling of inner well being.

Furthermore, you want freedom, physical freedom, psychological freedom which will save you from determinism, and moral freedom snatching you away from sin.

Finally, you need God. Whoever he is, man aspires to holiness, to see God even if the desire is covered by the mud of welfare society. You are made for God and you are only happy when you rest in Him: "Man's only problem, as far as I know" wrote Albert Camus "is how to be a saint without God."

It cannot be done... but there is Jesus Christ.

25. Christ satisfies and infinitely surpasses all man's aspirations.

Thanks to the Holy Spirit, you will understand in your prayer that Jesus is your Saviour. What does this mean? He fulfils and exceeds all your hopes and yearnings. Faith does not come from outside to show a way out, it discloses the meaning of what you are living, starting by the questions you ask yourself.

Certainly the salvation brought by Christ is supernatural, that is, over and above your expectations, but the divine life that He transmits to you is not foreign to your human life, but fulfils it perfectly. Your calling to the supernatural is not plastered on from the outside, it belongs to your human state, and is seen as its completion; by grace, it is fully accomplished. To believe in Jesus Christ is to encounter Him as the beginning and source of true life; it is to know in Him the ultimate meaning of your personal life in society and in history.

The communion, joy and holiness that Jesus brings you, go far beyond anything you might humanly expect. This is why man is astonished, stunned by the salvation Yahweh brings (Is 52:15 and Is 54). "They were amazed at what the shepherds told them." All who met Christ in the Gospel are filled with joy (Zacchaeus, the Samaritan woman, etc.), for they have found the pearl of the Kingdom. The salvation brought by Christ goes beyond but also responds to and fulfils your human expectations. He more than satisfies. How does Christ fulfil your aspirations?

He gives bread to nourish and fill you, in your hunger to live: "Whoever eats my flesh and drinks my blood has eternal life and I shall raise him up on the last day" (Jn 6:54).

Jesus brings His light in response to your desire to know and your need for meaning: "I am the light of the world; whoever follows me does not walk in darkness, but has the light of life" (Jn 8:12).

For your thirst for love and communion, He gives the living water of His grace and friendship, the drink which quenches your thirst: "Anyone who drinks the water that I shall give will never be thirsty again; the water that I shall give will turn into a spring inside him, welling up to eternal life" (Jn 4:14).

For your craving for freedom He brings a holiness which frees and divinizes, giving you fullness of joy.

Finally, He responds to your desire for God by leading you to the Father. Furthermore, He lets you share even here below in His experience of God the Father, He, the Son of Mary of Galilee, the Word, the same substance as the Father. Never forget that to believe means to enter with Jesus into the movement of the Spirit in His relationship with the Father.

This is our faith in Jesus Christ — human fulfilment in a relationship with the living, holy God: "I have not come to destroy but to fulfil and complete."

In prayer let yourself be called upon by Christ. He asks only one question: "For you, Who am I?" Have you truly met Him? Is He someone from history or someone alive now who gives meaning to your life? Could you say like St. Paul: "For me to live is Christ?"

Do you live the Gospel to your very depths? Is there any small part of you which is not influenced by His grace? In each of us there is a "last bit of earth" which has to be evangelized (Madeleine Delbrêl). In a word, do we believe that He can fulfil us completely? To believe is not just a change in our lives, to move from a lower level of existence to a higher level; it is to choose for or against life. The gamble of faith is: "to be or not to be."

Praying is answering Jesus, like Peter, from the depths of your heart: "Lord, to whom should we go? You have the words of eternal life. We believe and we know that you are the Holy One of God" (Jn 6:68-69).

When you discover that Christ fulfils you, it leads to a burning desire that all men meet this Savior Jesus. Can you live quietly and peacefully while there are men on earth who have not been caught by Christ? Are you obsessed by the desire to proclaim the Saviour? Do your lips burn with the name of Jesus?

It is in the light of this question that you find your mission in the world. Do you proclaim a Savior or a judge, salvation or the law, communion or organization, the Good News or the commandments? At the end of the Council, Father de Lubac asked the Council Fathers: "Are we still presenting the Savior?" Above all, do not think we are here outside of prayer, or that apostolic activity is a consequence of contemplative prayer. No, for to spread the Gospel is to pray and worship God. Paul said clearly that God gave him the grace "of officiating for Christ Jesus among the pagans, a priest of God's gospel, so that the pagans might become an agreeable offering, sanctified in the Holy Spirit" (Rm 15:16).

You are to manifest the Savior, for you cannot spread the Gospel without proclaiming it. You must mean the Savior to others and, for that, prayer cannot be enough. A contemplative man makes the world holy but does not spread the Good News — his activity cannot be replaced, but there must also be witnesses.

First of all, you must show and let the Savior be seen in your life. Your brothers must see Christ in you. Do Christians let others see that today salvation has come "to this house", that their bread is nourishing, their joy evident, that the Gospel is light and makes all holy? Sharing the life of all men, you have a special rôle since non-Christians can glimpse Christ through your life and all your activities: familial, political or social life. You spread the Good News through your own life, for there have to be living signs of salvation.

You have to convey your contemplation, your joy, your love and your freedom. The light of the Beatitudes must shine from your face and give light to everyone who sees your life. You have only one thing to do, to draw

63

your brothers into this contemplation of Christ which has gripped you and changed your life. The model of this type of missionary is the Samaritan woman; having found Christ she asked her fellow citizens to meet Him: "Come and see the man who has told me everything I've done. Could this be the Christ?" (Jn 4:29).

Last of all, show Christ in your speech. You don't convey a formula, an ideology, but a Person, Jesus Christ, a man of joy, peace, light and love. Jesus came to bring the fire of love and not a book. At some point in time, you must say that Jesus is the Savior, not Marx nor Mao. Above all, take care to talk of Christ at the heart of man's life. To do this, you don't have to be a hero, an intellectual or a fashion plate, but a saint who is in love with Jesus Christ.

26. Your life becomes consistent and firm in Christ; it is more simple.

You dream of a life when you will have long periods of solitude to pray, but when you do have free time, you scatter it in entertaining yourself. You are tugged about by your different tasks and your desire to run your own life. Don't blame outside events, a lack of time or many people around, but realize that the real problem is in yourself. You must make a synthesis between your inner life and your life with other people.

Each day you feel your time is broken up, "dispersed", without a plan, without freedom. You have trouble finding your own identity, for you are "dispersed", living on the surface. You want to unify your life both with regard to yourself and to other people and things around you. In other words, you want to feel like St. Augustine after his conversion. He says he went from being *drawn apart* to being *drawn together*, from being broken up to being unified, from a scattered feeling to a concentrated and united feeling.

There are no techniques that can bring about such a unifying process. Only a life given meaning and united around a person can rescue you from this feeling of being broken up which divides you inwardly. You must know your own identity to be able to accept fully and integrate the contribution coming from people, objects and ideas. As Emmanuel Mounier wrote: "Your inner dialogue must be such that you can continue it with the first person you meet."

There is a still higher unity, that which is formed around the presence of God in Jesus Christ. Here you escape distraction and dispersal. St. Augustine tells us that he had an invigorating period where, gathered up by Christ, he moved from being drawn apart to being drawn together. Christ picks up the dust of your moments to unite them in a history of salvation. In prayer, the presence of Jesus Christ is a window open on God. When you open a window, the dust floating at random is directed and unified by the rays of the sun. So, your attention directed to Christ, will unify the dust of the minutes and events of your life.

"There was my life, nothing but dissipation, and You gathered me up in my Lord, the Son of Man, the Mediator between your unity and our plurality... I bind myself to your unity. Forgetting what is behind me, not anxious about what must come, intent only upon what is present now, I follow in unremitting effort this crown of a heavenly calling. But I have been scattered in time, the order is unknown to me. My thoughts, the inner life of my soul were torn apart by many upsetting events until that day when, purified and melted in the fire of your love, I shall flow over into You" (St. Augustine).

You will find your unity the day you put your centre of gravity in God. Your life will take on a stability which is rooted in eternity. St. Augustine also said: "Then I shall be consistent and firm in you." There is a practical recipe to unite your life around the presence of God. It cannot be done by reading three books as one does to learn English in three months.

You cannot expect to live in this presence unless you take long periods of time to be there, in His presence, awaiting His visit and His Will. This goes beyond ideas, words and feelings. A little at a time, without doing anything, you will be penetrated and taken over by the experience of God and you will say with Mounier: "My only rule is to remain always in the consciousness of God's presence." The more you go forward into this dim cloud, the less you will be able to express it in words. Indeed, like St. Catherine of Siena, you will no longer be able to say anything about God without immediately denying it and feeling as though you blasphemed.

27. To follow Jesus is to enter into the mystery of the glorious Cross.

If you enter deeply enough into the mystery of the personality of Jesus you will understand that He came to free you by remaking you in the likeness of God. He does not do this in a dramatic way, but in the way of the suffering servant of Isaiah (ch. 53). Jesus saves you by love and hence by humiliation and obedience to his Father. It is in the mystery of the glorious Cross that Jesus makes you a son of the Father. Accept to be deeply frustrated by the folly of the Cross.

You cannot truly know Jesus except by entering the mystery of his Cross. Beware of knowledge which comes from ideas but which is not living and vital. We only know Jesus when we follow Him. If you give yourself to Him with all your strength, with all the love of your heart, it means you accept to be drawn where you do not want to go, into His Passion. It was in giving up His life that Jesus truly knew the Father: "Just as the Father knows me and I know the Father; and I lay down my life for my sheep" (Jn 10:15). True knowledge of God culminates in the acceptance of sacrifice, for God is essentially loving and giving.

When Christ invites you to follow Him, to carry His cross (Lk 9:23-26), He is proposing that you give up your life's dream in order to give yourself truly to Him. You are not giving your life to a cause, a system or an ideology, but to a Person: "... for my sake," said Jesus. You can turn away from His invitation like the rich young man. Christ then will sadly watch you walk away. You can also say like the sons of Zebedee: "Yes, we can drink your chalice" (Mt 20:22). This "yes" is in the same line as your baptism and your offering. It means that you follow Jesus wherever He goes, sharing His glorious death.

But it is not enough to accept to follow Christ just in words; the mystery of the Cross must be lived throughout your human existence by growing ever more close to the Lord. Here is the real giving of yourself to the service of the Kingdom. The mystery of the Cross, which is so frightening to modern man, watchful as he is for self-fulfilment, can be understood only through love, otherwise the Cross is considered as absurd, a foolish scandal. When you give, you deny yourself and to deny yourself, you must have a real existence. You cannot build self-sacrifice on the nothingness of human nature. Only he who gives and surrenders the things and people he loves, can hold them in a free and loving relationship.

The gift of oneself follows two movements. First of all, you must accept your own humanity. Before offering yourself to Christ, you must exist, at least. The Lord wants you to develop fully all the gifts He has bestowed upon you, body, mind, heart, will and freedom. All the strength which is in you must be clearly welcomed; it would be a bad thing to repress it under the pretext of self denial. Many problems arise when you cannot accept yourself as you are with all the powers within you.

True love of Christ implies that you do not close yourself in on your gifts, keeping them jealously for yourself or using them for your own enjoyment. (This is sin — that instead of using your gifts as a way to the Father and to other people, you use them for your own ends). Thus, you resume the whole natural order, all your aspirations, going beyond them to give yourself up to Christ, allowing yourself to be penetrated by the grace of divinisation. Give up your own ideas on the matter and accept the unexpected from Christ. This is a true conversion which means a "right about turn" on your part.

It belongs to Christ to purify the vital forces in you. By not interfering with Him, He will cleanse you of your tendency to grasp the things that belong to you. You must pick up your cross each day in those purifications that your life brings you every day. Take care not to build cross in your own workshop, let Christ lay upon you "His" Cross. When you accept to lose your life in this way, you will save it. You only own what you give up. In the daily Eucharist you profess publicly your desire to share in the mystery of His death and Resurrection. By eating His body and drinking His cup, it is Christ Who teaches you to give yourself up to the Father and to your brothers.

28. To follow Christ is to enter an upside down world.

If you wish to follow Christ each day, you will have to challenge the world in which you live. It is not that the world is evil, on the contrary, it is where we find the presence of God, where salvation is accomplished, but it is also the place of Satan, the Prince of this world. The world you challenge is one where money, power and impurity rule as masters, where the lowly and weak are crushed, where the lure of profit rots hearts. Be careful, your challenge of the world will be genuine if you challenge yourself each day, for you are deeply involved with the sinfulness of the world. As Paul Claudel put it crudely: "The world reeks with your foul breath."

In the midst of this generation you must be the poor man of God who lives completely in the spirit of the Beatitudes. This is the only path to holiness and it is in the light of this spirit that people see the excellence of your Christian living and your apostolic radiance. You spread the Gospel inasmuch as the light of the Beatitudes shines in your face. To live this way you will have to go against the present mentality, agree to be poor, humble and pure. Reread 1 Cor, ch. 1 and 2 and you will see that God has not chosen the wise according to our standards, nor the powerful, but what seems weak to us, so that

He might confound the mighty. God always shows His strength through weakness. To sum it all up: the Christian lives in an "upside down world."

When you carry your cross, you enter that mysterious wisdom which is incomprehensible to the powerful and well born. This was the way of Jesus, the poor man of Yahweh par excellence. Here you are in a divine climate which means it is impossible for you to acquire the spirit of the Beatitudes by your own ability alone. Only Christ can give it to you or rather, He alone is able to live and achieve it in you.

In prayer, stand before Christ as described by Paul in Ph 2:6. Beg Him to reproduce in you and in the community the feelings which lived in Him, and to clothe you in His poverty. Meditate on the Magnificat and ask Our Lady to let you follow in the footsteps of the poor of Yahweh of whom she was the living prototype.

The Beatitudes aim at shaping your heart into that of a poor man — open, willing, forgetful of self, and able to give. Poverty is a fruit growing on the tree of love. Begin by loving your brothers until you feel they are your equals — this love will take you far. As it led Jesus to strip Himself of His riches so as to enrich your life, you will become poor and humble and you will try to give to your brothers, not just your possessions, but yourself.

In itself wealth is not evil, it is neutral, even useful, but if you are not careful, it makes you a slave of yourself, encroaching ceaselessly. You are always threatened in being rich, by your culture, your spiritual and human values, your apostolic success. A poor man no longer has a centre of gravity in himself, he has accepted to give up everything for Jesus Christ. He is completely open to Him and dependant on Him. So, be one who is poor, that is a man of love, with a passion for justice and fellowship.

Let the Lord deepen your heart, taking from you your possessions one by one. This is the very meaning of the purifications described by St. John of the Cross. You do not know how much wealth can prevent His action, for you are often blind to the riches which take you captive.

Let Him go ahead; He will cut you free, rooting out gradually what belongs to you and binds you without your seeing it.

Prayer deepens in you a heart which is poor; makes your soul expectant and loving, able to discern between the true and false salvation and to recognize in the Cross of Christ the salvation of man. Otherwise, you might imagine yourself as the creator of your holiness and your apostolic success. Remember that poverty is a basic law of the supernatural world. God does wonders with instruments that are poor as they take nothing from His glory, returning it to Him intact and unblemished. Before this truth, pray intensely that Christ will allow you to follow Him in the humility of the truly poor, who expect everything from the Father and nothing from themselves.

29. Let nothing imprison you, but keep your heart free to love the Lord and do His will.

Following the poor Christ you are at the heart of the Gospel, ready to be seized by the Spirit Who opens you to the love of God. But a question arises: what is your position regarding those things which make up the fabric of your daily life? Are you to give them up completely or use them wisely? Too many Christians and religious today remain on a moral level when they seek an actual way of being poor. The position you are to take is not first of all on a practical and concrete level, but in the depths of your being and inner freedom; then the practical attitudes will follow naturally. Ultimately, evangelical poverty is not concerned with the object alone, but with your way of possessing or of being free of it. If you do not come to this complete freedom, you will be apt to despise things or idolize them, but one way or another you will not truly love them.

True spiritual freedom means that you stand a certain distance from things, not to identify with them. You may own them, but in your heart you want to be free before God concerning them. You are like the rich young man who observes the law of God but feels a certain lack of freedom when he surveys his belongings. It is not a matter of giving up everything, but to want what God wants for you. You are not to want what is best in itself, but what is best for you and according to God's will.

To do this, it is good to know what "things" you are dealing with. It is not only material objects, belongings and people around you, but also your activities, your abilities, your thoughts and desires, your real self. It would be a serious temptation to consider earthly things as insignificant, temporary, without value. You can only reach God through them, they are the place where you serve, love and adore Him.

Never forget that God grows in you according to the positive attitude you have towards people and things. Sin consists not in using things but in using them badly, a change in your objective approach to things. Instead of making them the means of relating to and loving people, you close yourself in on them making yourself the centre of the world. You must recognize them as good and valuable in the Christian life. Only this positive recognition will let you give them up properly, without resentment.

You must truly love both people and things if you want to give them up. Then, in giving them up, you will relate to them intensely since you are free from them and will want them entirely for themselves: "What has never been the object of a decision because it has never been truly encountered, cannot be abandoned by a free decision either" (K. Rahner). To give up people and things must mean a real choice, a real decision.

You can see in this movement the christological structure of the redeeming Incarnation. Jesus assumes the reality of the world and man, but this is exceeded in His Cross and death. It is only in going through both that all these realities are found, transfigured in glory. Love and giving up things are not two different attitudes side by side, but two phases of one and the same movement. In death, man is completely separated from everything but at the same moment the Resurrection reinstates him in a positive relationship to things as they are transfigured. This must be what Christ meant when he promised his Apostles a hundredfold of those possessions they had left to follow Him: "I tell you solemnly, there is no one who has left house, wife, brothers, parents or children for the sake of the Kingdom of God, who will not be given repayment many times over in this present time and, in the world to come, eternal life" (Lk 18:29-30).

30. "Take your son, your only child Isaac whom you love... you shall offer him as a burnt offering, on a mountain I will point out to you" (Gn 22:2).

To understand this movement of complete self renunciation, read in the Gospel the advice of Christ to the rich young man and what He said afterwards of the danger of riches. At the same time, think of Abraham's sacrifice and you will understand what willingness God expects of you. God asks the young man as He does Abraham for the best that he has, for what he holds most dear: "Give me your only child." All that you have is a gift from the Lord for you to give back to Him.

Such a sacrifice cannot be understood on the rational level. We must move to the level of faith and love. The attitude of Abraham, like that of the Apostles and the Blessed Virgin, is a total surrender to God in faith. The phrase that best expresses this willingness is: "Here I am." In prayer ask yourself if you truly want to belong entirely to God, to be given up, consecrated to Him through your very freedom. In this self renunciation you will give yourself without reckoning, knowing that God will provide everything. It is an act of complete trust in God, Who is able to raise the dead, but you must let go what you hold most dear.

You will find again in grace what you were not afraid to give up to God. In themselves, things are good but they can be possessed only in the grace and love of the Lord. This feeling of indifference towards people and things is not natural to you, for you are always tempted to hold tightly to what is around you. You must actively practise standing back, to free your will. Such a desire must extend to every level of your personality, including your affections, your actions, even your body. In his *Exercises*, St. Ignatius shows you how to behave when he describes the third group of people:

"The third group wishes to suppress attachment, so much in fact that they care not any more to keep than to give up what they have acquired; they want to keep it or give it up only according to what will seem to them best for the service and praise of His divine Majesty. Meanwhile, they want to look upon themselves as having given up everything from the heart, trying mightily to want neither this nor that nor anything else, unless the service alone of God our Lord moves them. They are thus moved to keep or give up some good by their desire to be able better to serve God."

You have to want all things in the will of the Lord. In this matter of renunciation, although an active attitude is important and depends on a free decision on your part, you must let yourself be acted on by God. St. Ignatius says that God will act through your will, which must welcome God's initiative. This active attitude must be included in a son's confidence in God. He alone knows what you need and the way to make your life poor. There are things which are so much a part of you that you cannot give them up of yourself. You must let God act Who will take them away in the happenings of your life. This is perhaps where acceptance is most difficult.

The day when you really give something up or when God takes from you someone whom you really love, then you might be really shocked. Only then will you discover how difficult it is to bear this beginning of emptiness, for the sake of God's love which apparently is not enough for you. True poverty means to give yourself like a child to the arms of God, loving Him enough to be happy that His will is done.

73

31. "Have I become a child again?"

Can you say like the little shepherd in *The Fearless Heart*: "Have I become a child again?" Have you noticed how closely Jesus relates spiritual childhood and the call to complete poverty? The two teachings follow each other in St. Luke (18:15-27), as though Jesus means to say that to enter the Kingdom you must become as poor as a child, who is not concerned about himself. The reason for true poverty is total trust in God.

Once you have accepted to be poor and to follow Jesus humbled to the very Cross, let God choose the things and people that He will take from your life. Above all, do not act as the master of this self-giving; let God take what He wants. Usually He hits you on the most sensitive spot in your life, something which really hurts. We all have a secret poverty which is our cross and suffering. To become poor is to accept life, with our wretchedness and our contradictions, so that the Spirit of God may penetrate that secret part of ourselves which has been wounded by sin.

The divine joy will overwhelm you and in the measure of your self-renunciation, you will be happy. Whatever your weakness, if you offer it to the merciful love of the Father, you will feel the infinite tenderness of God. "Unhappy are the rich, since their gold shelters them from the extraordinary kindness of God."

Above all, believe that God loves you personally and uses all the events in your life to draw you to Him. Your sin once acknowledged and told may be the occasion of feeling how much God loves you. As soon as the prodigal son returned, his father moved with compassion, ran and threw his arms around his neck and hugged him (Lk 15:20). Prayer is simply this loving embrace of God, holding to His heart and in His arms His rediscovered child.

When you pray, do not start to look at yourself or go back to be glad or sorry over past experience. Give yourself up to the Father in a confidence founded on a calm and tranquil daring. You must learn to give yourself lovingly and spontaneously to God in a blind abandonment to His caring providence. Let your faith be without calculation, or self-concern, waiting simply on God, in His love and mercy. God will let you love Him for Himself, to find perfect joy in forgetting yourself, knowing your own poverty and weakness.

Become again a tiny child, poor in spirit, wholly dependant — this is the only way to achieve fullness of sonship in God. God loves the humble, He gave them His revelation: "I bless you, Father, for hiding these things from the learned and the clever and revealing them to little children" (Mt 11:25). Never forget this, you do not give yourself spiritual childhood, it comes from on high. To live like a child, you must fit yourself to be born from on high, to let divine life flourish in you.

32. You see in Mary someone who is totally poor but overflowing with the riches of God.

Come before the Blessed Virgin in the attitude she had before the Almighty at the Annunciation: "Here I am". She is there uncomplicated, unaffected, frank, in the reality of her humanity received from God, open to His Love and Will. She was the first after Jesus to enter into the Kingdom of the Beatitudes, and that is why she is a model and source of grace for you. Listen to the words of Mary, look closely at her reactions. By contemplating her, you will become like her, a heart willing and poor, ready to be penetrated by God.

How happy Mary was when she found she was loved by God: "Rejoice, full of grace!" You are always moved when someone comes and says "I love you." At first, Mary did not understand, for she was in truth the work of the love of God. Reread the Magnificat and you will understand Our Lady's humility and poverty. Like you, she hungered and thirsted for light, love and happiness, but she refused to fill herself with the artificial and the sham. She is there, poor, empty-handed before God Who fills her with His very being. She sees God looking at her.

There was not the least complacency or self-concern in her, she was centered on God. This is the meaning of her title "Immaculate Conception."

This is why Mary is the opposite of the first Eve who looked away from God and was fooled by Satan. Mary wished to be completely dependant on God and His love. She did not, as Eve had done, snatch at the forbidden fruit and therefore she questioned the angel about his promise. She wanted to understand and discern which spirit spoke to her.

Then, she renewed the gift of her heart to God. In a sense, she did not wait to be fulfilled as a woman by a man, she wanted to give herself completely to her Creator. This is the meaning of true spiritual virginity: the complete gift of oneself to God. She could say with Isaiah: "My spouse shall be the Creator" (Is 54:5). This is why God could do wonders in her and make her the mother of His only Son. Mary exercised her motherhood in the very giving of her virginity. Once she had recognized God's call, she gave herself up to Him completely, in faith. She went still further, completely trusting in God in her life: "Nothing is impossible to God", she said. She believed in the almighty creative power of His Word, capable of begetting the Word in her. Thus does God change the barrenness of the poor into fruitfulness of extraordinary richness. Ask Mary in prayer for this grace of complete poverty, so that you may be filled with God who "fills the hungry and sends the rich empty away."

She is your model of self-surrender to God. You would like to plan this giving of yourself but, as long as you set limits, you are still too possessive of your offering. God asks an absolute willingness, often asking you for something you had not foreseen. Mary did not think of becoming the Mother of the Promised One, but she was willing and open, nothing in the call of God surprised her. Then she became the Mother of the Savior. Who can tell of the fruitfulness of her life, hidden in God with Christ at Nazareth?

You can ponder on Mary's willingness by going over the story of the Annunciaiton or by repeating the Magnificat. Or else, simply say the rosary going over in your mind the words of Our Lady, that she may reproduce in you what she herself felt so deeply. You can stop on a phrase in the Hail Mary which you especially appreciate or meditate on the mystery of the Trinity and Mary's part in the plan of salvation. The Rosary is an excellent form of contemplative prayer where you learn to go out of yourself to unite yourself with Christ in His mysteries and to be at His entire disposal.

33. You contemplate in Jesus someone who is all relationship: He comes from the Father and He is directed to man. To be a Christian is to be like the Son, totally open to the Father and to people.

The deeper you go in the contemplation of the mystery of God, the more you will discover that He is not only *logos* but *dia-logos*, that is to say that for God to be is essentially to declare Himself in His Word made flesh. The Gospel of Saint John which you should reread with this point in mind, simply translates the dialogue of Jesus with His Father and that of the Father with the Son. Discovering this dialogue in God, you are let to contemplate in Him an *I* and a *You*. God is a Trinity of distinct Persons, relative to one another in mutual action. To make us understand that, theologians use an outlandish expression; they say that in God the Persons are *subsistent relations*, for they subsist in a loving relationship.

The Person in God is relation. When you appeal to the Father, you cannot separate Him from His Son Jesus: "The Father is called so, not in relation to Himself, but in relation to His Son; in relation to Himself, He is simply God" (St. Augustine). In God there are only substance and relation, this latter is the original form of being.

When you turn to Jesus you find that He is completely turned towards the Father: "The Father is in Me and I am in the Father" (Jn 10:38). Jesus' life is completely open. He is a being-from-the-other, a being *coming from* and *destined* to others (J. Ratzinger). Jesus is all relation, He knows whence He comes and whiter He goes (Jn 8:14).

Jesus comes from the Father from Whom He has all He is. He continually refers to the Father Who is His primordial source. This is how He fulfils the will of Him Who sent Him. But He is also destined for man whom He wills to introduce into this primordial source, that is, into life of the Trinity. "I have come so that they may have life and have it to the full" (Jn 10:10). This life that the Son transmits to you is not foreign to human life but is it complete fulfilment in a movement of transcendence. Therefore, to be in relationship with Jesus is to achieve the fullness of your human calling, to reach genuine life. By creating you in Its image, the Holy Trinity has made you able to take part in a dialogue. Like Christ, you are essentially open to the Other — the Father, and to others, your brothers. You can only fulfil your human existence in a relationship of love and communion with the supreme Person Who is the foundation of your being.

If you are open to Christ at the heart of your life you cannot block your relationship to the Father, for Jesus is open *on high* to the Father and *on the earth plane* open to man. You will be fully human only if you relate to the Father through Jesus. If you neglect this relation of filial adoration, your life will be stunted, for man's life is to see and contemplate the face of God.

In prayer identify yourself with Christ Who is pure relationship to the Father and to men. To pray is to be like the Son, to become a son. Do not rely for this on yourself, but remain open in both directions.

The more you are a person, the more you are directed to the other, to one who is truly Other, that is, God. You are all the more yourself when you are closer to the Entirely Other, God. In the same way, the Father sends you, as He does the Son, to your brothers. You will be entirely yourself on the day when you stop being closed in on yourself and become completely open to God. "Eternal life is this: to know You the only true God and Jesus Christ Whom You have sent" (Jn 17:3). In these words of Jesus you have the fulfilment of your true vocation. Meeting you, Christ has brought you into eternal life which is the complete fulfilment of human life brought to perfection; but for you, to live truly, is to enter into a loving relationship with the Father. When you pray you are invited by Christ to share His dialogue of friendship with the Father. This is what gives your life its value for eternity.

34. Pray to discover God's will for you without illusion. Then, remain willing and give yourself into the hands of the Father.

You have heard the call to follow Jesus and you have accepted the challenge of love, serving in total poverty and humility. Like Paul, you want true wisdom: "During my stay with you, the only knowledge I claimed to have was about Jesus, and only about Him as the crucified Christ" (1 Cor 2:2). It is normal to feel within you a tremendous struggle between the desire to love Christ truly and the desire to follow your own will. Only the Holy Spirit can purify your heart so as to place it before God, to carry out His will.

In your life everything comes down finally to discovering the will of God and doing it: "It is not those who say to me, 'Lord, Lord' who will enter the Kingdom of Heaven, but the person who does the will of my Father in heaven." In theory you want to be more closely united with Christ in His total poverty, but you do not know what type of poverty Christ expects. What is good and perfect in itself may not necessarily be so for you. So you wait in constant prayer until God shows you what stands in the way of giving yourself totally. The important thing is not what you decide to give up for God, but what He wants you to give up for Him.

This is where deceptions can come into your best intentions. You think that the best thing for you is the most difficult. What matters, is not whether giving up something or an activity pleases you or not, but whether it demands more love. If, after earnest prayer, you see this work with peace and confidence as the will of God for you, it is a clear sign that God is calling you to respond generously. You can be sure that if you pray truly and take time over it (which is of great importance in making a decision), God will show you what He expects of you.

Now is the time to look at the work of the Holy Spirit in you. Simply consider the gifts of God you have received at different stages of your life, the calls heard in events and through people. Try to discover the vocation God has outlined in you which should stand out sharply. Each person has a mystery in his soul, his own mystery which is that of his individual name. All his anguish on this earth is to name it. Only Christ can reveal to each man the mystery of his name, hidden in the Heart of the Son of God, where He came into being eternally in the Heart of the Father.

At the same time, see how faithful you have been to the calls of God. Often you have used His gifts to promote your personal aims, good though they may have been in themselves. Is the vocation you glimpse, a gift of God or a fabrication of your own? How much self-deception is there in your desire for holiness and your work for others?

Be careful, don't give yourself up to psychological analysis and still less to rationalization, but let yourself be challenged deep within you. It is you yourself being questioned by this will of God. Pray earnestly and long then, to see yourself as the Holy Spirit sees you. Tell Christ over again that you want to be at one with the will of the Father. Only prayer can purify your motives and bring to light your real intentions.

Do not be surprised then to feel your great poverty, which lets you be malleable and limp in the hands of God. You are a little clay in the hollow of God's hand and you ask the breath of the Spirit to fashion you in the image of the Son. It is an uncomfortable position for you; it is no longer your decision to avoid something or undertake something else, but simply to let yourself be acted upon by God.

You give yourself up into the hands of God with complete unconcern. This is the basic willingness which makes it certain that your life harmonizes with God's designs. You fully accept to give up all to follow Christ, but you do not choose by yourself: put your strength into wanting neither this nor that, unless you are needed for the service of God Our Lord *(Exercises)*.

God can make saints of people thus divested of themselves. It is clear that prayer is more necessary than ever to reach this state of mind, which is so difficult since it involves the very roots of your freedom. Christ alone can teach you and give you the strength to offer yourself to God in this great sacrifice. He Himself opened the road for you in His Passover. Repeat often Father de Foucauld's prayer of abandonment: "Father, I abandon myself to you, do with me as You please. Whatever You do with me, I thank You. I am ready for anything, I accept all."

35. Let your heart rest in the Peace of God and you will perceive His will for you clearly and exactly.

When you have muddy water you have to let it settle in the bright warm sunshine, so that the impurities can settle on the bottom and the clean water will be seen on top. Your Christian life does something similar as it gradually settles in prayer under God's sight. If you live faithfully in the light of the Gospel, your heart's true intentions become clear and you perceive what really hinders the action of God in you. In the same way, the Holy Spirit inclines your heart towards one form or another of poverty, so that your life may come closer to the will of God for you. You will learn to be present, before God, for Him alone. When you work or rest, you act too much for a purpose. You forget the wonder of being, just being, without thinking. Prayer lets you be before God. It lets you reach your deepest self, beyond any thought, desire, image or act. You are alone with yourself at the source of your being. There where your soul came forth from the hands of its Creator. You are alone with the Absolute, alone in the solitude of the Alone.

Look closely at the difference between this spiritual choice made in the light of the Spirit and the moral decisions which you take to change your life on the natural level. For example, you may decide to struggle against a certain fault, or spend more time in prayer or take on some self discipline, to serve God better. You cannot disregard this work of self improvement if you want to become free, but it has its limits and above all it stays on the natural level. Furthermore, it can be done without prayer, with the help of someone who knows you well, for example. Ask your friends what they would criticize in you and you will know what to change in your life.

The spiritual choice you are invited to make here is on the level of the divine life. It is a matter of discovering God's will for you, at a given moment in your life, in order to direct it. So you cannot rely on the light of yor reason or the strength of your will — you need the higher revelation of the Spirit to understand God's loving design for you. Continual prayer and meditation on the Gospel will cleanse your heart and held you to surrender yourself completely to God.

To start with, it is certain that the Holy Spirit wants to achieve something in you which cannot be defined ahead of time. Usually, you come to prayer with precise problems for which you want immediate answers, reached by analysis or decision. You alone cannot discover the will of God Who demands the absence of all preliminaries and a disregard of what you are and do. So leave your problems at the door and open yourself to God submitting yourself to the active presence of the Spirit who wants to fulfil you. You do not make your own being, but receive it from God. Then you will understand the real and personal will of God in the recognition and acceptance of yourself.

In prayer become a channel for the Spirit, giving up your defences and safeguards. You become your true self, a free adult. Prayer lets you evolve to a higher level than your day to day concerns. There is no problem, no duality, but a personal and conscious taking over of your life in order to give it to Christ — you accept the play of love with no self delusion.

This is why the will of God does not usually seem extraordinary or thrilling. God works in the very fabric of your life, it is on the level of your daily life that He will show His will. Above all, He asks that you clearly accept your humanity, with its limitations and short-comings through which He purifies you.

Keep on praying, picking up from your life the specific calls and desires that the Spirit suggests to you; it is always through your deepest hopes that He speaks to you and shows you the will of God. Then, try to think how you could carry out this choice in reality, jotting it down if necessary. It could be that you end up expressing it in some sentence from the Gospel.

In any case, if you have chosen what God desires, you will feel great joy. Peace and joy are always signs of God's work in you, even if the joy demands a real sacrifice from you. Gradually this sense of spiritual understanding will grow in you and it will make you feel the will of God in all the events of your life.

36. God does not leave you to the light of your reason alone when He calls upon you to make a spiritual choice. In prayer, you will see His will take shape.

Here you are at the center of the Christian life, since in human life it all comes down finally to discovering the will of God and doing it. But even if you can perceive God's will through the commandments, often you have doubts about whether you are able to grasp what He expects of you, especially in your present circumstances. The deeper you go in authentic Christian living, the more choices you will have to make, answerable to your conscience, enlightened by the Spirit and the law of the Beatitudes, not able to refer to a code of law or a spiritual master "who should know" or holds the truth. Whether it is a political engagement, your state of life, a deepening of your prayer, or some other decision concerning the direction of your life, you cannot avoid onerous choices which involve your freedom and your loyalty. However, you cannot believe in God and His care for you if you think He would leave you without help in the decisions of your life.

If you want to know the will of God, the one essential condition is that you are at His disposal, that is, with a choice to make, you refuse any preference one way or the other, give up all preconceptions which might prevent God from letting you know how He wants you to commit yourself. In other words, you must have no ideas on the matter, accepting another's viewpoint even if it ruins your own plans.

Perhaps this is the fundamental frame of mind when you want to choose according to God's will. But you ask: "How do I become willing if I am not so already?" You must stop, step back from yourself and question your own judgment; put all your actions in the sight of God in prayer so that you may discover what opposition you might have to His will.

It may be that through such prayer God will show you clearly what He wants, but this is not usual. He prefers to speak to you through signs. Don't mistake your good intentions for the will of God. One way to discover this will is to analyze the various factors and elements that go into your choice. List the reasons you usually consider before making any decision, one way or another. If you do this in God's sight you will see the pros and cons fall into line according to spiritual criteria. If you want to follow Christ according to the Beatitudes, then you will see the human and selfish drives — for spiritual discernment uses objective criteria too: the wisdom of the Cross and the Beatitudes stated by Christ in the Gospel. On one side, the reasons will be clear, strong and sure, on the other worthless, inconsistent, hazy or doubtful. God does not seem to have answered your question directly, but He really has replied, enlightening and guiding your mind and your heart.

There is another way to discover His will and that is to look deeply into your own emotions. If you live in lasting peace and in true joy, you can be sure that the plans which produce these feelings are willed by God, since the Holy Spirit always acts in joy, peace and gentleness. If, on the other hand, you are sad, discouraged and anxious, you can know that the planned project is inspired by the flesh or the spirit of evil.

In this area what seems basic is the quality of the desire and how long it lasts. You can never be sure if you rely on the feeling of a moment. On the contrary, if during a fairly long time such a decision is associated with joy and the opposite with sadness, then you may believe that God is sending you the consolation of the Spirit and is suggesting that you take the appropriate action. Then, there is the free act itself which makes you choose for Jesus Christ. Quite often there is an abiding peace after this free choice. The feeling of consolation or sadness following your choice will confirm it and show you clearly if you are following the will of God.

Gradually, you will make truly spiritual choices, interpreting God's signs more and more clearly whether in major decisions which bind you for the life or in day to day choices. Besides, this training of your freedom must be followed all your life and, the more faithfully you respond to the demands of the Spirit, the more easily you will discover what He is asking.

To conclude this meditation you can read in 1 S 3:1-21 how God called Samuel. You will understand how God speaks to men to let them know His will. Samuel lived in the temple in the service of Eli and helped him at worship, but he was not yet close to God, that is, he had not heard the personal word that God was directing to him: "Samuel had as yet no knowledge of Yahweh and the word of Yahweh had not yet been revealed to him" (1 S 3:7). You are like Samuel when you have not heard personally what God wants of you. Like the young man, you ask Eli the high priest or for written laws to tell you what you should do.

But notice the divine way of teaching. Yahweh begins be calling the young man by his name three times "Samuel! Samuel!" This is both a personal call and a precise purpose that He wanted him to understand. Look at Samuel's willingness who, at the least call, sought God's will. Are you sensitive to the small promptings of the Spirit Who signals to you through apparently ordinary events?

Samuel goes to look for the high priest; the latter was not supposed to reveal the will of God to him — he did not know it, — but to put Samuel in touch with the word of God. So, in your own life, you question your spiritual father who is on familiar terms with the voice of God; and you ask him to help you connect yourself with the word of God. Only the Spirit can speak to your heart, but the spiritual guide is there to help you check on the reality of His call.

So Samuel is ready to hear the word of God for he had made himself completely willing, wanting only one thing, the will of God, beyond anything he himself desired. When you are called to make a choice in the Spirit, pray often in the words of young Samuel: "Speak, Yahweh, your servant is listening" (1 S 3:9). Then the Lord will reveal his deepest secrets and like Samuel "you will let no word of His fall to the ground" (1 S 3:19). You will become that true spiritual man of whom Paul speaks, who finds out the secrets of God because he is permeated by the Holy Spirit.

37. In Saint Peter's pilgrimage of faith, you will find the signposts for your own faith.

Remind yourself often of Clouzot's phrase quoted above: "I believe the real sin I committed when I was fifteen or sixteen years old was wanting to become myself by myself..." Don't you think this is your real sin? You want to conquer God by taking Him by assault while

His love presses you in on all sides He finds an opening so He can sweep in on you. You will recognize your own experience in three living scenes of Peter's pathway, his confession of faith at Caesarea, his attitude during the Passion and his confession of love after the Resurrection.

Reread Matthew 16:13-27 and you will see how, like Peter, you are led by a twofold spirit, the Spirit of Christ and the spirit of the flesh or Satan. With the inspiration of the Holy Spirit, Peter asserted: "You are the Christ, the Son of the living God." Jesus told him clearly that this revelation came to him from His Father in heaven. In the origin of this act of faith there is the magnetic strength of the Father who is acting in Peter's heart to let him perceive from the words and actions of Jesus that He is the Son of God. But Peter did not have full understanding of his act of faith; he would discover in the darkness of his life and especially in his difficulties, the depth of his hold on Christ. It is the same in your profession of faith. What is beautiful in a consecration to God is not the "yes" of the profession, but the perseverance in saying it every day in the reality of life.

Indeed, as soon as Christ began to tell of His Passion, Peter reacted involuntarily in a way which was far from being according to the Spirit: "Heaven preserve You, Lord" he said "this must not happen to You." Peter was willing to recognize Jesus as Lord and to serve Him in His Kingdom, but he refused a suffering Messiah who could accomplish the salvation of the world through the Cross. He received Christ's hard and biting words: "Get behind me, Satan, for you are a scandal for me, for your thoughts are not those of God but of men."

Peter was put in his place. He had to go *behind* Christ whereas he was ready to be with Him, but taking the lead. As on the evening of Holy Thursday, he needed to let Jesus wash his feet, that is to let himself be loved first. Without knowing it, Peter spoke as Satan did in the desert of the Temptation. He suggested to Jesus that He take an easy way to save the world, to refuse the Cross. Peter had to learn humbly with the other disciples the instructions of Christ: "If anyone wants to come after me, let him deny himself, take up his cross and follow me."

At the beginning of the Passion (Lk 22:31-62), Peter had a poor memory, he had already forgotten the words of Jesus. He wanted to follow Him to prison and death, but it was still a friendship caused by attraction and admiration and it needed to be purified. Then there was Peter's humiliating three-time denial as he saw himself surrounded on all sides. Three times he asserted that he did not know Christ. Actually, he did not know Him since he had not then discovered the infinite love that Jesus had for him — that knowledge would come to him along with forgiveness. Jesus would pour this love into his heart at the very moment when He gave up His Spirit to the Father. In your prayer put these two statements of Peter side by side: "You are the Christ, the Son of the Living God" and: "I do not know this man." How many times have you been through Peter's experience, practically denying the face of Christ?

It was in a glance from Christ that Peter was converted. His humiliation was changed into love. The first confession was one of faith, the second was to be one of love: "Simon, do you love me?" At the third repetition of the question, Peter could not hold himself back and told of the depth and strength of his love for Christ: "Lord, you know everything, you know well that I love you." Peter was no longer afraid to assert his love for Christ since he could see in Him the source of love and forgiveness.

When Peter was young he "put on his own belt and led his life as he pleased." When he was old he had to let another lead him where he did not want to go. Earlier, Peter spoke under the inspiration of the Holy Spirit but he did not know the full import of his words. The time came when he had to turn around and abandon himself into the hands of the Father, so that He could work wonders through his poverty.

You want to follow Christ all the way but, on your own, you are not able to catch up with Him and to go into the mystery of the Cross. You must suffer many failures and know the trial of the desert before you can understand Christ's boundless love for you. Then, this love will be poured into your heart by the Holy Spirit and you will be able to say to Jesus with Peter: "Lord, you now I love you." First, however, you must give yourself up to the love of Christ.

III

The Working Out of Salvation

38. **"The life I live now is not my own; Christ is living in me" (Ga 2:20).**

You must measure the mystery of Christ in your human life. You try to reach Him in prayer and to imitate Him in your life, you yearn to find Him in the events of your life and the faces of your brothers. In a word, you want to be bound to Him in friendship, to know Him better, to follow Him carrying your Cross and to enter into the Kingdom of the Beatitudes. Isn't this why you look at Him throughout the Gospel, not to know His story, but to *recognize* Him in faith and love? Then Christ still remains someone outside of you, who has an indirect influence, but who has (pardon the expression) "not yet got under your skin."

You don't read the Gospel like the Little Red Book of Mao. You read the latter to know a man's thought, take it in and put it to work in the life and history of the world, but Mao remains a man outside his readers. It is different with Christ, the Son of God who, by His Incarnation and Resurrection, has entered the heart of both man and the world. Since Jesus became man and rose again, the face of the world has changed. He truly lives in our midst in such a way that we can no longer speak of God and man without thinking of them in relation to each other.

So, your relationship to Christ is not just knowledge, nor outward imitation as you might admire some hero, reproducing his words and actions. Since you have been plunged into the glorious death of Jesus, His life has filtered into you and so, in Paul's strong and wonderful expression, we have become *one being* (Rm 6:5). A radical transformation has taken place deep within you so that the ties which bind you to Christ are stronger than any earthly tie. You believe and live in Christ in His complete mystery.

You know Christ so deeply that you are one with Him. To help you to come to this reality which cannot be expressed in human words, theologians speak of "identification" or incorporation. So your life is a long labour of love to be "incorporated" into Jesus. Such an identification is brought about by the Holy Spirit Who is endlessly shaping the *person* of Jesus in you.

You understand how your prayer changes when you discover that Jesus lives in you (Ga 2:20), so much so that He is more real than you are to yourself. He lives in you not only by identification, but by a gradual assimilation of His Word and His body. "You really become", as Augustine says, "what you eat."

In prayer, go deeply within yourself and into the heart of the world, so that the Son of God hidden in you, may rise up. You are one with Him: why look for Him outside as if He were foreign to you? To be Christian is to be involved in your inner life with Christ; it is to let Him think, will and love in you. You are, as Paul says, Christ's imitator *(mime)* in the full meaning of the word: to reproduce, to bring to life.

To pray is simply to set your daily life in its least significant moments in accord with Jesus, so that He will bring to you His redeeming Incarnation. Unceasingly you live through Him, with Him and in Him in the fabric of your daily life, in communion with all men, your brothers.

The more you contemplate Jesus, the more you are

transformed into Him, provided you live as He lived, giving yourself completely to the Father and to your brothers. This mystery of communion with Jesus is the only source of prayer and through it you reach the depths of the Trinity. Through the humanity of Jesus living in you by the power of the Holy Spirit, you penetrate the depths of God. Stand aside more and more, so that He can take possession of you and be at one with the Father in you. This is an inexhaustible mystery for your prayer which plunges you into adoration and thanksgiving.

39. Your life takes on eternal value as it becomes one with the Body of Christ dead and risen.

Jesus is not simply the one who teaches you the way of salvation, he also carries it out and fulfils it in His Passover. He said himself that He is the Way, the Truth, and the Life. You must follow Him, carrying your cross, that is carrying out the exact will of God for you, but also you must let him relive His own life in you. Every decision you take in your Christian life takes its meaning and value in the life of Christ. He is the first to have made His whole life an offering to the Father. This is why you must contemplate Him in His Paschal mystery so that He may pour out His divine life on you in the gift of His glorified Body.

In your previous contemplations your mind and heart had to undertake unaccustomed work. You had to accept the teaching of Our Lord on the mystery of the Cross and the Beatitudes. Usually, you take the Gospel and you build a doctrine from the words of Christ. But here you have to enter into another's thought and pattern your life to it. It is natural that you would feel a violent struggle, enduring both consolation and desolation, for it is not normal for man to enter into the wisdom of the Cross. Now you are calm, for you have found the will of God for you. However it still remains for you to taste the inner part of the mysteries of salvation and to beg Christ to relive them in you.

Now is the time to live Christ's Passover in prayer. This means to take the event fully in all its dimensions, seeing it not only in its historical reality, but in its universal and real dimension. Christ dead and risen is present to all men and all times; He is also present to man's inner reality. Today, He reaches you in the Eucharist. The Eucharist is thus at the very heart of your Christian life, but it attains its complete substance only in the reality of the Passion-Resurrection. If today we can celebrate the Lord's Supper it is only because there was Good Friday and Easter. You can never separate the three panels of this triptych, but in prayer you can contemplate them one after another, to absorb them and move them from the realm of theoretical truths to those practical truths which involve your freedom.

In approaching these mysteries of salvation your prayer will change its aspect. You are no longer preoccupied in receiving the teaching that Jesus gives you about entering the Kingdom. If you have followed the course, your heart has been enlightened by God's Word and you have found what He expects of you. Now you must drop your immediate concerns to contemplate Christ alone, not in His outward actions but in His state of being. You can summarize it in one of Jesus' sayings: "A man can have no greater love than to lay down his life for his friends" (Jn 15:13).

At the very centre of your contemplation there must be only one reality — the love of Christ for all men. At the Last Supper, as on the Cross, there is no doubt of the love of Jesus Who gives himself up to the Father and to you. Make yourself into simple acceptance so that you can welcome this love. In this way your daily life is taken into the life of Christ and takes on an eternal dimension.

Recall all that was said of the prayer of praise and adoration which is going out from yourself, keeping your gaze on Christ alone. Try to be hidden and disappear, so that you can contemplate the infinite love of Jesus in thanksgiving and in sharing His cup. This is unselfish prayer where you express all your heart's love to Christ — or rather the small love you have for Him, for this is the paradox of such contemplation: the more we try to find the love of christ, the more our hearts are broken by our indifference and ingratitude towards Christ. This is the very essence of prayer. You will soon discover how little you cling to Christ, your heart will feel heavy and dull, unable to contemplate Him for long, since you love Him so little. The benefit of such a contemplation is to let you find out by a test how hard and dry is your heart before the infinite love of Jesus which shines in His passion.

If you have these feelings it is a sign that your heart is being softened and you can see the gulf that separates you from Christ. Accept being at a loss, poor and powerless before Him. Above all, make this suffering into an entreaty that when the time comes, He will let you sense the love He has for you. Your prayer must become more and more simple — read the story of events in the Gospel, but leave out the details so that you can focus on Jesus alone. Ask the Spirit Who moved Jesus to give Himself up to the Father to show you a little of His love. It needs years for His love to spring up in your heart and to leave you no rest. Then, you will love Christ with the same heart that He loves you.

40. Discover through the act of breaking bread and the wine poured out, the deep commitment of Christ Who gives up His body and sheds His blood for the multitude.

You can understand nothing of the Last Supper if you separate it from the agony; they are two complementary actions bound together with the theme of the "cup". In the first, the cup is offered during a meal, in the other, it is lived by Christ at the very moment when He asks the Father: "Take this cup away from me" (Mk 14:36). In prayer, try to read of this, not only on the level of symbols, but on that of the heart of Christ.

Without speaking of the supernatural awareness He had of His mission, Jesus was aware with His human intelligence that He was going to His death. In going up to Jerusalem, Jesus mentioned His death frequently, in declarations brought on by the rejection by the people and those in power. The officials of Israel were to arrest Him, one of His own would betray Him and the greatest believer would deny Him. It is in the understanding of death that Christ sat at table with His disciples for the Last Supper.

Reread what happened in Mark 14:22-25. Jesus carried out a prophetic gesture: the bread given and the wine poured out show that He will give Himself to death for his own. It is the prophetic gesture in the great tradition of Isaiah (i.e. the episode of the broken jug), of Jeremiah and Hosea. He taught with gestures the way to emphasize the reality of what He was doing. His body will be emptied of its blood. The words of Jesus bear out His actions and the apostles well understood the meaning of His words. Speaking of the blood of the Alliance, He evoked Exodus 24:8, a ritual which created the people and united them to Yahweh. The sacrifice of Jesus will conclude a new Alliance in His blood which will be shed *for all*. Jesus alluded here to Isaiah 53:12 whereby no one is shut out from salvation (cf. Mk 10:45), another allusion to the Suffering Servant Who offers His life to expiate the sin of the people. Jesus looks at His sacrifice in the perspective of the atoning sacrifice of the Suffering Servant. By the double reference to the sacrifice of the Alliance and the atoning sacrifice, Jesus gives us the meaning of His sacrifice. He will obtain the forgiveness of sin and create a new people who will live in closeness with God in eternal joy.

When you receive communion your sin is atoned for and you live with the Father in an association of matchless friendship. The Eucharist is the highest point of union with God, it is the strongest expression of God's espousing his people. But it is still a union which is lived symbolically. The reality will be infinitely more rich; that is why the Eucharist is directed towards the Parousia, when we shall know complete and final union with God.

Look carefully at all the dimensions of the Last Supper, contemplating in your prayer the innermost purposes of Jesus. The physical offering of bread and wine is the symbol of a mysterious reality which can only be grasped and understood on the level of the Heart of Christ; it is a mystery of love. The Eucharist is the reaction of Jesus to his coming death. He did everything possible to avoid this murder so that Israel should not be condemned for a crime (cf. the parable of the murderous vinegrowers). But Jesus did not endure it as an outside happening; He would change the substance of his death and make it an act of love.

Think of these words of Jesus: "... I lay down my life in order to take it up again. No one takes it from me, I lay it down of my own free will" (Jn 10:17-18). Jesus Himself gives meaning to His death. It is a crime on the part of his enemies, but Jesus makes it an act of free love: "There is no greater love than this: to lay down one's life for one's friends" (Jn 15:13). You can reflect on the deep meaning of the Last Supper while slowly reading St. John, chapters 13-17. Choose a free evening when you have some hours to spare and silently go over these chapters of the will and testament of Jesus. Unite yourself to the words of the sacrificial prayer and listen to them as if Christ was telling them to you. Don't read everything; appreciate various phrases. This form of prayer is especially good on the night of Holy Thursday.

Here you discover the true meaning of the Passion: it is not an act to appease the anger of the Father, for God does not desire suffering. The will of the Father is the Act of love of Christ Who abandons Himself to the Father completely (He 9:11-14). It is Jesus' awareness of His mission which leads Him to offer Himself to the Father in love. He did everything He could for His people; sadly enough, they rejected Him.

Jesus had one thing left to do: to take His life and offer it in an act of trust. You would think that this offering could have taken place in peace and calm, but the episode of Gethsemane will bring to mind all the tragic anguish of the sacrifice. You can only understand the Lord's Last Supper and the Eucharist if you contemplate, before the Blessed Sacrament, this loving action which led Jesus to give Himself up to the Father for the salvation of His brothers. Only then will you be able to commit yourself to Christ, but the love urging you to offer yourself comes from One higher than you — it is a sharing in His impulse of love. You cannot desire to bear the fruits of love before you have planted the tree of the Cross at the centre of your heart.

41. It is not enough to go through the gestures of the Eucharist; you have to commit yourself to Christ by giving up your life.

In the Lord's Supper there is another important gesture: "Take this and eat, all of you... drink, all of you." By inviting you to eat His Body and drink His Blood, Jesus involves you in His Sacrifice. He invites you to enter into and with Him in the offering of His life that He makes to the Father. It is the very meaning of the words that you prayed earlier: "If anyone will come after me, let him take up his cross and follow me." This is what Jesus meant when He asked the sons of Zebedee. "Can you drink my cup?" If you agree to share His cup, then you must go all the way in the gift of yourself, as Jesus did: "Jesus, knowing that His hour now had come, to pass from this world to the Father, having loved his own who were in the world, He loved them to end" (Jn 13:1).

Having meditated on the Lord's Supper, you must discover the meaning of your own daily Eucharist. You cannot eat this bread and drink this wine without wanting to share wholeheartedly in the sacrifice of Jesus. One might wonder if years of liturgical life, with all the reforms you have known, have not made you lose the spiritual fruit of the Eucharist, the gift of Christ in the shape of His Word and His Body.

The sacrifice of the Alliance is the Lord Jesus, for the Eucharistic meal is that of a body given up and blood shed. Going through the gestures is not enough; you must be part of this commitment where Jesus gives up His life to the Father, loving His own to the end. Otherwise, you are living the symbol but not the reality.

Have you become aware of the gift of Christ to you of His glorified Body? It is the strength of His love which pierces you in the depth of your being. He gives you His life and so you share in the dialogue of love which unites Him to His Father. Jesus said it clearly in His talk on the bread of life: "Just as the Father Who has life sent Me and I have life because of the Father, so the man who feeds on Me, will have life because of Me" (Jn 6:57).

But there is still more — the way in which Christ meets you and gives you His Body. He does not come in a static way. He comes to renew in you His redeeming incarnation and to reproduce in you the movement which leads Him to His Father, bringing back the humanity which has become His Body. In the Eucharist, the unity of the Body is carried out and becomes in Jesus an offering to the Father. In this meditation you must ask the Holy Spirit (such is the meaning of the second epiclesis) to make you part of the sacrifice of Jesus, teaching you to give up your life to the Father: "May the Holy Spirit make of us an everlasting offering of praise to your glory" *(Third Eucharistic Prayer)*.

Jesus teaches you to give yourself, not only at mass but in every detail of your life by a complete abandonment to the Father in all the events of your life. The Eucharist is the supreme act of the love of Jesus which transforms your heart, to make your life an act of love for the Father and your brothers. Reread what St. Thérèse Couderc said about "self-surrender" (cf. Annex III).

In the Eucharist, your life become the true spiritual sacrifice that Paul speaks of: "And now, brothers, I beg you through the mercy of God to offer your bodies as a living sacrifice holy and acceptable to God, your spiritual worship" (Rm 12:1). Your life takes on an eternal dimension when it is offered to the Father, with the life of Christ. The least of your actions, when it really expresses your love of the Father and man, is a prayer of praise, adoration and intercession; it is a spiritual sacrifice. But remember that the eternal is not made with the insignificant; if your life is to become a prayer, it has to be genuine and an expression of the true gift of yourself to others.

All your life then becomes a prayer. The prayer of Christ was the offering of His life in the sacrifice of the Cross. Christ prayed everywhere and always, for in doing the will of His Father He was simply showing to man His unceasing and secret dialogue with the Father. You know that your life is welcomed by Him Who glorified His Son, that it is closely united to the mystery of the Trinity. In the Eucharist, you offer yourself completely and in your daily life you give yourself drop by drop in doing the will of the Father. Be genuine in your offering and do not cut down on the sacrifice.

42. "My soul is sad unto death; remain here, and stay awake" (Mk 14:34).

The tragedy of Gethsemane has always strongly attracted the saints — they were unable to stop contemplating it. However little you love Christ, you cannot remain unmoved when you think of that night when He sweated in agony at the thought of what was to come. By your sin, you are involved in the agony and death of Jesus. It is because of you and your brothers that His soul knew agony and sorrow even unto death. You understand anguish when you have lived through something similar. It is in times of affliction, when you suffer and cry, that you need your friends with you. Jesus also knew in His agony the terrible loneliness of unappreciated love.

Let these words echo in you, words He spoke to His disciples as He went to Gethsemane: "Stay here and watch." It is an appeal to abide with Jesus, looking at Him silently as He appears to you in this scene, as Paul said: "Let us not lose sight of Jesus Who leads us in our faith" (Heb 12:2). Only just at that moment when you want to pray, you feel it is impossible. Like the apostles who were friends of Jesus, you are overcome by fatigue and you sleep.

It is not just a matter of physical fatigue, of being unable to focus your attention, which would be quite normal if you have prayed for a long time. However, the difficulty in praying is due, not just to tiredness, but reaches deeper and is rooted in your fundamental selfishness. I think it is normal to feel a great discomfort before someone in agony, as Fr. Loew says: "It is an area where you cannot go." "Remain here" said Jesus, "while I go over there and pray" (Mt 26:36). Between the *here* where you want to stay and pray and the *over there* where Jesus went, there is an unfathomable, immeasurable gulf.

You see why you have trouble praying, it is because you are unwilling to cross this chasm. Yet you are asked to contemplate His confusion and His agony. We shall try to draw near to this scene later, but you will always remain on the threshold for you cannot share in this. The reason for your discomfort is that you have discovered the hardness of your sinner's heart. You are reduced to the helplessness of sleep for you are weak, heavy with the sleep of your sinfulness. You are like the Apostles who also slept with the sleep of the oblivious. But opposite you is Christ, the man alive Who goes wide awake into the mystery of His death. Fundamentally, you suffer from loving Jesus so little while He has showed you boundless love. It is His agony. He is alone when He might wish for a friendly, comforting presence beside Him.

But your suffering is good since it puts you in touch with yourself. It is a reverse appeal to the Holy Spirit that one day He may let you know the mystery. Then you will be repaid for the years of dryness and barrenness about the Passion. You are simply asked to stay in complete silence, to be there and stay there with Jesus. In the agony there is a mystery you cannot share nor understand, you can hardly imagine it. This is why you must continue watching, in prayer.

Do not try to understand the agony of Jesus, nor His sadness which is that of the Word Incarnate, the Suffering Servant, the Lamb crushed by the sin of the world. But simply stay beside Him awake in your faith and love. When you meet a friend in pain, you don't start to talk about the meaning of his suffering, but you stay there, near him, silent, trying to share in love what he is enduring.

Do the same in the Garden of Gethsemane. Leave yourself and your preoccupations, think only of Christ and His sadness. Such a prayer, free, simple and selfless, is the hallmark of your choice to follow Him, to be genuine. It is a difficult prayer since it demands deep silence and great calm. It is Christ alone Who must occupy your whole attention and your consciousness. So read the scene over again quietly and let each sentence and each word echo in your heart throughout the day. If you can stay a long time in this prayer, Christ will flood you with His presence and His sorrowful radiant face will draw you from your sinful wretchedness.

43. "Going on a little further, He threw Himself on the ground and prayed" (Mk 14:35).

In the Agony you can only follow Jesus at a distance; how could you understand this mysterious dialogue of Jesus with His Father: "He threw Himself down and prayed." At the Last Supper Jesus faced death serenely; at Gethsemane it is the reality of the *cup* that Jesus accepts to drink in agony. The story of the agony raises the question of the humanity of Jesus, for there is no other scene in the Gospels where Jesus loses His air of self-mastery to become instead close to despair. Jesus is still a man, a being with free will who knows agony before a choice for the future. Man never knows what will happen tomorrow, otherwise he would not be free. Endlessly, he has choices to make and it is he who makes or destroys his own life. In the struggle of the agony you see Jesus freely choosing the will of the Father.

The eagerness of His prayer is shown by His posture: "He threw Himself on the ground." Then you must consider His dialogue with the Father. You have two prayers of Christ which have the same aim. The first is indirect: "He prayed that, if it were possible, this hour might pass Him by" (Mk 14:35). The second is more abrupt, in direct style: "Father! Abba. Everything is possible for you. Take this cup away from me. But let it be as You would have it, not as I" (Mk 14:36). Father George thinks that the first prayer (14:35) offended the primitive church — they did not understand why Christ would go back on what He had given, once and for all, at the Last Supper; so they added a reassuring sentence.

Now the most basic point was certainly v. 36. The rest of the text shows that Christ renewed this for a long time, certainly over several hours (Mk 14:39-41). Here you have a foreshadowing of the mystery of the agony. Jesus was not in a situation where everything was settled ahead of time by an unchanging will, since He said to the Father: "Everything is possible." There was still room for freedom, either to accept or to refuse.

You are in the middle of the struggle between acceptance and refusal: "Take this cup away from me. But let it be as you would have it, not as I." This is the only time that Jesus made an involuntary movement against the will of His Father. Jesus is not cut off from the tragic human condition. He was not bound by a will forced on Him from without. The life of Christ is not that of a robot with everything programmed ahead of time. He was torn apart, He had to choose between Himself and the Father; the victory was not settled beforehand and Jesus could consider that this cup might be set aside.

You might think that Jesus seemed to have the appearance of a man, but that in the final reckoning, victory was taken for granted. To understand this struggle, you can look back on your own experience where you have had a tragic debate between your will and that of God. Such a struggle may last hours, especially if it has any bearing on basic choices in your life. You have to forget those story book situations where such a decision can be taken easily, with no second try, no going back. But, in the depth of this struggle, Jesus manages to say "Father". Torn apart by the vision of the cup, He put himself, with a Son's confidence and a loving abandon, into the hands of the Father.

It is in this scene that the love of Jesus for the Father comes through most strongly, a love which gave up its own will and embraced that of another. In the agony, Jesus always saw Himself in relationship to His Father and cared for His own. It is from this contemplation of the love of God and men that He found the strength to accept and to persevere. The Gospel is silent about the response Jesus made, not saying that He accepted, but at the end of a tragic struggle, He made the Father's will His own and it broke Him. He stands there with a noble dignity, waiting for Judas and the cohort of soldiers who come to arrest Him. From then on, you will find Jesus unhesitating in His decision. His will is to go on to the bitter end. His last words on the Cross were: "It is accomplished."

This struggle is valuable for you. When you endure temptations and trials, when you face death, you sometimes feel that God is asking too much of you. Since Gethsemane, whatever your sorrow or trouble, you know that a man, with the same nature as you, has gone through the same thing "even unto death." Ask Him in continual prayer to come and live again in you all the way to victory.

44. Contemplate the transfigured face of Christ in the "departure from Jerusalem" — you will feel the joy of the Resurrection.

Invited to follow Christ in His passover by an act of complete self-denial, you must also contemplate Him in His glory. Christ did not desire death for itself, He passed through it as a shining expression of His love which gave birth to His resurrected life. If you are called to die to yourself, it is so that you can share in this new life of the glorified Jesus. This is why, before you enter the mystery of salvation, it is good to contemplate Jesus in His Transfiguration. Here He has given you a foretaste of His Paschal glory, even now in your natural life. If you do not enjoy the glory of Easter in prayer, your Christian life will remain harsh and tense.

To help you meditate on the Transfiguration you could reread Luke 9:28-36, stopping after each sentence to let the words sink one by one into your heart. Look at a painting of the Transfigured Christ, something similar to a Byzantine icon. But beyond this, put your inward gaze on Jesus Himself, shining with the glory of the Father. May the Holy Spirit enlighten your eyes so that you may contemplate the face of Christ. You have to tear away the veil of words and ideas to reach the heart of reality. This is a grace you must ask for constantly, praying intensely. It was when Christ was praying that His face became transfigured. He lived in such a close and loving relationship with the Father that it shone out openly and lit up His face, just as you might turn pale when you are inwardly upset. Here you could pick up the saying of St. Augustine: "Give me a heart which has seen and loves, and it will understand what I'm saying."

The Gospel tells us that His face seemed quite different. You know how the face discloses the soul, how it reveals the inward emotions. With all your soul, look at the face of Christ, but through this face recognize the heart of Christ. His face shows the infinite tenderness of His heart. When you feel very happy your face lights up and shows your joy — something like this happened to Jesus at the Transfiguration.

If you examine closely the Heart of Jesus in prayer, you will find that the divine life, the fire of the burning bush, is hidden deep inside Jesus. In the Incarnation He "humanized" the divine life, so that He could communicate it to you without destroying you, for "no one can see God and live." At the Transfiguration this divine life flashed forth for a short time in broad daylight and irradiated from the face and clothing of Jesus. It is the Glory of God that you see in the face of Jesus.

In the Transfiguration all the power of the Glory of Yahweh, that is the intensity of His life, radiates from Jesus; Moses and Elijah meet Him. There is no mistake: the very being of Christ shows the presence of the thrice Holy God of the burning bush, and the God so intimate and close of Horeb. The Glory of Jesus must be seen in its fullest dimension as it shines forth in a mysterious way in His leaving Jerusalem, that is, in His Passion. It is in His glorious death that Jesus frees the intensity of the divine life hidden in Him.

Don't stop just at the death of Christ, but go deeper and discover the act of loving obedience that Jesus gave to His Father; you will understand why God consecrated and quickened Him by His holiness. Dying on the Cross, Jesus carried out an act of perfect love in giving up His life to the Father, and that is why the Father glorified Him. The Spirit which moved Jesus to abandon Himself into the hands of the Father penetrated and wholly transfigured Him, just as inchoately it had shone forth from Jesus' face at the Transfiguration. In accepting the sacrifice of love of His Son, the Father gave Him the seal of His supreme testimony: "This is my beloved Son, hear Him."

So the contemplation on the Transfiguration lets you go deep into the mystery of the Trinity where the cloud is the most striking symbol. You share the loving kiss that the Father gives His Son, if you accept with Jesus to abandon your life to the Father in love. Everything goes together, you cannot separate the Cross from the Glory. Meditate on the Glory of Jesus Transfigured, sharing in the Departure from Jerusalem: "All of us, gazing on the Lord's glory with unveiled faces, are being transformed from glory to glory into His very image by the Lord Who is the Spirit" (2 Cor 3:18).

45. One with the whole of creation, you suffer with Christ, so as to be glorified with Him.

The agony and the Cross are not events which are finished, cut out in stone. Pascal said: "Jesus is in agony until the end of the world, He must not be left alone." Christ indeed does relive His Glorious Passion in all mankind. As long as anyone suffers, wherever it might be, the agony of Jesus brings His Cross to life again and fulfils the Redemption. You are not alone when you go with Jesus to Gethsemane and Calvary; you are one with the universe and your brothers. Your suffering is not felt primarily as individual suffering, but as sharing in a vast suffering, vast as space and time. It is that of all mankind, and even more it is that of the whole universe, conscious or unconsious.

The whole of creation groans for it has been subjected to sin and pride. As Kafka said: "There is something broken in the world." If you do not live as irresponsible, or a trifler, if you are really in the world with love, you cannot remain distant from suffering humanity. Everywhere there arises a mysterious cry, that things are not what they should be, that suffering is more bitter because we are aware of man's dissatisfaction with his state. Your faith does not make you invulnerable, unfeeling — on the contrary: "Creation groans" says St. Paul, "and not only creation but all of us groan inwardly" (Rm 8:22).

Christian experience implies an element of pain, sharing the agony of the human condition, and this is not just on the surface — it is in your very self: "We groan inwardly." Along with your brothers, you question yourself, you struggle and often endure death. In prayer, let this groan arise, recall those faces and situations where men are in agony and dying. At the heart of the world, you will truly find the Cross of Jesus.

In prayer, you beg the Christ in agony to take upon this vast suffering. With Him, you offer to the Father and celebrate the true Eucharist, and so you concelebrate in the agony and in Calvary. But know too that in suffering with Christ, you are glorified with Him. Your Christian life is an experience of suffering and of glory, a Passover experience since you are a joint heir with Christ.

Paul said: "There is no comparison between suffering and glory" (Rm 8:18). You have the certain knowledge that the suffering of the present time are nothing compared with the future glory. They are not two separate realities to be put on the same level. There is no proportion, no comparison. The relationship is more inward, more vital since it is at the core of death that life is born. Do not say that the groaning of which Paul spoke is joyful, that would be a contradiction. Say, rather, it is glorifying, that it is already raised up by the victory for which it is preparing.

For there is in reality groaning and groaning, suffering and suffering. There is the groan of man crushed, overwhelmed, beaten, the groan of agony. Then there is the groaning, still painful, but heralding life, the groan of a woman giving birth to a child. You know that your suffering, united to the suffering of the world, is not that of agony, "but of birth", as said Paul Claudel. You know that your own suffering, your own groan, is a sign of life rising, life coming. You are a son of God by faith and baptism, son of God by the indwelling of the Holy Spirit really present, but in a way which is in the earliest stage of development.

Each day you give birth to yourself as a son of God. Your very body, your vital powers which bind you to humanity and the universe, must share in this quality of being a son: "What we are to be in the future has not yet been revealed" (Jn 3:2). The spirit of God has yet to take over your whole person and the whole world. Total salvation in its fulness is yet to come. You are drawn to this new man to whom you give birth each day. Your groan is similar to that of Christ in His agony and on the Cross, giving up His Body to suffering and pain, but a dignifying suffering which carries in it the seed of the victory of the Resurrection.

46. At the heart of your faith and your prayer is the experience of the Risen Christ, sharing with you His life and His joy.

You did not know Christ according to the flesh, but you can recognize Him today in the power of His Spirit. As John says at the beginning of his first epistle, you can hear, see, contemplate and touch Him in faith. Meeting Him, you will share the joy and peace of Easter. In great interior silence, all taken up by the indwelling Spirit Who lets you experience the presence of the Glorified Christ, reread the accounts of the Resurrection. Your faith as a believer rests on the witness of the Apostles, handed on today by the teaching of the Church.

First, be convinced of the actual presence of the Risen One. He is alive, the Glory of God has pierced His being, He can die no more. Before His death, the body of Jesus Christ was limited by the density of His flesh, from now on He shows Himself by a body that Paul calls "spiritual." The risen Christ becomes, as Father Xavier Léon-Dufour calls it, a "pure hyphen." It is why He can show himself at the same time in places distant from each other, so that His disciples can understand that He had abolished the boundaries of space and time.

The Risen Christ is present to all men of all times. You can thus establish a personal relationship with Him. You know yourself and you feel yourself relating to the Risen Christ as someone other than yourself, on Whom you depend completely; you feel that living without Him would not be living, but with Him everything becomes love. The Risen Christ looks upon you and those around you whom you love. So He has a special relationship with all men. If you leave out this universal presence of Jesus you maim Him.

Now this universal presence of the Risen Christ also makes it possible for you to unite with others from within themselves; to make them understand what your words are unable to say. You can act on them and love them with all your heart's love, whereas in personal contacts your body's limitations prevent real communion. "Christ binds us together", Teilhard de Chardin says, "and shows us to each other." In Him you find every man and everything, in order to impart the best of yourself to them. All creation, enlightened by the presence of the Risen One, resumes its movement towards the Father and becomes a sign of the presence of God.

But you can only make this discovery insofar as your vision is enlightened by faith. In every appearance of the Risen One, He was at first disbelieved. The apostles saw Jesus and did not recognize Him. It was as if a fleshly veil prevented them from seeing Him. This is what happened with the disciples at Emmaus — Christ was not changed, but He was unrecognizable. Because of Good Friday, the apostles were unable to believe that Christ was present. So Jesus took the first step in meeting them. He did not come, He let Himself be seen. He "appeared and stood suddenly in the midst of them" (this is the language of the theophanies). Each time, He grappled with the reason for the disciples disbelief — the shame of the Cross. Peter had already refused a suffering Messiah after his profession of faith at Caesarea.

The disciples found that knowing the Risen One was not the same as the earthly knowledge of Jesus. He was not a ghost, it was truly Jesus, but He was "other." He had a spiritual body preserved from the normal conditions of life on earth. To know Him, one had to commit oneself and decide for Him, that is to believe in Him.

It is the same in prayer. You will know the Risen Christ when you welcome His presence, committing yourself to Him in free dialogue. To recognize Him, you must make a step towards Him. At the same time that you lovingly put your trust in Him, He will disclose Himself to you: "Come to me with your heart" says an Arabian proverb "and I will give you my eyes." The Risen One can only be known by believers.

The Risen Christ does not give Himself to you as a spectacle. He pushes you towards others in the future. From now on, you must proclaim that Christ is present and alive at the heart of the world and in every happening. The presence of the Risen One is not static but dynamic and evangelical. You are sent to all your brothers to tell the good news. Do not forget that Matthew was chosen to be an apostle because he had been with Jesus from His baptism to the Resurrection. Unless you have known the experience of the Resurrection in prayer and your daily life, you may preach a truth and an ethic, but you will not proclaim the mystery of a living person which is, in the end, what your brothers expect.

47. "You have never seen God; the only Son, Who is in the bosom of the Father, has shown Him to you" (Jn 1:18).

Without knowing it, you are threatened with spiritual starvation if you limit your contemplation to the person of Christ. Certainly, Jesus is the ultimate meaning of your life and it is in Him only that you will fulfil yourself as a man, but Christ is not an end in Himself. You can be Christ-centered in a way that borders on shortsightedness and deceives you insofar as it obscures your relationship with the Father. Jesus is the way, the truth and the life. His only aim is to let you cross from this world to the Father. Without this openness to the Father your baptismal vocation cannot be understood.

You must go even further: your human life is damaged if you are not open to a loving son's relationship with the Father. Placing yourself in the life-giving Christ Who directs your life towards the Father, you will know a new fulfillment and a transcendent humanism (*Populorum Progressio*, no. 16). You are all the more yourself when you remain in the Father through Jesus.

So you cannot be indifferent about entering with Christ into the Glory of the Father. Following Jesus in His earthly pilgrimage, you enter into the mystery of His Glorious Cross. His fundamental desire is for you to be with Him in His Father's dwelling, where He has prepared a place for you: "Indeed, I promise you, today you will be with me in paradise" (Lk 23:43). The night before He died He prayed for you in this way: "Father, I want those you have given me to be with me where I am, so that they may always see the glory You have given me" (Jn 17:24). To show clearly that He wants to bring you into the life of the Trinity He said to Mary Magdalene: "Go, find the brothers and tell them: I am ascending to my Father and your Father, to my God and your God" (Jn 20:17).

In your meditation on the Gospel you must never underrate this dual attitude of Christ, wholly turned towards men to save them, but no less turned towards the face of the Father. If you let go one of the poles of this definite orientation, your prayer will no longer be Christian; you will see nothing but a man in Jesus. You will have lost the Son of God Who wishes to make of you a son, in the power of the Spirit.

It is good sometimes to fit in your prayer this deep and secret part of Christ which came to his awareness in His nights of silent adoration. You will be helped in this meditation by reading St. John, chapters 13-17, where you see Jesus living intensely in the joy of contemplating the Glory of the Father. He quivered with joy at the thought of living fully in the sight and love of the Father. The Easter Sunday introit has Jesus say of this experience of union with the Father: "I am always with You." Take time to savour this joy of Jesus, the beloved Son in Whom the Father finds all His pleasure.

Only intense, prolonged prayer can let you see, from within, moved by the Spirit, how much Jesus is *turned* towards the Father *(ad Patrem)*. Did you notice in the synoptic gospels a phrase of Jesus in which the Father is seemingly absent, but which clearly shows Jesus looking with love and admiration at His Father: "No one is good but God alone" (Lk 18:19). If you persevere in prayer you will undestand how Jesus and the Father are one in their very being. To pray is to share in this loving relationship where you are in the Father.

The plan of Christ is to bring you into the relationship of love with the Father, of which prayer makes you more and more aware. When you pray let this life of the Trinity, which is the very foundation of your life, rise to the surface of your heart. Then go close to Christ in faith — tell Him of your desire to be one with Him, by the power of the Spirit: "No one can come to the Father except through Me" (Jn 14:6). The more you see Christ, the more you will also see the Father. "Do you not believe that I am in the Father and the Father is in Me?" (Jn 14:10).

Do not try to understand this life of Jesus with the Father, it is beyond your human intelligence in every way. Acquiesce to the reality in your being and enter more and more into the movement of life and love which carries you like a wave to the heart of the Trinity: "Adoration of the Trinity is our sole purpose" (Fr. Monchanin).

48. You will become a truly spiritual man, that is, a man of prayer, when you live completely in the present moment.

There is in you a secret desire to live in a state of unceasing prayer. You feel that to live in the presence of God is the source of joy, of peace, and true happiness. If you gathered together all the minutes and the hours that you waste each day, you would have plenty of time to pray. Now and again, take five minutes to stop and rest in inner silence. Let your only concern be that you be there, speechless, motionless, in the presence of the living God. Throughout your day never let an hour go by without going deep into your heart in the presence of the Most High. You often have the chance to call on God for help, a cry of love or recognition, even in the taking of a breath.

You will be a man of continual prayer if you know how to accept the present moment as a gift of God. You well know that your life becomes prayer on the day when you give yourself up to the Father in the same sacrifice as Jesus. Your life becomes a spiritual sacrifice to the Glory of the Trinity. But the gift of yourself is not true or real unless God draws you where He wishes you to go. Usually, you want to make your offering yourself, while God is asking you for something else, very often the thing that you consider as the apple of your eye. Let God take from your life what He wills, to make it the subject of your spiritual sacrifice. In this way, you will be completely open to the work of God in you.

This is just how you lay hold of the present moment, the pivot, says Father Loew, between eternal life and daily life. You want to give yourself up completely to God, but you must leave to Him the way of obtaining this gift. He carries out His will of love in you through the labyrinth of your individual history. Each moment of your life is a small fragment of this sacred history and it comes to you just as God wills it. It is here, in this very moment, that you must live this gift of yourself to the Father.

Do not choose the event, it comes to you unforeseen and will surprise you by its strangeness. If you endure it passively you will live your life as fate; if you accept it fully as the will of God, you will make your life a sacred history. As Christ made His death, apparently enforced from without, a free act of love for the Father, you are called to make of each happening in your life a spiritual offering. This is the ultimate basis of your continued presence before God.

The present moment is the only point in your life where, discerning God's will, you can unite yourself to Him in His very being. You no longer have any power over the past which belongs to His lovingkindness, and you have no idea of the future which is entrusted to His Providence — all you have left is the present. The present moment is a window open on to eternity, it is the "blink" of God in which you live (R. Guardini). You can reach God only in the present moment, this one and the next one; it is the everlasting sacrament of the presence and the action of God.

When you are on a train and you pass beside fields perpendicular to the track, it is only at one precise moment that you can see them clearly down their entire

114

length. Before or after, you see only a confused tangle. In the present moment are centered all your human experience and all the love of God for you. God is no longer in your past, He is not yet in your future, He is only present for you where you are.

If you want to make your life an unceasing prayer, a constant union with God in everything, live fully in the present moment. You will discover there, hidden under the ordinary appearance of everyday things, the living presence of God. At this very point you will meet God; if you look elsewhere, you will miss Him. It is here that He waits for you, to give Himself entirely to you:

> "He who has the present moment has God...
> So whoever has the present moment has all...
> Sufficient is the present moment...
> Let nothing bother you..."

> (Saint Teresa of Avila)

49. To pray is to sink deeper and deeper into that abyss where the Trinity lives. The Spirit lays hold of you, to give you to the Son and the Son gives you to the Father.

You began this prayer experience by contemplating the thrice Holy God; you will complete it, or rather continue it, in the mystery of the Holy Trinity. Going through the stages of the plan of salvation can give you a better idea of the unfathomable riches of the mystery of God which Paul compares to an abyss. "You will, with all the saints, have strength to grasp the breadth and the length, the height and the depth, until, knowing the love of Christ which is beyond all knowledge, you are filled with the utter fullness of God" (Ep 3:18). One last stage is left to pass through, since the paschal mystery is not an end in itself but flows into the love of the Trinity. Leaving this world for the Father, Jesus draws you behind Him and brings you into the mystery of His relationships with the Father.

The life of the Trinity is the very essence of prayer and the contemplative life. To pray is to become aware of the new relationships which exist between the Persons of the Trinity and yourself, it is to let yourself be drawn into the very movement of the life of the Trinity. St. Irenaeus said: "The Spirit comes and lays hold of you and gives you to the Son and the Son gives you to the Father." In prayer, do not stop in the intermediate zones of thought and feeling but go deep into that abyss where the Trinity lives, come join the Trinity which is in you. Whatever your worries, your sins and your needs, re-unite yourself first with the Trinity and after that you will rediscover everything in another way.

Here you are at the heart of prayer. With your mind and heart you can reach the existence of God, but the secret of His inner self remains out of your reach; only the Holy Spirit can actually reveal this mystery of love. You well know the saying of St. John: "God is Love" (1 Jn 4:8), but have you taken in all the dimensions of the word *Love*? For you, love is often kindness, a concern you have for someone, or an attraction you feel for him. God in His essence is Love, that is, He is a community of Persons or rather a communion. His very being, His life, is to love. In other words, He personifies Love.

For God, to be is to love, that is to go out of oneself, to give oneself, to live in another. Each Person of the Trinity lives in the relationship that He offers to the Other. When you say that God is Father, you affirm at the same time that He lives only to go out of Himself, to give Himself and to find Himself completely in His Son. Jesus Himself exists and lives only for the Father to Whom He gives Himself completely. Their mutual love is expressed and becomes creative in the Person of the Holy Spirit. Prayer is the real discovery of this immense flow of love between the Persons of the Divine Family.

At the heart of the Trinity you are at the source of love, both in the world and in the Church. When Jesus proclaimed the greatest commandment (Mt 22:34-40) and invited His disciples to love God and their brothers, He did nothing more than place you at the heart of the

Trinity. You cannot obtain the love of God and that of others, it is not a love that you can bring to birth in yourself by your own power; it has nothing in common with feelings that you have for God in prayer or a certain benevolence towards your brothers.

Contemplating the Holy Trinity, you ask that the love which comes from above and which intimately unites the Three Divine Persons may come to you. "The love of God has been poured into our hearts by the Holy Spirit which has been given to us" (Rm 5:3). This love is created in you by the Holy Spirit and it is given to you by Christ Who died and rose again, received by you as food in the Eucharist. "Pour forth in us, Lord, your spirit of charity, that having been nourished by the paschal sacrament, your fatherly love may keep our hearts perfectly united" *(Easter Communion Prayer)*.

If you try to get closer to this mystery of the relationships of the Trinity you see that they are distinguished by a dual movement, welcome and communion, gift and reciprocity. The Divine Persons possess one another only to give One the Other. God never stops showing His love in the gift of Himself whether it be in the love of the Divine Persons among themselves, or in the love for men which burst forth in the Creation, the Cross and the Church.

Simply try to become aware of the love of God for you. It is an invitation for you to remember the wonders God has done on your behalf, so that you may grasp their significance and unite yourself to Him. He created you and keeps you alive with all the riches of your personality, body, mind, heart, talents, etc. By your baptism He has recreated you and made you His son. He has fed you with the Eucharist and He has forgiven you. Remember all the graces in your life, in your vocation, your prayer, your mission...

In prayer, go deeper into the meaning and secret of these gifts. Too often you are like the oldest son in the parable whose mind is clouded by his father's riches: "You never offered me so much as a kid goat to celebrate with my friends" (Lk 15:29). Seeing such wealth and possessions had stopped him seeing people. He no longer saw his father who was the source of these gifts, and the latter reproached him gently: "My son, you are with me always and all I have is yours" (Lk 15:31). Becoming aware of the gifts of God, you find that through them the Father becomes more and more present to you. He will go still further bringing you His loving and gracious presence. The supreme gift He offers you is centered in His Son Jesus.

Becoming aware of the *mirabilia Dei* is an invitation to praise and admire God's work in you. Here you see what is at stake in every Christian life. On one hand, you can use these gifts of God for your own selfish enjoyment instead of using them as tools to create relationships to God and your fellow men; this is the sin of the younger son who wasted his goods in prodigal living, far from the Father. He has no relationship with His Father and cuts himself off from his family. On the other hand, you can offer yourself to God with all that you are, redirecting to Him your gifts, your riches, your heart. The aim of this contemplation is to lead you to make this offering to God, your true self.

As with the whole of creation, you are called to join with Christ in the heart of the life of the Trinity. "All things are yours, you are Christ's and Christ is God's." To pray is to be admitted by grace into this dialogue of love between the Three Divine Persons: it is to share their life and their union, and finally to be able to speak to God as a friend.

You will discover forthwith what demands this being taken into the Trinity will make on your life. You can only enter this stream of love if you are prepared to live and love as do the Persons of the Trinity. This demands a total surrender of yourself, that you become absolutely poor to give yourself to others. You will prove the word of the Beatitudes — spiritual poverty is an essential condition of love. In this way, all we own is put at the service of God and other people.

Then you understand why brotherly love is rooted in communion with the Trinity. In communion with your brothers, you are called upon to reproduce on earth the love which unites the Divine Persons. It is from the mystery of the Trinity that brotherly love finds its beginning. In the same way that the Father loves the Son and gives Himself wholly to Him, and the Son loves the Father, giving Himself up wholly to Him, so this same love which flows in the heart of the Trinity will teach you to give your life for others. Brotherly love does not lie in techniques, but in greater communion with God. In a sense, you do not try to love your brothers, for you are likely to have many illusions, but living poor, without anything, you are filled with the love of God and made able to love others: "That they may be one as we are One" (Jn 17:22).

This explains why little has been said on the apostolate and brotherly love in this book. Too often brotherly love has been reduced to a vague moralism or a skin-deep sentimentality whereas it flows primarily from the mystery of the Trinity. Each time married people give themselves to each other, or friends really love one another, they live and reproduce on earth the mystery of the Trinity. Then, the foundation of all prayer and of all true love for others, lies in the contemplation of this mystery. Nicholas Berdyayev used to say to his Communist friends: "Our social doctrine is the Trinity." Your sole purpose on earth is to contemplate and to adore the Trinity, opening to that love the whole naked surface of your being, even to its most sensual powers, so that the love can penetrate you and carry you away in its current. Isn't this the absolute fulfillment of your eternal vocation? Why do Christians take so little nourishment from this mystery of the Holy Trinity? They would find in this "contemplation to win love" a rising spring of eternal life. You can contemplate the Trinity unceasingly as it is the very essence of prayer and the life of prayer. At the end of a retreat, designed above all as a prayer experience, it is a good thing to go over it for several weeks to keep in mind the mysteries you have contemplated.

The last stage sets you at the heart of the Trinity, to

see how everything flows from it. "Consider how all good things and all gifts come from above... as the sunbeams from the sun and water from its source" (*Exercises,* no. 237). The day you understand that everything comes from God you will truly be collaborating with Him, exercising the priesthood of the baptized. With Jesus, you offer yourself to the Father as a "holy, living and pleasing sacrifice" (Rm 12:1) and you offer the whole of creation at the same time. As Jesus in the bosom of the Trinity endlessly raises up to the Father all that He is and has received from Him, in the same way you give back to God all the good things He has given you. It is the act of complete surrender which Jesus performed on the Cross saying to the Father: "All is accomplished."

This contemplation of the Trinity should unify all your life for it thrusts you into the reality of love and teaches you to search for and love God in all things. The day you understand that God loves you, that all is included in love, your life changes and you find Him everywhere, in your meetings, your daily work, your studies and your prayer. There is no opposition between prayer and action, between being with God and being with men; the real struggle is between the old man and the new man, sin and grace, selfishness and the giving of one's self. If your heart is open and willing, you will be carried in the flow of love and your life will be a favoured spot in the knowledge of God.

A note concerning
the experience of the believer

Considering the importance we have given in this work to spiritual experience, it might be useful to be precise about this idea. We are, in effect, speaking of a prayer experience in which one enjoys the presence of God or of an experience of spiritual understanding through our desires — all expressions which seem to emphasize feelings. We are aware, too, of the importance given to experience in the life of faith, which is often defined as real and vital knowledge of Christ. Turning to religion, modern man often asks: "What worthwhile experience can you offer me?" The present interest in oriental religions is often motivated by a vague desire for undemanding religious experience, without any real conversion on the part of the individual.

We know how vague and doubtful, and even dangerous, can be this idea of experience when it deteriorates into violent, irrational and anarchical demonstrations. Some definition is needed in order to speak more freely and spontaneously in these pages, refining the idea of experience from its counterfeits. One must always distinguish the essential from the accessory, the unchangeable from the temporary, the authentic from the deceptive, so that readers are not misled about what we really mean. We would like, therefore, to be very precise about Christian experience itself.

The word *experience* has several meanings, in the

secular vocabulary as well as in the religious vocabulary. It means scientific or philosophical experience, and in religion, the experience of the believer or the mystical experience. The experience we speak of here is not that known by the exceptional mystic nor the extraordinary charismatic, but the normal Christian who tries to live fully by his faith. It would be interesting to study in St. Paul the different degrees of the believer's experience; there would be beginners in spirituality who are like children in the faith, called upon to grow and become mature. Then there are the spiritually adult whom Paul calls "the perfect" that is normal Christians, faithful to the graces they have received. It is the experience of these Christians that is discussed in the Epistle to the Romans.

Elsewhere Paul alludes to the "spiritually stunted" who stay at the beginning, who do not develop their faith and their Christian life or who lapse into ignorance and sin... which proves that in his mind, these categories were not static. The spiritual can indeed become sensual again and the sensual can become spiritualized. This is an important difference from some religious ideas for which everything is predetermined by an inflexible and unchanging God. Lastly, Paul alludes to a very exceptional kind of experience: "I was taken up" he says "to the seventh heaven" on which he does not elaborate, neither need we. These different degrees of experience should be gone over again in detail, but that is beyond our study. Here we take the word *experience* in its broad sense, concerning the believer, that is the man who holds fully to the word of God and who is a spiritual person because he has received the Spirit of God. Paul clearly distinguishes between the two categories of people, the "psychic" who remains on an entirely human level and the "spiritual" whose spirit is transformed by the Divine Spirit and who enters into the wisdom of the Beatitudes and the Cross.

Here we shall discuss only the experience of the normal Christian. We might add that until recently, Catholics did not look favourably upon the word *ex-*

perience. It has begun to find its place in the religious vocabulary only in the last twenty years. It used to evoke so many variations (all types of false mysticism, both individual and collective) that theologians and spiritual directors avoided it like the plague.

At a time when feeling and states of mind induced by esoteric techniques are made so much of, wariness can be helpful. It is not a question of being afraid but of forming a wholesome idea of what the word implies, avoiding all deviations. When we speak of experience, we are threatened by several temptations, either to reduce it to mere emotion or to overestimate the action of man. The biggest risk we run is of depersonalizing experience, splitting man into various levels. It is the whole man, a part of his community, who knows experience.

First of all, Christian experience must not be reduced to its emotional elements; this is a strong temptation for many today threatened to be overrun by not properly ordered feelings. It must not be confused with feeling, even of a higher or religious type as Bergson rejects this in his works. In Christian experience there is more than a stirring of emotional faculties. This does not mean that the emotional part is foreign to the experience, but you must not confuse emotion and sensitivity. Sensitivity in us is a faculty which tests, receives and transmits, and therefore has a place in experience as long as our real emotion takes on the movement of our sensitivity.

In Christian experience and particularly in prayer, there is first of all an element of knowledge, of clarity and intellectual belonging. Man must stand before God's truth and in the truth of his own being. This is why there is an objective contemplation of God, as He is revealed in the Bible. God does not exist just because I have met Him, but because He revealed Himself objectively to a people, to witnesses and in His Son Jesus Christ through actual historical events.

Then there is the emotional element. The God Who revealed Himself is also He Who is love, kindness, goodness and mercy. According to Pascal, He is the God of

123

the heart. It is normal then for our emotional faculties to be stirred, and for us, to thrill deeply with gratitude, joy and praise when we become aware of this personal love of God.

But it does not stop here in the true Christian experience; it must include a voluntary, free and active element. Whoever talks of love does not speak only of the affection felt, but also of the gift of one person to another. When we speak of love we must never separate emotional love and actual love, receiving and giving, otherwise we fall into sentimentality. To love is to receive the other's affection in our sensitive faculties and to give ourselves to the other in an actual gift of our self.

We only become aware of the presence of the love of God in us, that is, His grace, when we get out of ourselves to give ourselves to Him. "It is not those who say 'Lord, Lord'" Jesus said "who will enter the Kingdom of Heaven, but those who do the will of my Father." We truly feel the presence of grace in us only in the free gift of ourselves to God and to our brothers. It is the same on the natural level, we can only know our intelligence and freedom in performing free and intelligent acts. It is in the free action that I know that I am a spiritual person.

This is why genuine experience of God must be real on the level of our daily life and our relations with each other. It is the only norm to go by, far more sure than emotions felt in prayer. Have you ever loved a brother unselfishly, for the simple joy of helping him as a free man? Are we able to forgive someone who has hurt us without expecting any return except secretly doing the will of the Father? Do we do our daily work conscientiously, only wanting to give ourselves completely and lovingly to the Father, without anyone knowing? Have we given a free hour to pray to the Father, listening to His Word in the secrecy of our room? This should not be done simply as an act of will, but to feel joy and happiness in the free gift of ourselves. I think that it is on this level that we can experience truly the love of God and His grace.

This is why Christian experience is not a sensitive or

intellectual passivity. If it were that we would become people who are entirely sentimental or entirely intellectual. It is for this reason that throughout these meditations we have insisted on the authenticity of our prayer with regard to free praise and self-effacement in the gift of ourselves to others. It seems more consistent to restore its active meaning and character to Christian experience: "Thus, whatever the appearance, being active in experience is surer than being passive, what is willed surer than what is lived, what has been done than what has been felt" (J. Mouroux). In the same way, you must not confuse the passivity of someone who merely submits with the passivity of one who receives. There is a Christian passivity which both receives and gives. It is an active passivity or a passive activity.

Christian experience is part of a certain becoming, for it unfolds all through life. If it implies a certain dimension of depth, for it concerns the whole of man (mind, heart, body, will, freedom), it also implies a dimension of length and breadth. This means we experience God in the unfolding of our personal and social lives. The Christian experience fits within a dialectical and historical movement, implying a *before* and an *after,* detected only in the unfolding of our personal history; but the instant it occurs escapes our notice, for it is God breaking in, that is eternity in time. Like Jacob, we can say after this experience: "God was there and I knew it not!"

It often happens that after years lived in faithfulness and aridity, we discover the action of the Spirit in us. Newman said: "We do not recognize God's presence when it is with us but afterwards, when we look back towards what is past and gone." Time is therefore a factor of prime importance in both prayer and our spiritual life. Suddenly, we know that Christ has visited us and that He is really a person to us; we could not say exactly when this encounter took place, but we have the evidence that something spiritual occurred. It's the same for our spiritual choices, which time proves true.

Without our knowledge, the Holy Spirit enlightens

our minds and moves our wills along a specific line, and when we look back at the constants in our life, we see God's will for us becoming clear. This is why a prayer experience should not be assessed on the spur of the moment, but over the duration of our spiritual history. As St. Bernard often observed, we cannot foretell when Christ will come or go, but we can experience Him day after day by our self renewal and the spiritual progress in our lives.

Finally, let us remember that Christian experience is never simply that of an individual. Truly personal, of course, but nonetheless it is part of a community, closely related to a Church in which it is known, fostered and verified. The Church is the vital and maternal environment of Christian experience. No one can stand before God except as a member of an immense family, and there is an experience of prayer and community life which celebrates prayer and brotherly life in everyday experience.

Christian experience is a complex experience; we might say a complete experience or an integrating experience. It concerns the whole man, his emotions, activity, insight, will, freedom, personal history and openness to the community. It is neither pure passivity nor pure activity: "Experience is when a person sees one's self in relation to the world, to one's self and to God" (J. Mouroux).

IV

The Dialogue with God

I. If you want to know what your life is worth, judge it by the measure of your adoration.

In prayer, you are particularly drawn by the movement of God's love which comes to save you in Jesus Christ. So you risk placing yourself in the centre and enclosing yourself in a spiritual utilitarianism. Break this circle and dare to move upwards in the opposite direction, in a gesture of free adoration. You are made to adore God and your life will find its true centre of gravity when you prostrate yourself in the dust before the thrice Holy God, in the vision of Isaiah (ch. 6).

Christians still talk a great deal about God; they even do many things for Him, but they are losing the sense of adoration and this is why they are threatened by atheism. A God Who is not adored is not a true God. You must acknowledge that God alone is God and that adoration is your first duty. This act is only a foretaste, an anticipation of what you will be doing forever in the heart of the Holy Trinity.

To adore is not only a duty which springs from your state as a creature; it is the highest form of human life. In adoring God, you affirm His holiness, and at the same time, you affirm your importance as a free man before Him. "A life's value" says Father Monchanin "is its measure of adoration." When you want God for God's sake, in adoring Him, you have found your natural freedom.

It is true that the Chruch must ceaselessly recall that Christ came to save man and that Christians must serve their brothers, but she should be unfaithful to her mission if she reduced Christianity to a mere brotherly stewardship, for the faith would be reduced to mere humanism. Today, men are stifling in a consumer society, they have a definite right to see the Church in her true mission: turned towards men to save them, but first towards God to love and adore Him.

Ask the Holy Spirit long and earnestly for a sense of adoration and then prostrate yourself before God in the attitude of one who at the same time realizes the holiness of God and his own sinfulness: "To adore God" writes Father Geffré "is to lower one's eyes before His glory." When Moses heard God's voice, he covered his face "afraid to look at God" (Ex 3:6). Christ alone praises the Father in perfect adoration. Ask Him to reproduce in you the movement which drew Him *to the Father*.

To adore, you must glimpse the glory of God that is His unapproachable grandeur and His matchless holiness. But God never shows Himself as the Entirely Other without at the same time revealing Himself as the all near, for He is Love. The God of Holiness is also the God of love Who lets you share in trinitarian life. God is to be adored because He is Love.

Your very body is called upon to express your heart's adoration. At times, you will be unable to do anything but prostrate yourself on the ground (Ezk 1:28), for the holiness of God is a mystery which always eludes man's grasp. You will hide your face in your hands but you will hear God call you by your name. You will become aware of your sinfulness, facing God's holiness. But the God of holiness does not destroy the sinner, He purifies him. The angel touched the mouth of Isaiah with a coal from the altar to purify it.

It is in contemplating Jesus Christ that you will find the holiness and nearness of God. In Him you have the intimacy of the Entirely-Other God with man. He is the only adorer of the Father: "The hour will come when true worshippers will worship the Father in spirit and in truth, that is the kind of worshippers the Father wants" (Jn 4:23). When you pray, you are caught up by the Spirit Who models you in the pattern of Christ. In turn, the Son brings you to the depths of the Father and lets you share in His loving embrace. Ascending from the lips and the heart of Christ is the perfect adoration of the Father. Sink ever deeper into Christ.

II. Desire God with all the strength of your heart but never try to lay hold of Him. Then only He will come to you.

Do not believe you can conquer God by sheer might or seduce Him by the beauty of your words. You cannot take one step towards Him unless He has come to meet you. It is He Who wishes to conquer and seduce you: unfortunately your heart is often closed to His call. God goes round you and He waits until you make an opening in your heart so that He can rush in with all the power of His love.

This opening will be your desire, turned towards Him. It is the only force able to make Him come down. But your heart must be entirely filled with a burning desire for God Who will suffer no sharing. Ask the Holy Spirit often to dig deep into your heart so that this desire for God may spring from your depths.

Only desire compels God to come down. You cannot go up to Him for the upward direction is essentially forbidden to you. "There is no ladder with which the mind can reach up to God" (Saint John of the Cross). If you look long and intensely at heaven, God will come down and lift you up. It is always He who seeks: "Tired, you sat down, looking for me..." You cannot seek God, you cannot even take one step towards Him unless you have been inwardly asked or called specially."

If you beg Him to come, He will come to you. Better yet if you ask Him often, long and earnestly, He cannot

129

help coming down to you. You must understand that prayer is unmistakably like friendship between two people. Meditate often on these words of Simone Weil who wrote about friendship, and apply that to your relationship with God: "Friendship is the miracle by which someone accepts to look from a distance, without coming close, to the very one whom he needs like nourishment. It is the spiritual strength Eve lacked, yet she did not need the fruit. Had she been hungry when she was looking at the fruit, yet, in spite of that, had indefinitely remained looking at it without coming any closer, she would have performed a miracle similar to that of perfect friendship."

You cannot attain to union with God by your own effort. The work which is required is to look, to listen, to desire. You must be attentive to God's gift of Himself and consent to it, as Mary did at the Annunciation saying "Fiat". Prayer is an act of attention and consent to God Who is always near your heart.

Prayer, like friendship, is a joy given freely. You must not seek it for itself. You must wait, poor and stripped, to be worthy to receive it. Prayer belongs to the order of grace. If you spend all your prayer-time desiring God, not striving to lay hold of Him nor take Him for yourself, you may be sure that a great grace has been given to you, for you would not desire God if He were not present and acting within you to arouse this desire. If you do not have God in you, you could not sense His absence.

If your heart is dry, if you are like a log or dumb animal before God, with no desire for Him, cry out your suffering with loud cries. Knock on God's door until He opens it to you. Know that the Father will not give you a stone if you ask Him for bread. He wants to grant what you ask Him, but He waits for you to persevere as long as you can.

III. To experience God is to go deep into that silent mystery you call God, apparently receiving no reply, except the strength to go on praying, believing, hoping, and loving.

How many people turn to oriental religions today, asking them: "What experience do you offer us? Christians themselves frequently speak of experiencing God by which, unfortunately, they too often mean a pious feeling or some religious emotion of a higher order, whereas spiritual experience is far better and quite different. God never offers Himself to men as a sight to see or to excite their feelings.

Yet, there is a true experience of grace, a penetration of our human nature by the Spirit of the Trinitarian God which was realized in Jesus at the moment of His Incarnation and His sacrifice on the Cross. Yes, it is possible to experience this grace in your human life but it is obscure and mysterious, never matching what you expected. It is always an experience of giving, a freedom in which you give yourself up in self-abandonment to let the infinite God act in you.

To get a little idea of this divine life in you, look how Christ really knew Himself as Son of God and how He knew the Father, that is, what experience He had of Him. Certainly, Jesus lives in great intimacy with His Father; in His hours of nocturnal prayer, He heard the words: "This is my beloved Son," but He truly knew the Father in His agony and on the Cross. He expected direct help from the Father, one of those visible consolations which would have taken away the cup from Him; the Father did not grant this for He always refuses this consolation to His best friends. Christ truly knew this grace at the moment, when abandoned by man and plunged into dreadful solitude, He nonetheless drank freely from this chalice, out of love. Christ linked together this experimental knowledge of the Father with His giving up His life. "I know the Father, and I lay down my life for my sheep" (Jn 10:15).

If you want to experience God you cannot ignore the

experience of Jesus. At the moment when the silence of God weighs heavily on you, and you need to be helped directly by Him, if you keep on believing, hoping and loving, you will experience the true miracle of faith and the presence of God in you, for you could not do this unless God had intervened directly.

Karl Rahner thus describes certain situations in which we experience grace: "Have we ever obeyed, not because we had to, under penalty of punishment if we didn't, but simply because of this mystery, this silence... that we call God and His will? Have we ever once been truly alone? Has it ever happened that we take a decision simply because of the call of our conscience...? When we are absolutely alone and we know we are making a decision that no one else can take for us and for which we are forever responsible... Has it ever occurred to us to love God without any wave of enthusiasm carrying us... when it seemed like a frightening jump into the abyss, when everything seemed incomprehensible and apparently absurd? Have we sometimes been good to someone from whom we expected no echo of gratitude or understanding?"

It is in this free gift of yourself to God and to others that you truly experience grace and this comes not in intellectual theories, but on the level of your daily life. In the same way, when you suffer and you see your suffering dragging on, if you go on believing in the love of God, then only are you close to God.

Tell yourself this: you have a real experience of God or, to put it more simply, you are a man of prayer when you are brave enough to throw yourself, all through your life, into this silent mystery of God, without seeming to receive any reply other than the strength to go on believing, hoping, loving God and man, and through it all, you go on praying.

IV. Do not pray with your intelligence or with your feelings, but breathe out your heart before God.

You must keep on telling yourself that the place of prayer is the heart, the centre of your being, where you are completely free, where you open yourself or close yourself to God. Your heart is the very source of your conscious, free, understanding person and above all, the place where the Spirit lives in you. Go ever deeper into this silent abyss where you share the very life of the Trinity.

Too often you think that to pray is to develop fine intellectual thoughts before God. You are wrong. God has no need of your ideas, His are infinitely finer than yours. In the same way, your prayer cannot be made up of your feelings or moral resolves. You have to pray with your heart, your whole self. To pray is above all to be before God, in His sight. If your heart is with God, the rest will follow and you will know what to say and what to do.

Set aside all sham. Get rid of your mask so that from your heart's depths you may fly to God. It is not easy to be honest before God since you often play a rôle in your own eyes and before your brothers. You have made "skin clothing" to protect yourself from the consuming fire of the burning bush. You must first free your inner self and bring it to life. Then you expose yourself, poor and naked, to the radiance of the life of the Trinity. Perhaps then, after years of cleansing prayer, you will be drawn into the great current flowing between Father and Son.

Your being is what you are. You are worth more than your words, your thoughts, your actions. It is your self that you must bring to God, stripped of all you have and all you do. How many times have your possessions stopped you from living freely? The more you develop in your prayer life, the more you will become poor, plain, empty. You will pray then with your very self, beyond words. Like Charles de Foucauld, you will breathe out before God, losing yourself.

Learn to stand there facing the Father in complete silence, particularly aware of His love. What good to tell Him what He knows already and sees more clearly than you? Come simply to pray, with a strong calm desire to be there with God, for God, in the presence of God. Sit at the feet of the Lord, open wide your heart and your hands to receive the gift of His loving presence. He does not ask you to make intellectual meditations or to put on special behaviour, but simply to be aware of the presence and friendship of Jesus Christ.

You will feel that you are wasting your time, doing nothing and you will be tempted to leave. If you accept to stay in silence, poverty, fervently praying without losing your desire to contemplate the face of the Lord, be certain that the Holy Spirit will merge with you and carry you away.

When you leave on vacation, you are tense and tired, you are not yourself, in fact your heart is torn apart, divided, dispersed. Yet, after a few weeks of fresh air, relaxation and sunshine, you return calm and recollected. You see people and events differently. You could not say how this resurrection came about, but it is real and noticeable. In the same way, if you show yourself as you are to the sun of the love of God in the healing of prayer, you will clear the air you breathe and you will find a great peace. Never forget that those who pray are the lungs of humanity. If prayer were to disappear from your life and that of your brothers we would be threatened with suffocation.

V. In prayer, open the floodgates of your heart and let the living water flow into the innermost depths of your being.

When you read the Acts of the Apostles, you see the Spirit penetrating and transforming hearts and giving health to the sick. It seems like a flame which gets closer and closer and no human power could make it turn back.

Today you are deep in a world from which God is absent and often you look odd because of the demands of your faith. There are days when you wish that God would grant you one of those unexpected visits of the Spirit, which would reassure you, "one of those exhortations with which your soul, incarnate in the flesh, might somehow replenish itself and regain strength" (Moeller).

Do you believe that today God's arm is too short to perform such wonders? Do you not think that it is your human wisdom which is too short to allow God to manifest such signs? If your faith were a little stronger, just the size of a mustard seed, you would again see God breaking into your life and into the world. So, open your heart to the power of the Spirit and leave behind your doubts, your sorrows, your delays. Trust in the Spirit and He will act in your heart.

Prayer is that unique, favoured moment when you open the gates of your heart to the impetuosity of the Holy Spirit. Yes or no, has your baptism made you into a new creature, one being with Christ, has it poured into you the life of the Trinity which can change the face of the earth? The message of the Risen Christ is disconcertingly simple — a true meeting with God will convert your heart, transform you completely.

Taking hold of you in baptism, Jesus brings you to a new life and He promises no reward nor happiness for tomorrow, but a totally different life — His own life: "I tell you most solemnly, unless a man is born through water and the Spirit, he cannot enter the Kingdom of God; what is born of the flesh is flesh; what is born of the spirit is spirit. Do not be surprised when I say: you must be born from above" (Jn 3:5-7). The good news of transformation is at the heart of the gospel message. It is not through your own efforts that this change takes place — it is the work of the Holy Spirit in you.

There is no area in you which is not influenced by this new life, even your unconscious is reached by it. You know how this mysterious part of your being takes over, directing and stimulating your behaviour. Christ truly lives in you and His life penetrates your whole personality, even your unconscious. Within your life, you will feel painful struggles, sin has left deep scars, even in your psyche, which no doubt you will never be able to erase.

Remember the power of the Spirit: He is the originator of the first creation as also of the second at Pentecost. He is the Spirit of strength and sweetness, He asks you to give Him all your life, work, rest, joy, suffering, even your struggles. He will never interfere as with a magic wand since He respects your freedom, but He will let you recognize the presence of God in the midst of your natural life, and will give meaning to your life.

In prayer, ask the Spirit to come into your life, so that you may become a new creation in Jesus Christ. If you believe enough, you will see greater things than you had hoped for. The Spirit will not upset you, but He will give you a new insight so that you agree to accept painful crosses taking them as part of the Death and Resurrection of Jesus. He will give you the strength of His love so that you can reduce your struggles as much as possible. Above all, He will take sin from your heart since it is the cause of your suffering and He will give you peace, to live in harmony despite your inner tensions. In prayer this new man will grow to the measure of Christ: "We are already the children of God but what we are to be in the future has not yet been revealed; all we know is that, when it is revealed, we shall be like Him because we shall see Him as He really is" (1 Jn 3:2).

VI. In prayer you go deep into God and you free unexpected depths within you.

There are within you "ends of the earth" still unexplored, virgin territory where any creation and any resurrection might be possible, if you let yourself be carried into this mysterious world.

Those who have dived in the depths of the ocean have been fascinated by the marvels they have seen. This silent world, even if they stayed there only a quarter of an hour, becomes unforgettable. When in daily life they find themselves dragged into the sterile uproar of fighting, quarrels which men can hardly escape, bewildered, they can in a flash go back to the ever fresh memory deep within them, of that great silence; they can find quiet and peace and face difficulties with a higher view, with serenity and greatness of mind.

In your confused life is there not something similar missing? Sometimes you do feel something of this inward calm in a friendly talk where the darkness and obscurity in yourself fade away. You have an intense feeling of lightness, of sharing, which cannot be put into words, a feeling of complete joy. Two people come face to face sharing each other's presence in a way that goes beyond what words can express.

Such an experience is a hint of what depths might be revealed when you hold a dialogue with God. There is no comparison between the silent world of human experience and the silent world of God. In fact, Christian inner life is not of the psychological or the spiritual order, but is that which God creates in you. He hollows a deep, wide place in your heart so that He can impart His own inner life. To be born of God is to have been taken back as it were, formed anew in the very womb of God. It is coming back to the world having been washed in a deep, shining water, the water of the truth of the God of Love.

When problems and difficulties occur in your life, when you seek God's will for you, or when you want to recover unity in your life, you must be able, in a flash, to reopen the memory of the depths of God where you were born. God gives you the grace of sharing His own inward life. You cannot approach Him by digging out your own depths — only God can let you in by His grace. In other words, you must be born again in the womb of the Father, to become "a child of God" (Jn 1:12).

Prayer is the special means of immersing yourself in this light in which you were born. You join the current of this universal life, flowing into the life of God. If your prayer is a genuine face to face with God and not just an enjoyment of one's own self, prayer must bring to your consciousness the unsuspected depths of your being. You will discover areas of knowledge and love as yet unexplored which will come to life in God's sight. God is the true source of your being, closer to you than you are to yourself.

To pray is to let yourself be carried into the depths of the Trinity where God kneads and moulds you to His likeness. Do not be surprised that your natural self finds a fullness of joy and fulfilment. Your being, your thoughts, your words and actions are a little like more or less well woven baskets. To hold the truth of God which is living water, you must ceaselessly dip them in this spring where you were born, otherwise the water runs out and you are left with a dried up self. Do not be a broken basket!

Set aside in your days some time to be deep in God, no matter how short it may be, even if it is just the time to take a breath, so you may give God access to the secret depths of your life. Never let a week go by without setting aside a long period for silent prayer and a lengthy contemplation of the Word of God. If you do not spend enough time in prayer to test the limits of your strength, you will never be penetrated by the prayer of the Holy Spirit. This is why prolonged prayer is a necessity in Christian life. It is important to create a pattern of these encounters with God on Sundays and rest days.

VII. "Whenever you pray, go to your room, close your door, and pray to your Father in secret. Then your Father, Who sees what no man sees, will reward you" (Mt 6:6).

Listen to the invitation of Christ to withdraw to your room. Jesus speaks here of a *tameion,* a storeroom that is a place where food is kept. This is your desert. It is a remote room where no stranger is allowed and which is filled with solitude and silence. He went on to insist on the secret nature of this place where people cannot see you. Your only concern must be to stand in the sight of God so that your prayer is unnoticed. What matters is that you pray with a pure intention. You can set aside in your room a place kept for God alone. Have a fine painting there with a lamp burning in front of it to be a symbol of your continual prayer.

The true place for your prayer is in your heart, not your intelligence or your feelings. Few people reach this deep level of their being, many don't even suspect its existence. The Holy Spirit rests and lives in the bottom of your heart to bring you into the depths of the mystery of God and to reveal His secrets (1 Cor 2:10). Unfortunately, you are bound inwardly by these *heart's knots* which tangle you as a person. You find difficulty in prayer because you cover up your face with a mask. Prayer is the act of a free man. Put yourself honestly before God, such as you are and above all with what is best in you.

Then lock your door. Let in no unwanted presence. Find a place which is permanent and solid, where no one can enter to find you or disturb you; you need silence in the heart, the imagination, the memory, the understanding, the will. Often you suffer in the deep silence before God because you see yourself as poor. You do not know what to do because you have no personal life. To make ready for prayer, you must silence your bitterness, your cares, useless regrets, difficult conditions, too sensitive feelings.

It is most important to silence your overwhelming *ego*, which unconsciously demands recognition from God. In the light of Jesus' teaching on prayer, meditate on the poem printed in the supplement of this book (Annex II). You are not meant to experience the void, but to go into the depths of your own heart and commune with the living God in you.

For the aim of prayer is not to find your own inner life but to stand as a son before the Father, Who penetrates your secret self. Between God and yourself there is a stronger link than you have with your earthly father.

139

He gazes at you with love. Cherish being in this silence. Be silent before the Father. Above all, don't add words, for silence is a guardian of love. Anyone in love stays silent before the other, just looking, with all his heart, not wanting to touch. You need say nothing to God since the Father knows what you must have before you ask Him (Mt 6:8).

What does the Father give to those who keep silent and pray? He will give you the Spirit to teach you to pray: "If you, who are evil, know how to give your children what is good, how much more will the Heavenly Father give the Holy spirit to those who ask Him!" (Lk 11:13). You do not know what to ask in order to pray as the Father wills (Rm 8:26). Then the Spirit comes to help your weakness, joining with your spirit to make you call out "Abba! Father!" (Rm 8:15).

To pray is to let Christ say within you "Father" in the movement of His Spirit. You have to go through various levels of your being to find this life of the Spirit in you, buried beneath layers of possessions and show. Go deeply to find this vein of living water which flows from the heart of Christ to you.

VIII. Become like Christ and repeat each phrase of the Our Father to breathe out the love of a son.

If you are looking for substance in your prayer, you will find it within your reach in the Gospel: "You should pray like this: Our Father..." Since Jesus taught His Apostles the Our Father, you no longer need to rack your brains to invent new prayers. No prayer is more pleasing to the Father than the one taught to you by His Beloved Son. It has been used by generations of believers to express their faith. Keep repeating these words of Christ to make them your own and take them deep within you. They nourished Jesus' long hours of night prayer.

To say the Our Father well in the company of your brothers, you must have prayed it deep within you in silent prayer. There is a continuous interplay between words and silence, that is why there is no community prayer without the deep silence of prayer. Vocal prayer has no meaning unless it is lived and understood. It is silent prayer which lets you grasp the meaning, otherwise you have just the outward form. On the other hand, inner prayer finds it is regulated by vocal prayer and this avoids falling into sentimentality or illuminism.

Your silent prayer will be satisfying if you nourish it with spoken prayer. Here the Our Father can help you to remain attentive to God. It is useful to have some prayer formulas which you know by heart and which can support you in prayer.

As always, be careful over the beginnings, do not be in a rush to start your mental film machine — say one thing alone in your prayer but play a hundred variations on the theme. This is where you will discover how important and useful is repetition. Be aware above all that the Spirit of Jesus is drawing you eagerly to the Father. After the Resurrection, the traditional prayer of the Our Father was completely renewed by the action of Jesus, because the Kingdom of God, in some degree, is there.

When Jesus taught the Our Father, He clearly made a distinction between it and His own prayer: "When you pray, say..." This was to be the community prayer. No Jew would dare to say to God: "Abba, Father"; it was a phrase kept for an earthly father. He would say: "Abbi, my Father" or "Abbinou, Our Father." Since Jesus rose again, He has sent you the Spirit which allows and permits you to say "Father" to Him. Jesus renews in you His prayer of Gethsemane (Mk 14:16). When you say the Our Father you do not copy the prayer of Christ but you are to convert your heart using the very prayer of Jesus Who clothes you with His humanity.

Calling the name of Father, you bring into your awareness your desire to be a son, which is alive in your heart. The saints knew this well and they alone can say the Our Father well. When they say it they stop at the first phrase — they cannot go on as they are so overwhelmed by the experience of the Divine Fatherhood. Go deep into the word *"Father"*, tear back the veil and you will know the sweet abandonment of being a son of God.

This is why prayer does not consist of thinking over the words of the Our Father — such research must be done apart from prayer, but remember it is limited, it can only take you to the threshold of the mystery. In prayer, say each phrase of the Our Father, not just to find the meaning but to desire with all your heart that it come into effect: "Hallowed by Thy Name", "Show yourself as the Most Holy God", "May your Kingdom come — let Your Will be done." May the power of our love give life to this supplication and make it your own.

As you say these words the Holy Spirit will take them deep inside you. You will grasp them with a spiritual knowledge. Above all, you will show your full affection as a son, begging the Father to listen to the prayer of the son. The Our Father is the model of all other prayers for it puts the glory of the Father in the centre, never forgetting the humble realities of daily life for it is of these that the Kingdom is built.

Praying the Our Father in this way, you will shape in you the heart of a son, more concerned with the holiness of the Father than your own concerns. Allow your mind and heart to be shaped by this prayer of Jesus. Some days you will not be able to say it — this prayer is so demanding. Then call Jesus to you, so that He may renew His prayer and transform your wretchedness into a cry for help and an opening of yourself to God.

IX. **If you spent all your prayer time begging for the coming of the Spirit, you would not have wasted your time.**

If anyone asks you about your prayer, say: "I simply call upon the Spirit." Likewise, if anyone asks you to help him begin to pray, do not confuse him with complicated methods. Say simply: "Ask for the Spirit" and help him to find this deep energy, hidden inside him. You cannot say "Jesus is Lord" — which is the basis of prayer — without the help of the Holy Spirit. If you receive the Spirit, your prayer is perfect.

You can draw the features of the Father and the Son, but the Spirit has no face, not even a name which might evoke a human face. You cannot imagine the Spirit, nor touch Him — you may hear His voice in your conscience, you may recognize His passing by dazzling signs, but you cannot know "where it comes from nor where it is going" (Jn 3:8).

Yet He alone can make you pray. He is at the beginning, the middle and the end of each prayer, as in all spiritual decisions. You must ask for Him as the supreme gift which contains all other gifts. Holiness is the Holy Spirit filling the Church and the hearts of all the faithful. You can only call Him and beg Him to come. He is the source of all ministries, the sacraments and prayer.

Do not call Him to come upon you or upon others or even upon the Church in any special way, but call Him purely and simply in a long appeal: "Come!" If you spent all your time in saying this little word, recognizing His presence in you, adoring Him, thanking Him for all His gifts — you would be deep in the prayer of the Trinity and you would not have wasted your time.

You do not have to call Him from without; the Spirit of the Risen Christ lives in you, deep in your heart. To pray is to become aware of His presence, reviving the spark which burns beneath the ash. His action starts always from within and it is within you that you will know Him: "You know Him because He is with you, He lives in you" (Jn 14:17). Recognize His presence in you, and beg Him to manifest all His dynamic power. The symbols used to indicate Him (water, air, wind, fire) call to mind "the inrush of His presence, its irresistible and ever deepening expansion" (X. Léon-Dufour).

When you call upon the Spirit, be like someone dying of thirst in the desert; he does not think of drinking, he thinks only of water, but this image of water is like a yearning of his whole being. Without knowing it, you

143

thirst for the Holy Spirit. Come to the side of the Risen Christ for the rivers of living water will flow from His heart. Call upon the Spirit with all the strength of your heart, in a long appeal: "Come." You will need years of waiting and patience to discover the presence of the Spirit in you.

All the actions of the Spirit are to win you over to the Father and to the Son. He wants to have you in living communion with God so that you may taste and enjoy His presence. Let Jesus communicate His Spirit to you so that in Him you may name God "Father."

You may prove His presence by His kindness which is life and peace. He will help you praise Him for His great achievements in your life, He will deepen your heart and your thoughts, granting you true freedom. Above all, He will instill in you peace and joy, enlarging your heart. He will go into your body and change it, giving it the glorious seed of the resurrection which will change you into the likeness of Christ.

Cry out always to the Spirit: "Come." Turn also to the Father knowing that Christ intercedes for you before Him. You cannot enter into a relationship with one of the Persons of the Holy Trinity without having a relationship to the other. If you have truly cried out to Him, do not be afraid, all the love of Father and Son has come to you.

X. Let Christ pray in you. You reach His prayer when you share the same thrust of love which unites Him to the Father under the influence of the Spirit.

The only prayer truly pleasing to the Father is that of His beloved Son in Whom He finds Himself and is pleased. Your prayer will be welcomed by the Father if it is that of His Son Who prays within you. Be with Jesus in His long lonely nights of prayer on the mountain. Stay at His side, so that He may bring you into the loving dialogue with the Father.

It is only when you discover your fundamental inability to pray, when you know your limitations by reaching your lowest point, that you can understand the prayer of Jesus. But you can look at this prayer in several ways, for example join your prayer to that of Jesus when He told His disciples to pray in His name: "I tell you most solemnly, anything you ask for from the Father, He will grant in my name" (Jn 16:23). But you are close to an equivocal position which is to think that the prayer of Christ, perfect in itself, makes up for your poor prayer. In this sense, you are still in a dual situation where you are outside and ask Christ to pray with and for you.

But Christ has said there is a second way, deeper and more inward, to pray to the Father in His name: "I do not say that I will petition the Father for you. The Father already loves you because you have loved me and have believed that I came from God" (Jn 16:26-27). There is no longer any duality between His prayer and yours but you must let Him truly pray within you.

Jesus remains always the only mediator but His disciples are not outside of Him, they are to remain united to Him and their prayer is not on this side of His prayer but part of it. In faith and love, the disciples of Jesus are one with Him and the Father loves them and listens to them because He finds in them the features of His beloved Son.

More precisely, let us say that the prayer of Christ in you presupposes a deeper belief, that you are identified with Christ. To say that Christ prays in you is not to try, through a psychological effort, to remake the different parts of the prayer of Jesus to make it yours. On the contrary, it is to know through a total conversion that you are one with Him, by baptism. All that is His is yours and His prayer becomes yours.

When you pray, try to reunite with this prayer of Jesus, living within you by faith. You are not aware of it, but Christ truly prays to the Father through the babbling of your poor prayer. To reach the prayer of Jesus, is to be part of the thrust of love and life which joins Him to the Father under the influence of the Spirit. You can understand nothing of the prayer of Jesus if you take it

145

out of the mystery of the Holy Trinity. Jesus is always aware of the living bond which unites Him to the Father and gives Him life. He takes His being from the Father and in return offers Himself completely to the Father: "All I have is yours and all you have is mine" (Jn 17:10).

You are seized, held by the Spirit so that you can be shaped like the Son. In his turn, Jesus brings you back to the depths of the Father. It is the life in Christ which lets you share in the relationship of a son and you cannot reach God except through Him. At the beginning of your prayer life you are not aware of this life of a son which is buried within you, and you remain outside the prayer of Jesus.

Little by little, you will grasp the relationship of love with the Father in Jesus, and His prayer will take the place of yours as He is in you in an increase of humanity. Only then will you feel a sense of joy and satisfaction in prayer, for Christ will adore and love the Father in you. At certain moments you will be so much taken over by the love of Christ that you will be aware of loving the Father with the very heart of the Son. Know too that your prayer is fully accepted and heard by God Who refuses nothing to His beloved Son. Your daily life, put into the life of Christ, becomes a spiritual offering to the glory of the Father. When you are reduced to the silence of poverty, it will be Jesus Who will give you the riches of His dialogue with the Father.

XI. Feast upon and ruminate the Word of God.

Today you live in a civilisation which is based on consuming rather than absorbing. It is normal for you to be bewildered when you enter the world of prayer with such a mentality. But prayer is based on quality, not quantity. One single truth of the faith meditated and assimilated in peace and calm opens the way to all the others, just as one point rejected in the Creed shuts the door to the whole Gospel message.

Avoid such a race to pile up texts from the Gospel.

Do not be on the watch for novelty inducing to superficial feelings, but be the fertile ground which received the good seed of the Word. The Word of God is bread that you must relish in calm absorption. Pick up a word of Christ's and sit in a corner to think it over calmly, silently.

Be like the bee which returns to the same flowers until they have no more pollen to give. In the same way, exhaust the meaning of the text until it has nothing more to tell you. Do as the prophet Jeremiah did when he took the scroll of the Word and ate it, as a child might eat bread and honey: "When your words came, I devoured them. Your word was my delight, and the joy of my heart" (Jr 15:16).

We all have a series of texts to which we like to refer, to nourish our prayer. You must know your range of selections. If you do not return to the same text in Scripture or in spiritual writers, you will never know how to pray well. You will be like a tourist who wants to see everything and who does not take the time to contemplate, that is to look with love and admiration at what he sees. Do not be a spiritual glutton.

The world of prayer is a world to welcome, to discover but not one to be snatched at. The ideal in prayer is to simplify it to the point where you no longer need a subject to pray about. It will be enough, for example, to let yourself be taken up by this firm belief of the love of God, to fill up all your prayer time. Simply take a prayer from the liturgy, or a psalm, and pray this text, murmuring or singing it. Or read a text slowly and stop when it starts to mean something to you. Then you will understand how well founded was the saying of Saint Ignatius: "It is not indeed knowing many things that satisfies and fills the soul, but to feel and savour them inwardly."

Take half an hour to recite a part from the Liturgy of the Hours. Learn to savour a beautiful passage from Scripture, just as the lover of fine wine sips and savours his glass of wine. Above all, do not complicate the matter, prove to yourself that it is a good thing to pray calmly this way. Little by little you will take on God's thoughts, they will become your own and your life will reflect the ways of the Gospels found in the Beatitudes.

If, in the busy life you lead, you have not found time to pray, it is a sign that your love of God is growing cold or breaking down. It should be obvious then that you should make some major changes, planning your days so that more time is set aside for spiritual needs. Truly, do you enjoy the Word of God? When you have a free afternoon, do you think of sitting down peacefully to spend an hour listening to the Word?

In order to relish the Word, you must read it, reread it, meditate on it and contemplate it in silent prayer. Repetition is an essential law of prayer. Restrain your desire to know, but satisfy your deep hunger for God. Always keep some good saying from the Gospel to ruminate, so that you do not starve to death in a time of spiritual drought.

XII. When you are looking for a simple way to pray, look at the gospel in stone of the great cathedrals.

If you ever go to Chartres, stop in front of the north door of the cathedral. On the left opening, on the second row of arching, the sculptor has carved six scenes of "Contemplative Life." The Virgin is seen communing with herself, opening her book, reading, meditating, teaching and going into ecstasy. In the thirteenth century, the Bible taught people the knowledge of prayer in a very simple way. Go beyond the material reality of the sculpture and adopt the spiritual attitude which animated the heart of the Blessed Virgin in her prayer.

First, she collects her thoughts before beginning to pray. She has her left hand on the book of the Scriptures and her right hand is raised to her heart as if she wants to teach you that to pray, you must keep your heart pure and silent. She gathers all her thoughts, all her affections in her heart (Ps 131:1-2). She is ready to listen to the Word of God and keep it within herself. Like Solomon, ask God for a silent heart which knows how to listen (1 K 3:9). The first requirement for prayer is one of acceptance, of listening and receiving the good Spirit, the spiritual gift that the Father gives to those who ask Him for it (Lk 11:13).

Her second step is to open the book of the Scriptures; an action which seems just an ordinary, physical movement, but which reveals an important spiritual attitude. When you open the Bible it is not a matter of having theories or ideas about God, but you open the Scriptures to receive the thought of the Other One and not our own thought. We do not create true life and prayer, we discover it and receive it from God. This does not mean you need not read a good explanation of Scripture, but that there is another threshold to cross, that of free gift and mystery.

Mary reads then, not to know but to penetrate the deep meaning of the words. In the Bible, there is something beyond the words alone which lets you discover a hidden truth, a sweetness for the heart. When you have found what you are looking for, imitate the Blessed Virgin by closing the book and meditating inwardly on the Word, letting it sink into your very heart. "I have placed the Word within your hearts" said St. Paul. The spirit lets you penetrate intuitively into this Word whose truth you know by experience: "You give both to it from the depths of your heart like natural feelings which are part of you" (St. Cassianus). A lively, enjoyable reading of the Word makes you ready to find God in contemplation. Let these things come to you and stand before the mystery with wide open hands. Reflecting on the Scriptures, you will hear the Word speak to your heart. This is the doing of the inner Master who is the Holy Spirit.

Then the Virgin teaches the Word she has savoured and meditated. In the Church, all teaching of the Gospel begins in an attentive, prayerful meditation on the Word of God. The apostle is one who helps his brothers know God in Jesus Christ. It is not just a knowledge of Christ in a vivid personal contact, but the passing on of the very experience of Jesus Who, in His human awareness, knew Himself as Son of God: "Christendom is first of all experience. It is the experience that Jesus had of God His Father — He, the Son of Mary of Galilee, the Word, of the same substance as the Father. It is the experience of the Father in Christ and the Holy Spirit. Christendom is life, the very life of God in the heart of the Blessed Trinity, given to man by grace" (Dom Henri le Saux). How can you transmit this experience if you have not had it yourself? The words you speak take their strength from the inner word, the Spirit, planted like a seed deep within you.

Lastly, the Virgin goes into ecstasy. She goes out of herself to find her joy and happiness in God. She does not look for the tranquillity of contemplation for itself, but for God Who is the final end of her prayer. All true prayer must bring you to the point where you find joy only in God. You will pray truly on the day when all your attention is focused on adoring God, meditating on His love, and thanking Him, not only for the gifts He has given you but for the coming of Christ on earth. In prayer, do you think of God's concerns, His glory, the building of His Kingdom, are you happy over His happiness, His joy, His beauty?

A great contemplative Robert de Langeac wrote one day: "Only in ecstasy does one pray well." If you practise keeping silence in prayer, you are getting ready to be carried away by the action of the Spirit. You are hidden in your own prayer and you are no longer aware of praying. "True prayer" said St. John of the Cross "is always at night." But this gift of contemplation does not depend on your merits but on the mercy of God. He grants it when He wishes and to whom He wishes, often when you least expect it. Pray that God will grant you this sight of His face, promised to the pure of heart.

XIII.   Man keeps his balance only in love and self-giving. The desire for God in prayer is needed to balance a Christian life.

The goal of prayer is not to have beautiful ideas about God, but to find joy only in Him and in doing His will. Let us repeat, the place of prayer is in the heart, that is that part where you are yourself and where you give yourself completely. In the biblical sense, the heart is the place where God is known; it integrates every level of your being, intelligence, will, feeling and freedom. This means that Christian experience implies insight, a loving unity, freely given. Prayer thus raises the question of the emotions since you must come to enjoy God.

It would be hard to imagine a mayor making a bylaw that all the lovers in town must meet once a week. Why do so many Christians go to the Eucharist and prayer as if it were a duty or just observing a rule? What would you think of married people who only met out of duty? Habitual dryness is not a normal state. It is often a chance to love God for Himself but if it goes on, you should be concerned and find out the reason. God wants to be loved in the fulfilment of joy and inner freedom.

It is normal to ask for spiritual gifts which will let you enjoy God deep in your heart. The liturgy has you asking for them continually: "Fill us with your delights, grant us the taste, the joy, the love of your law." Even in the matter of sin, the Church has you ask for sorrow, that is a loving regret for your faults which is another way of knowing the merciful love of God. The goal of prayer is to satisfy the heart, tasting God within you.

To enjoy God in your prayer it is necessary to balance your Christian life, all the more if your life is wholly dedicated to God in chastity. Man is only balanced in love and self-surrender; all the more when the object of this self-surrender is the Creator and no one else but Him. The Creator of man is able to satisfy the human heart in the mystery of that eternal marriage, begun here in the intimacy of grace: "Your Creator will be your husband" (Is 54:5). Perfect chastity brings you into the secret garden of intimacy with God. In prayer, you live in close and personal union with God. If you give up human love, it is because you are looking and have found the fullness and perfection of love.

This is not easy for you to understand since your education has been centered on your intelligence and the observance of the moral law. To pray well, you must have genuine affection which is founded on the deepest powers of your very self. Do you accept to love others with your human heart and to let them love you?

You know that to pray is to be in a relationship with God through Jesus Christ. If you find it difficult to relate to others because your love is possessive, you will find it equally hard to go to God with your very self and especially to find your emotional balance. Many people cannot pray because they have not been taught to meet others in truth.

If you suppress your feelings, they will demand their due violently. This results in a feeling of dryness and of not being real as a consequence. In prayer, put yourself before God with all your strength. Do not be afraid of loving Him with your human heart and feel real joy at being with Him. May coming close to God be your real wealth (Ps 73:28). Let this love be true, an oblation, not self seeking.

XIV. Do not be disturbed if your prayer is unrewarded, for in this way you learn to love God for Himself and not for the joy you find in Him.

In prayer you need not be afraid of sensitivity but you must train and purify it. Accept its evidence and expression but avoid all self-satisfaction. The joy that goes with self-surrender is good and willed by God but, if having enjoyed it, you try to revive it for itself, with no reason, you are impure.

You must learn to seek God for Himself in prayer. From this point of view, difficulties and dryness are useful since they reassure you that you do not pray for ideas and feelings but for God alone. So, the most desolate prayer develops this deep affection for God which moves you to pray, to be with Him and to give you more of His love. What you are asking is not a feeling of love but true love which moves you to give yourself truly to God. When you come to pray, you have only one thing to bring — the desire and will to be there, before the Father, and to persevere for love of Him. Then you must call the Holy Spirit to grant your poor human heart the love with which the three Persons of the Trinity love each other.

In this way, you perform a work of discernment and verification. In your relations with God as in your relations with others, you can distinguish true love from mere emotion in which you too often surround your prayer and brotherly affection. You cling more and more to God, loving Him for Himself.

If you are given a real experience of prolonged prayer, you will learn to persevere before God who is sought and loved for Himself; you will know then great poverty and forgetfulness of self, and when you return to daily life, your prayer will be the gage of your right relations with others whom you will desire and love for themselves.

The law of all love, and particularly spiritual love, is the forgetfulness of self in order to seek one's joy and happiness in the other. What counts in prayer life as well as in community life is to cease to be self-centered and to direct all your attention to others. Your look must be full of sacrificial love and centered on others. Here we are at the other extreme from André Gide who wrote: "Let the important be in your view, not in the viewed."

So, far from becoming self-centered, prayer like true love is a going out from the self to go towards the other. It is a gift of oneself to the other, freely and in praise and adoration. Only the prayer of thanksgiving can help in this shifting of your centre. If your prayer makes you narrower and more self-centered, it is an obvious sign that it is not a true desire for God but self seeking, whatever may be its emotions and sensitive outpourings.

153

The greater your capacity for human love, the greater is your need for balance and purification. Without the desire to pray and know God, there will be a great imbalance between your capacity to love and your spiritual life and the latter will stay thin and adolescent. Go to Christ in simple love, and look for dialogue in prayer. Do not look for ideas about God, but look for joy and peace near Him. Your difficulties in this area will be overcome by love itself. The times when you meet God must be joyful even if He seems far from you: "Love should be in works more than in words" (St. Ignatius).

XV. Do not pretend when you come to pray, but show yourself to God just as you are. If you spend a long time before Him, you will go away in joy and peace.

Sometimes you don't pray because you are afraid of contact with God, you are afraid of showing yourself to Him as you really are, as if He didn't see you all the time, deep down. Your prayer slows down when you recognize yourself to be sinful and poor, just when it should be more intense. Then, you put on the appearance of a very good, clean little child and you leave your cares and sins at the door. You offer Him a plaster face and a cottonwool personality — how could you expect Christ to impress His features on a mask or give His life to a ghost? He can colour it or dress it but He cannot change it profoundly.

When you go to pray, you are very heavy while God seems unreal, light, far away. You come weighed down by heaps of anger, disgust, bitterness, pessimism, impurity. You wonder how you will ever lift all this up to free the tiny flame of love of God which glows inside you, since you are there, before Him, to pray. Stay there before God with your real self in your hands.

Above all, don't lie, don't pretend, don't pretend that everything is going well, saying lofty things like: "My God, I love you with all my heart." You know it isn't true, you would rather God left you alone since you love His will so little. You have tried so often to love so and so, to make a special effort, but you have given up and accepted defeat. Breathe out before God your poverty, your suffering, your sin.

Do not try to restore the balance by sheer will power; the scale of your sins outweighs the scale of God. Do not put your hand on the balance to change things in your way — you are apt to spoil everything. If you persevere in prayer, going deeper and deeper into the mystery of the Holy Trinity, God Himself will intervene. This means a long time in prayer, and so, little by little, you will come out of your monologue to listen to God. God replies, works and acts during this time: "My father works always" Jesus said. What is God doing in your innermost heart?

He calms your anger, changes your bitterness into love, your pessimism into joy, your impurity into holiness. In a word, He lifts you from mediocrity, so that you are amazed to find that the mountain has disappeared into the sea. A great contemplative, the doorkeeper for the Jesuit's house in Majorca, who could calm hearts with a simple glance, said: "When I feel bitterness in my heart, I set it between God and myself, and I pray until He transforms it into sweetness" (St. Alphonsus Rodriguez).

Yes, everything has melted under God's loving gaze and you will be joyful and happy in His presence. You will begin to love the will of God and above all, you love the life He gives you today since it is the visible sign of His tenderness. You understand that these insuperable obstacles frightened you because you looked at them by yourself. Now, you dare to look at them closely with Him and everything has changed. Your problems remain the same, but seen with God's eyes, they are transformed.

A girl with many problems once said to me: "Since I've met my fiancé, my friends don't recognize me any more, I'm not the same." Her difficulties hadn't changed but she had changed and she saw her problems differently.

God will disappoint you in your natural hopes in

order to open the way to divine hope. He makes you give up *something* that seems the magical solution to your problems, so that you might encounter *Someone* and you will open yourself to Him. To pray is to die to your own ideas, your judgments and your selfish wishes, to be reborn to the ideas of God, that is to the love that springs up in His heart. To reach this point, you must stay a long time in the sunshine of God.

XVI. Filter your heart through the name of the Lord Jesus.

Whatever you say or do, may it always be "in the name of the Lord Jesus" (Col 3:17). You sense that these words of Paul could unify your life in continual prayer. This is the reason why you should rediscover this basic, traditional attitude of the East. Filter your thoughts, your desires, your affections and your meetings in the memory of the name of the Lord Jesus. It is in this Name, that is, the person of Jesus that you must clean and filter your heart and all your life.

There is a whole wave of desires, impressions and memories inside you and these plunge you into a whirlpool and yet, you are baptized, the Lord Jesus lives in your heart by faith and His divine life wishes to flood your being. Bring up from the depths of your heart the name of the Lord Jesus and allow His consciousness to take over your deepest thoughts.

Let these thoughts surface in you, do not repress them but make them objective by the spoken word in order to take them upon yourself completely, lay fast hold of them. You know your weakness, accept to see yourself as you are, and stand confidently in God's sight. Then you will feel inside your weakness, the presence and the strength of the Lord Jesus. From this practice comes the unceasing repetition of the Jesus' prayer in the Eastern tradition.

In prolonged prayer the Lord will show you a short,

simple prayer, which He expects from you all day. One of these sets us right in the heart of the Trinity and unites us to the Lord Jesus in the power of the Spirit. It is essentially evangelical and that is why you can adopt it for your own: "Father, in the name of Jesus, give me your Spirit" (Jn 16:23-25).

The Lord Jesus must be present in everything you live, as Teilhard de Chardin so well expressed it: "Let your human nature become a medium of expression for the Holy spirit." When you experience bitterness, temptation, sorrow or joy, bring it out of your heart, hold it in your hands before the Lord and pray to Him until He transforms it to peace and sweetness.

You must never count on your own strength. On the contrary, when any disturbance arises, you must turn immediately to the Father and keep calling on Him until the Spirit comes to calm your anxiety. There are days when you will have to pray for hours to regain your peace but if you accept to face reality, God will use the hindrances to help you find it. Never forget the words of Christ which will enable you to remove mountains into the sea: "Whatever you shall ask in prayer filled with faith, you will obtain it" (Mt 21:22).

Let this attitude be your usual approach in life. Here you lose yourself, your thoughts, your ideas, in order to follow Christ, carrying your cross. This is the spirit of the Beatitudes which goes deep into poverty and adopts the spirit of a child. Coming to your heart this way, Jesus will share his essential gift, which is a giving up of Himself to the Father, in order to offer Himself to the movement of the Spirit. This is where you will find true springs of refreshment, and in this continual giving of yourself to God, you will free new sources of energy, you will find Him in all things, and you will look beyond people and events and live a little already in eternity.

In life, you may be deprived of the sacraments, of prolonged prayer and all the normal means that God uses to give you His grace, but you are never excused from giving your heart inwardly to God so that He can purify it by the Spirit. This will cleanse your heart in the continual remembrance of the Lord Jesus; it is the only way to examine your conscience. In this way, you will be united with God in your life and you will pass on to the Father, in Christ, with nothing to stop you.

XVII. Prayer is the act of a free man. It means that you put in order all the areas of your life, taking your difficulties within you.

It is when you begin purely contemplative prayer, made up of praise, adoration or compassion that you find the need for human well being in prayer. Until then your mind was given over the feverish activity, your will worked out more projects, all your strength was put into the intelligent area of your being. Then suddenly everything was calm in this upper part of you; you find that your human existence has a real stability and that it would be dangerous to repress its needs under the pretext of praying with your spirit alone.

Many people want to pray and cannot do so because they are not balanced in their personalities. Do not be too quick to say this is a matter of spiritual tests or the dark night of the soul. There is a great temptation to move onto the spiritual level the unknown areas of your being which you do not want to see. There are normal psychological problems which prevent or upset prayer. Thus, people who have not accepted or discovered their sexuality or, what amounts to the same thing, cannot master or control it, seem incapable of emotional maturity. This means they cannot come out of their own personal point of view, to see the other as he really is. Often their strong sense of logic makes them intellectualize these conflicts and shift them to the level of faith. Their difficulty in meeting Christ as a person rises often from their difficulty in having any relationship. Prayer is impossible for such people, who are unable to give.

Reading this, do not point the finger at others, for in some ways we all bear a certain resemblance to this portrait. You feel the need to pray and you cannot do so, because of your human limitations. Above all, try to understand, do not be afraid of the truth and do not become discouraged. Do not imagine just trying will be enough to help you over it, or that you can leave the problem, as it is a trial that will go away tomorrow.

You must try hardest where it is needed. A sickness is not healed by fighting its symptoms, but by attacking the cause. Often you are advised to take up a different attitude; you must use your reason to try to get out of this weakness and learn to pray. Then you forget to change yourself in your depths. Do not believe that everything depends on the reason and the will, the problem goes deeper. Common sense resolutions often run the risk of bypassing and ignoring an essential question. Deep within you is a living reality, a real emotional drive which fuels your inner life and gives it meaning. The meaning of your life is the daily work of God in you. You must turn to this, understand it and serve it and not try to bypass it. It is not a question of deciding but of understanding.

If you want to get over a difficulty or free yourself from a painful situation you must stay in it and suffer, not rejecting it nor trying to remake yourself from without. For example, say you have an emotional difficulty — you must let come into your awareness all those instinctive drives which lie within you, without trying to dam them up. You receive them, accept them and live in them directing these powers in an offering of love to God and your brothers because it is a present reality and holds the hidden meaning of your future.

Experience shows that you cannot evade a problem. If you succeed in avoiding it psychologically, it will come back in other forms or through outside events. It is useless to sidestep it since the difficulty means that a part of human reality must be accepted and integrated. You must hold this difficulty such as it is, go deep into it, suffer it to the end. Usually you will come through it.

This does not mean that prayer is only possible for well balanced people. Besides, they don't exist; all men have trouble keeping their balance and we all have inner crosses, which are very heavy to carry. But you must accept this human reality with all its weaknesses and conflicts. If you live with them inwardly, without ignoring them, you allow Christ to take them up, as powers of resurrection and salvation. Your prayer life must be rooted in a constantly checked balance and when this adjustment has not been made, you cannot truly pray.

XVIII. So that your prayer may not be an indulgence of your ego, but a true love of the Father, go into the world of praise and adoration.

Many people neglect their prayer life to dedicate their time to duties they see as more urgent. They are also against personal experiences which might lead people away from an objective meeting with the person of Christ, in the liturgy or the service of people. This reaction is prompted by a dislike of pious dreamers, of men who live tuned into themselves rather than the Word of God.

You who pray, you are not beyond this reproach. You are always tempted to center on your own experience in the middle and to judge the quality of your prayer by the intensity of your feelings. While it is good that your whole being is involved in the relationship with God, you must know that the true law of prayer is to forget yourself completely, so that God may occupy all your awareness. You will truly be praying *in the night*, that is to say, when you are no longer aware of talking to God and this movement has become *natural* for you. Prayer must become part of the unconscious layers of your being and it must live there even when you sleep. When you wake in the morning, it will come to you before any other thought. When you really talk to a friend, you do not bother him with questions but you are centered on him, on all his joys and his sufferings.

In your prayer you must continually move from a pleasurable egocentricity to a loving contemplation of God's *You*. Movement towards God can only be a going out from yourself towards the Entirely-Other God. Nothing is less subjective than the real experience of prayer if you know how to free it from the clumsy language in which it is often expressed.

True prayer begins when you go deep into the objectivity of God, when you stand aside before the object of your love. You are drawn towards Him with all the strength of your being. Above all, do not listen to those who say that service of others is the highest and purest form of prayer. You know how so-called realistic and altruistic work for others can be self-seeking. Prayer will allow you to be certain whether you are really serving Christ, in events and with your brothers. When you pray solely for God's sake, you will no longer have any difficulty in loving others for themselves.

If you want to break out of the circle of your subjectivity and avoid all spiritual self love, enter the world of praise and thanksgiving. You will be bewildered at first, for your own little self will no longer be the central point of your prayer. In prayer, let the God of Love be the only object of your contemplation and desires. Put away the *I* and the *me* in order to open yourself to God, to the redeeming plan of Christ and the intentions of the Church.

When you discover the infinite love God has for the world, you will no longer think of your narrow feelings; you will be busy admiring, singing and praising this love. You will live in Him and you will lose yourself in this boundlessness. Prayer is truly born in the contemplation of Love, don't pretend to draw it from your own depths.

This is why the Divine Office where you sing of the wonders of God for his people, must become the heart of your prayer, even your most secret prayer. This praise should begin your day, offering yourself to God as a spiritual sacrifice. It brings you into the silent prayer of night. Afterwards, you can respond to the love of God, expressing your own feelings, but here again your prayer will be a thanksgiving for you send back to the Father the divine life that He has put freely into your heart.

May your prayer not be a falling back into yourself, but a presence, an opening, a communion with God. Love to pray using the Gloria, the Sanctus, the Magnificat; they sing of God's glory and love. You celebrate in this way the great things that God has worked in the poverty of His servants. In your prayer, do not talk about yourself to God but let Him talk a little about Himself, of His love. In a word, be happy over His joy, His happiness, His beauty. Love prayer which only talks about God.

XIX. When a man has been taken over by God, no one can meet him without being inwardly transformed.

Have you ever met a real man of prayer, a man who has taken God seriously and who has gone through the initiation of the burning Bush? If you have, you will understand what I am saying, even though it is awkwardly expressed. You cannot meet such a man and have anything to do with him without going through the same initiation. "Nothing human" wrote Simone Weil "is so powerful in keeping one's sight every more intensely set on God than friendship with the friends of God."

Such people are rare because few contemplatives know how to live with their heads in heaven and their feet on the ground. This demands so much purification, so much silence and prayer that most men flee from contact with God; they are afraid of losing themselves, their security. But if God lets you have the joy of meeting one of these men, do not miss the chance of being in touch with him. If you only meet him once seriously, you would go away transformed and for the rest of your life you would live in this meeting and this memory.

The service these people give to the Church and the

world comes from their communion with God. They are present to the world and to men, in the very place where men find their beginnings. The world has never needed these witnesses so much, rooted as they are in the eternal which gives stability and firmness to our lives.

It is the Holy Spirit Who leads these people far from everything, beyond everything, set in the depths of the Trinity. They are rooted in God at the heart of their being. Each day, they go further into the mystery, and that is why they reach you so easily since they go beyond your facade of possessions, power and knowledge to show you your real self, a reality you sometimes don't know at all. They dive into the ocean of the Spirit to bring back the finest gifts for troubled people. The service of a saint, hidden in God, is not some humanitarian or social service, but a true spiritual ministry.

It is enough just to meet them, to discover your true self and above all to know what you should do. You do not even have to ask for advice, just let them look at you, for they share in the look of God and they show you your true identity. Some days you ask yourself questions; you are burdened by sin, you are crushed by misery; come to this man of God, don't tell him your story but be there, open before him, in silence. Henry Bergson wrote, concerning Christian mystics: "They only have to exist, their existence is a call." A saint understands you without talking, he looks at you as no one else can, and in his gaze you understand everything. Your questions, your doubts, your worries disappear without your knowing how or why. Dom Le Saux said this of Father Monchanin: "When you met him, even just once, you couldn't forget his direct, penetrating gaze which let you too reach his soul. He drew you into the depths of the interior life, to the very centre of divine life, to the heart of the life of the Trinity. And he did this, with an astonishing simplicity."

Essentially, it is the look of God reflected in the eyes of one of His friends. You can truly say you have seen God in someone, but such an experience is not possible unless you are open to God and want to see Him. At least, this is what Meister Eckhart tells us: "When someone is surrounded by God and radiates an unselfish love of God, no one can meet him unless he himself has already met God."

Our world has a pressing need of these men of prayer, witnesses of God. We don't expect them to solve our problems, just that they live is enough. Their lives are a reply to all our questions. Christians talk a great deal about God, they even do things for Him but very few accept to live only for Him, in a life of adoration and praise. If you are lucky enough to meet one of these men of God, perhaps this is a call for you to be a relay runner of God among your brothers. Certainly you would not be exempt from working for them, but your real steward-ship would be to show them God, within a man.

XX. Walk resolutely in the evening and abandon your-self to the night's rest; night, like prayer, is a trustful entrance into the realm of God's love.

You belong to a civilisation in which people begin to live at 9 o'clock at night, but keep some evenings for yourself each week and above all, the evenings on days off and during vacations; these times are to be kept for living with God alone. First, learn not to put up with time but to master it, going into the night as if you were going into a silent temple. At nightfall, give expression in your heart to this choice of being in the presence of the Most High, with a burning desire to contemplate His face. Perhaps this evening He will come to meet you, to invite you to His everlasting wedding feast. The night is sha-dowy with the silent presence of God. It is a time when you let in only what nourishes your prayer; all other unnecessary things must be mercilessly banished.

The later it is in the evening, the more you must simplify yourself so as to be calm and peaceful in the night's rest: "In peace I lie down and fall asleep at once since You alone, Yahweh, make me rest secure" (Ps 4:8).

Your body itself shares in this inward peace, for night should be entered as one enters prayer, relaxed and peaceful. After a day's work, the night is a time of deep relaxation. Scripture teaches you to watch for the Lord as He often comes to visit you during the night: "Therefore, you too must stand ready because the Son of Man is coming at an hour you do not expect" (Mt 24:44). Night time lets you share in the agony of Jesus in the garden of Gethsemane, if your are able to watch and pray with Him.

Above all, be watchful and prepared to let God instruct you, for the night is a favoured time when He speaks to you: "In vain you get up earlier and put off going to bed, sweating to make a living, since He provides for his beloved as they sleep" (Ps 127:2). During this mysterious sleep, you can speak from the depths of your heart things which otherwise might be repressed.

Then too, the night's sleep reveals a profound truth of your spiritual life. All through the day, you direct your own life taking free decisions and exerting your power. Now, at the threshold of night, you must give up and let yourself be overcome by this powerful impulse of sleep, that you cannot command but welcome. It is the image of your spiritual life which above all means to be submissive in the hands of God. There too you must submit and let God love you without wanting to direct things.

This is why your sleep should be part of the way you conduct your life; make it part of your inner life. When you pray, you do nothing except make yourself open and available to God's plan which will transform you without your knowing it. You know that to pray is to let Christ live and pray to the Father in you. So, when you sleep, put yourself completely into the hands of God: "Into your hands, Lord, I commit my spirit." If you pray to Him, He will send His Holy Spirit and your night's rest will be turned into prayer.

It is not surprising that when you go to bed, you feel a strong urge to pray, to thank God for the graces of the day, to purify yourself of your sins and to entrust your sleep to Him. Thus you abandon yourself to the mystery of love which never ceases to surround you: "You know when I sit and when I stand; you understand my thoughts from afar" (Ps 139:2). Do not forget that if your spirit is immersed in prayer when you go to sleep, your first thought in the morning will be of God. As you lie down so will you wake: "Spend your night in quiet meditation. Offer just sacrifices and trust in the Lord" (Ps 4:5-6). Sometimes God will give you long watches in the night so that you can continue your dialogue with Him. With the example of Christ and all the great saints, prayer at night is an integral part of an intense life of prayer.

If you fall asleep while praying, you will escape the shadows of the night, forerunners of death. The angels of God will watch over you. Your peaceful, relaxed sleep will link up with your very depths where God lives and will go on building your real personality.

XXI.   You will have no trouble praying if you have real relationships with your brothers.

Prayer is easy when you know the tragic meaning of your life or you are in danger or you know yourself to be poor and a sinner. Doesn't the same thing happen when you truly share in the life of your brothers? On the day when you saw the grief of your brother or his joy, didn't you really pray with him and for him? At that moment your prayer springs spontaneously to your lips like a cry of anguish or joy, sent towards God.

Often your prayer is lifeless because you are cut off from those around you. You go on acting, even being helpful to others, but you have not discerned their real condition. You are still at the stage when people are entertaining or are acting a role. Be silent with them but be alert to see what they are really asking. They may be asking for bread, material help or they don't need anything, but if they talk to you they are hungry for your smile, your friendship and ultimately for God.

You will truly pray when you guess that under their

words they are hungry for love. When a man suffers, you can say nothing to comfort him, for you do not know his real suffering — he does not know it himself, in fact. He asks you simply to be there, in silence, beside him, to look at him and to love him. Your prayer begins on the day when you are aware of this suffering, when you cry out to God in appeal and intercession.

If you want to pray, start by being attentive to your brothers. Be welcoming and silent with them, truly listen to them, discern, beyond what they say, their suffering or their joy that they cannot express. Lose sight of yourself as you let this go deep into your heart. This is what it means to lose your life for your brothers. Your brothers should live in you as a vivid presence, warm and active. In prayer, you will gather the voice of all men to make them rise up to God.

Do the same for your distant brothers. Do not read the newspaper as a tourist might, don't watch the television as a pleasure seeker, but each time try to share in the real life of these people which is echoing to you through the media. Your prayer will be enriched with the life of the world.

Pray first in entreaty for men who suffer, both spiritually and materially. You will understand that what they need most is not the means to live but reasons for living. They are hungry for the light and the life of God. Intercede and entreat for them that they may receive the Father. Having seen the suffering of your brother, you cannot be satisfied with prayer alone, but in order that your prayer be true, you must commit yourself to their service.

You will also see their discoveries and their joys. Every advance in love and knowledge, even on the secular level, must overwhelm you in wonder and gratitude. St. Thomas said that each spark of truth, wherever it comes from, is stirred up by the Holy Spirit. If you listen to your brothers and contemplate the world, you will see God's glory throughout creation. Then you may sing His praises, glorify Him, thank Him. You will not become proud as if you had done something great. The man of

167

prayer sends up to God the wonders that He has granted him to do.

If you are able to become one with all men and the whole world in depth, not merely being curious about the surface of events, you will turn your life into unceasing prayer; for you will know the hidden presence of God in all events and when you pray, you will only have to enter ever deeper into these happenings to make yours the voice of your brothers. "Never say or do anything except in the name of the Lord Jesus, giving thanks to God the Father through Him" (Col 3:17).

XXII. When you pray, do not leave your body at the door. It would make you rudely aware of your discourtesy.

As prayer means a continuing progressive re-education of your psychic powers, at the same time it means an integration of your body in the act in which you place yourself before God. It is an essential element of prayer. You will never pray well unless your body shares in the deep feelings of your heart and helps it to prolong them. Your body does not only express your feelings; it gives them stability and reinforces them. Your prayer takes shape in your physical attitude. When you are tired and you cannot settle your mind, do not make desperate efforts for a well built prayer, but be content to be there, in the sight of God and for Him. Be entirely in every part of your body; or walking quietly, breathe deeply for God.

Some simple conditions foster prayer. It presupposes a well-ordered life, not hectic, with emotional security. To turn your thoughts continually to God, you need some relaxation, sleep, a healthy well balanced diet. Do not pray when your mind is disturbed or worried: "Rest your mind a little, either sitting down or walking about, whichever seems best, considering where you are going and what you are going to do" (St. Ignatius). St. Ignatius advises those in retreat who are going to pray to calm their bodies and minds first, by going for a quiet walk and breathing deeply to clear the mind and heart and direct their whole attention to God.

Choose a peaceful, silent place, sheltered from prying eyes. The ideal place for prayer is, of course, your room but you might like to pray in an oratory where Christ is present in the Eucharist. Some days you need this real, actual presence of Christ so that your prayer does not wander off into emptiness. This is when you must make every effort with your body to enter truly into prayer.

You could stand still for five or ten minutes, your hands beside your body, waiting, ready for God, or you could stretch up your hands in the manner of the early Christians or you could kneel, sitting back on your heels, or rest your back against a wall, or if tired, sit with your open hands on your knees, like a poor man who begs God to listen. The essential thing is that you find a way which helps you settle yourself firmly in God's sight and feeling His presence. On your side this means a state of great humility, knowing your sinfulness.

Look upon God inwardly, in contemplation; your whole being gives itself, surrenders to God, so that nothing escapes Him. With your body gathered into quietness your mind will not be distracted by things around you. Above all, be careful not to move too much when you have a satisfactory position, otherwise you might lose this fragile sense that God gives you of His presence. But this silent attitude must not be rigid or uncomfortable. When you meditate on Christ in His mysteries, especially in the Eucharist and the Passion, do not walk. Walking helps reflection when you must settle your mind to receive a higher truth of the Gospel, such as the Cross or the Beatitudes. Contemplative prayer needs silence and calm or it can be done in peaceful, tranquil walks.

This is the time to think of what you want to contemplate, say, Christ offering Himself in the agony to His Father, for your inner gaze must be on a definite reality, but one truth meditated on, will feed your prayer and open you to other aspects of the mystery of Christ. St. Gregory Palamas advises you to find the place of the heart, so that the Spirit may go down there. St. Ignatius advises you to pray "rhythmically, as it were, from one breath to another", a prayer going forth with each breath.

All this may seem much too artificial. But don't say too quickly that these things are useless; try them out and you will gather the desired fruit. In the beginning, they will need a certain effort but later you will find them easy, even relaxing. You will realize that there is no distinction between body and soul, for you are praying in your wholeness.

XXIII.   Go deep into the heart of the world and you will find God. Go deep into the heart of God and you will find your brothers.

"Goodbye", said the fox. "Here is my secret, it is very simple; one can see well only with the heart. The essential is invisible to the eye" *(The Little Prince)*. Unfortunately, you stay always on the surface of things, on their outward appearance, that is why you are not present to God, present to men. When you stay on the surface of the world, you are torn apart by departures and quarrels. Your very body which lets you meet other people, is also something which cuts you off, separates you from others. The darkness of the flesh makes it difficult to be transparent to other people. The same is true if you stay at the visible aspect of prayer which means you might be deceived by a false impression. All this belongs to the deceptive aspect of the surface.

Leave the surface and cross the visible outward areas to be with people from within. Beyond words and physical grasp, on the deep level of self, you may share love together. The darkness of the body is lessened, distances are suppressed and time is no more. When you reach this source of being, this universal home where all thought, all free activity flourish, you discover that this inward gift of people and things is not your doing, but the continual gift He offers you of Himself, He Who is. When you are detached from all transitory things (this is true Christian detachment) and you go down into these depths, you will find yourself outside fortuitous, the fleeting, the trivial, and you will savour the peace of God.

Reaching this point where man is rooted in God, you reach the source of the creative act and you are working for its real fulfilment. So, going deep into the heart of the world, you do not neglect earthly realities; just the opposite, you build upon their true being. This is why true love of man, in his very reality and in the depth of his being, should open you up to the meaning of God.

Your prayer receives something from this. Certainly you must pray over the events of the world and people, but do not measure the value of your prayer and the quality of your relations with others by the interest you show in newspaper items and newsreels. The essential thing is to be with others in their deepest yearnings: "This true giving of ourselves to others throughout our life counts more in assuring a place for them in our prayers than all the moving pictures we make of their faces" (Besnard). "He alone enters into true communion with his brothers and with the world", wrote Dom Le Saux, "who has penetrated within himself, beyond himself, to his place of origin, to God Himself, to the eternal birth of the divine Word within the Father, for he has at last discovered them not where they appear and seem to be, but where they truly are."

Likewise, when you go deep into God in prayer, you do not leave this world, at least not if your prayer is true and if it is deep in God. Do not believe those who tell you that the service of God stops you from being dedicated, body and soul, to your brothers, this talk belongs to the "religious parrotry" of our epoch. In God and through God you are in real contact with men and the world. As Teilhard said, you are united with them "by the most vulnerable, receptive and enriched point of their substance."

In your relationship with God, you rediscover your relationship to others, in a common source. Really believe this — only those who are jointed to God can give real value to earthly realities and personal relationships. If you do not reach the core of these realities and relationships to find God in His creative source, you will be overcome by a certain agony because of the trivial and temporary aspect of what you are doing. GOD ALONE IS, in Him you exist, you live, you love.

XXIV. To advance in prayer is to know the radical poverty you have in all areas.

It is especially in prayer that you will know this law of poverty which is at the heart of the Gospel message. The more you advance in prayer, the less you will feel you are progressing; some days you will feel you are going backwards. You will be like the diver who, when he goes deep in the ocean and enjoys its beauty more intensely, finds at the same time with amazement that it is unfathomable. This is how deep sea explorers speak. The deeper you go into God, the less you are conscious of the distance travelled. God alone is the Holy One, unknown, beyond all. Whatever you do, He will always be beyond your reach. Reread the poem of Dom Henri Le Saux, *Kingfisher My Soul* (Annex I) and you will know what I want to say. Every prayer life, sooner or later, will know the painful experience of the long tunnel and the endless night.

In the beginning you had the experience of the presence of God, now you will know His absence. God asks you to seek Him for Himself and not for the joy you have in His presence. But, at the same time, this produces another experience, which proves the authentic quality of your search for God. The more God is distant, unknown and unreachable, the greater the emptiness within you; you miss His presence and long to find it again. You do not cut down the time you give to prayer, you even add to it and you begin to live in the presence of God throughout your days. This is a sign that you are advancing, and not that you are far from God.

It is now that a strange and puzzling phenomenon takes place. Progress in prayer means a steady impoverishment. In other areas, progress means adding new friends, whereas in prayer everything is gradually reduced to a single insight or a few words endlessly repeated. For example, the mere sense of God's presence keeps you silent all through your prayer time or you murmur a single prayer — such as the Jesus prayer — for hours.

To know prayer is like knowing a friend. In the beginning you feel the need to tell your friend what you think and feel, then gradually the words get fewer and you stay silent, facing each other. It is the same in prayer, as you progress, silence begins to be more important than words. Everything goes on beyond the range of words and a short phrase from the Scriptures is enough to nourish your prayer.

From now on you will feel a great need to keep silence before the Lord. You are there, mute in His sight or you murmur simple words, taken from the Psalms or the Gospel. Do not be anxious about this silence, it is the proper course of development in prayer. Don't try to read or to reflect nor to produce great thoughts. Prayer normally evolves this way. It is good sometimes, in a retreat, to ask yourself this question: "Have I simplified my prayer enough?" A life of true prayer is not made up of a series of prayers, always just the same. Proof of progress is seen as your prayer becomes more simple. Your prayer today is not that of yesterday, nor that of tomorrow.

Learn to give yourself up humbly to this experience of total poverty. Be like the blind beggar at Jericho, seated at the side of the road and stretch out open hands to the silence of God. There are signs which will show you this is neither laziness nor poverty. In silence, you will hold all the misery of humanity, and your prayer will take on the voice of your brothers. In the same way you live continually in the presence of God. This is the sign that you have reached the limit of your human powers and, without your knowledge, the Holy Spirit bears witness with your spirit that you are a son of God. True prayer is always made at night while you are hidden from your very self, as St. John of the Cross has said so well.

XXV. **God never ceases to speak to you in the events of your life. In prayer, learn to make out the meaning of your own personal story. In this way you will gather the will of God like a ripe fruit.**

To have the Spirit free to speak to you, you should not be bound to any single form of prayer. This is why you must pull out all the stops in the spiritual experience. One of these is especially appropriate for what we just mentioned, praying about what has happened in your life. It is constantly said today that God speaks through the events of both personal and collective history. It is true, all through the Bible you see the prophets deciphering the events in the history of Israel, enlightening them by the Word of God.

It is still the same today. So that an event in your life may become a living word of God, you must read it in the light of the Word which has been uttered, in other words, the Bible. "Press the event" is often said "and Christ Jesus will come out." It is true, provided it is lighted by faith in the action of the Holy Spirit, for Christ always comes from above, not from below. He comes from the Father but we are of earth.

You only understand the meaning of the events in your life after prolonged contemplation of the Word of God. So your prayer and Scripture reading must feed you in your day to day life. In the same way you live Easter, not just in the celebration of the liturgy and sacramental life, but you live the mystery in your daily life when you die to selfishness, impurity, sin, to be reborn to love freely given, to purity and life. This is why in prayer it is good for you to imitate Our Lady, by silently going over all the events in your own history. Much later you will discover their meaning. Thus, you will need to reach a peaceful plane of consciousness to understand the crises which have clouded you for years.

In the evening, at the end of each day or at the end of a week, you can examine your prayer life. As usual, put yourself in the presence of God Who knows you completely and loves you. Now there is an act of faith to make: your life is not fate or the result of chance, but a love story in which the happenings are disposed by the fatherly hand of God. Make a fervent act of confidence in God Who directs your life. Make yourself totally available asking what He wants to show you through these events: "Speak, Lord, Your servant listens." Usually the meaning of the events is hidden, and God can only reveal it to you in the light of His Holy Spirit. Do not impose your own thoughts and desires, but let God show Himself to you.

So, go over each one of these events in your memory, recalling the people taking part. Search the Gospel and ask Christ what He thinks about them. It is always in the light of the Beatitudes that you must judge your own life. Then, pray intensely that the Spirit will give you spiritual understanding of your life. Then you will see that a certain friend with whom you could share and be silent, was a sign of God's love for you. That suffering, that failure or that success will appear to you as invitations from Christ to enter more deeply into His friendship.

This way of praying is particularly important when you have crucial decisions to make in life. We shall come back to this when we will speak of spiritual choices. God never refuses His Light to anyone who prays with humility, trust and perseverance. Here again do not look for a solution to your problems using your reason alone, nor by sheer moral drive, but let divine life unfold in you, let the Holy Spirit rise from the depths of your being to enlighten your mind and heart. There are certainly ways to distinguish the ways of the Spirit but you will not find the answer through your own efforts; it is a gift of God which is "assigned" to you, a vital impulse that you cannot take like a ripe fruit that you pick. It's like the feeling of completeness felt by a fiancé before the young girl he loves: "She's truly the one and nothing could make me change my mind."

Such a prayer can close only in adoration and praise. Seeing yourself so loved by God, you will feel a pure hymn of thanksgiving rise up in you. Be certain that the wonders God accomplished for His captive people in Egypt are renewed for you today, provided you are poor and trust in the Lord alone. Then you will be able to sing with the great Hallel: "His love is everlasting."

XXVI. Seek, knock, ask, plead. Cry out night and day until He is tired. You shall receive all that you pray for with unwavering faith.

We have so often said that irrigation has replaced the Rogation days, that men have become too rational in their prayer. They are timid and fearful, they talk to God in faultless forms of prayer and they ask Him for favours that they could very well manage for themselves. You have to be really desperate so that, from the bottom of your wretchedness and anguish, will rise a real prayer.

If you have not reached the limit of your strength, if you have not shared the material or spiritual needs of your brothers, your prayer will stay polite and respectful, but it will not go beyond the stage of worldly requests and it will never reach the ears of God. If you have time before praying, reread the parables where Christ talks about prayer — the sterile dried up fig tree (Mt 21:18-22), the importunate friend (Lk 11:5-8), the little picture of the mulberry tree (Lk 17:5-6), and then all that Jesus said of the efficacy of prayer (Lk 11:9-13).

Compare your prayer with that of the importunate friend or the widow and you will know how timid and fearful you are in your prayer. You wonder how you should pray, what sort of ideas you should develop before God — you would think it was a composition or a poem. God knows you, He knows your wretchedness, He shares your unhappiness. He doesn't ask you to think up flowery sentences or launch out on a wave of useless words.

Before knowing how to pray, you should know how "not to give up, not to be discouraged, not to surrender before the apparent silence of God." "He told them a parable about the need to pray continually and never lose heart" (Lk 18:1). Be bold as the widow before the judge was bold. Find God in the middle of the night, knock at His door, cry out, beg, plead. And if the door seems to be shut, come back again, ask and ask until His ears ring. He will listen to your continual appeal for it shows your absolute trust in Him: "I tell you, even though he does not get up and take care of the man because of friendship, he will do so because of his persistence, and give him as much as he needs" (Lk 11:8).

Let yourself go with the violence of your agony and the strong drive of your impetuosity. Sometimes the Holy Spirit Himself will express the deepest petitions of your heart. Have you ever heard a sick person groan when he feels great pain? No one, unless he has a heart of stone, can stay indifferent to this pitiful sound. When you pray, God expects you to add this violent, vehement imploring note so that He can break down and grant your request.

In the end, you are only touching infinite love, pressed down in His heart, which is waiting for your prayer to release all His tenderness and mercy. If you knew how God is aware of your slightest cry, you would not stop importuning Him for yourself and your brothers. He would rise up then and fulfil your expectations, far beyond what you asked. Anything can come to someone who prays without tiring, who loves his brothers with the very tenderness of God.

Such a prayer implies faith. How could you pray with such perseverance unless you have a boundless trust in God, Who listens to you and Who loves you. Here again Christ reminds us that there is no comparison between what you ask and what the Father gives: "I tell you solemnly, if you have faith and do not doubt at all, not only will you do what I have done to the fig tree (withered it), but even if you say to this mountain, 'Get up and throw yourself into the sea', it will be done" (Mt 21:21). Some days you will say foolish things, you will want to be cursed on Jesus' behalf, but what does human wisdom matter? It is madness in the eyes of God. You cannot see the wretchedness of your brothers without being the importunate friend who knocks at God's door, "in season and out of season." Weigh these words of Christ: "If you have faith, everything you ask for in prayer, you will receive" (Mt 21:22).

XXVII. A prayer experience which goes on all your life.

A genuine prayer experience will transform you completely. True, you have learned nothing new, you have made no definite resolutions, you still have problems in yourself and with others, and your outward life hasn't changed — but your heart has been changed by the presence of God. All that you think, live and do, is brightened up in a new day. Your prayer has unified you in the person of Christ and His work, and all your strength is directed towards the Kingdom. Turning back is no longer possible when you have given yourself to Christ, to discover real meaning in life. Your renewal is not on the intellectual or moral level, but in the depths of your heart, penetrated by the love of God. This is why you do not feel this immediately but, as your life unfolds, you will see the benefits of your prayer experience.

The same holds true for brotherly love and the apostolic life about which we have spoken little. Too often you think loving others is the result of your own unaided efforts, when it comes primarily from an emptied heart, with nothing of its own but penetrated by the love of God. Basically, it is Jesus who loves others through you. If you do not ground yourself in divine love, you are likely to have many delusions, mere caricatures of genuine love. If you have carried out this experience of prayer, your heart will be taken over by the Holy Spirit and you will be able to love others for themselves.

Above all, you have found out from your own inner experience how prayer is vitally necessary. This is why St. Ignatius advises retreatants who become slack, to return to the Exercises, that is to be faithful to the prayer that you have practised. It aims to foster in you a demand for unceasing purification. It teaches you, in the light of the Holy Spirit, to purify the real motives in your life and behaviour, it aims to unite your prayer and your life.

Briefly, it teaches you to welcome outward events within you. It integrates all the contributions of the outside world within your purified heart. This movement towards God within the depths of your heart is never made without the help of exterior things, just as interior prayer is fostered by vocal prayer. The dangers in your life are distractions and dispersal; you cannot integrate within you the things brought from the outside, so you feel uncomfortably heavy, a sort of "spiritual indigestion." The book you find, the man you talk to, the physical work that you do, do not all these form your spiritual unity? Never talk of a purely inner life, for there can be no opposition between your interior and exterior life. Your spiritual life is not a flight from the world, but an improved ability to be present to others. A question arises: what sort of welcome do you give to people and outside things?

You can welcome people and things with the superficial approach of curiosity — for example, the interest shown in a book you enjoy. Your reception of a book is authentic when you go beyond the ideas to create a dialogue with the author, about deep questions he raises: the meaning of life, the experience of God, sharing with others, betterment of men, etc. When ideas and people make a deep impression on you, in such a way that they can be accepted and integrated with a Christian viewpoint, then you are truly being centered on God. How do you react to another person — do you welcome him, reject or fight him?

If you welcome things in the depths of your being, you have no need to be afraid of being torn apart or scattered. The whole issue is to be on the same wavelength as others. Your inner dialogue with God "must be such that you could carry it on with the first person you met in the street" said Emmanuel Mounier. It is in prayer that you settle your ideas about other people, so that you find out on what sort of level your talks and meetings take place. Otherwise, you are apt to start acting and not be honest towards others.

The same thing happens in your intellectual life where you are more concerned about piling up ideas than discussing things with thinkers. You must learn to be selective in your reading, not to accept what you do not want to integrate within your heart and mind. You need people and meetings to balance your life, but you must be careful to choose only what you can best integrate within your life.

This is the aim of prayer which brings together a pledge of yourself to God and other people. Prayer is the place where the unction of the Holy Spirit flows over into your decisions and your actions to unify them in the person of Christ. You learn to make genuine promises, genuine relationships, so that they are consistent with Christ's way of thinking and living.

To do this, you have covered the main stages in the plan of salvation. You are called to relive this experience throughout your entire life. Daily prayer finds its nourishment in the Holy Scripture read, meditated prayerfully throughout the liturgical year. Little by little, you will enter deeply into all the mysteries of Christ and you will learn from Him to become involved according to the will of God. The unity of your life is not a matter of technique nor formulas, it is a matter of being taken into Christ, to live always before the Father, in harmony with His will and service for your brothers. May your only rule day and night be to have the sense of the presence of God.

Conclusion

**Remember God's goodness and give Him thanks
for His love is everlasting.**

Yahweh often told the people of Israel to remember, to recall the wonders He had performed for them. As this prayer experience ends and those pages are finished, it is good to contemplate God's mercies in a prayer of thanksgiving. Looking back on the past, gives you confidence for the future and demands fidelity now.

We thank You, Holy Father, for having rescued men from their loneliness, sending them your Word of love. Teach us to listen to this Word in silence and to watch night and day in unceasing prayer.

We thank You, Creator of the universe, for having called men to life with a loving look. You never cease to create him by granting him your gifts — let us live in your creative presence in adoration and love.

We thank You, Holy Father, for the gift of your Beloved Son. He came to tell us of your infinite love and make of us adopted children. Give us your Holy Spirit so that in Jesus we may say: "Abba! Father."

We give You thanks, most merciful Father, for having shown us our sin, giving us a Saviour at the same time; teach us to confess that we have turned away from you and our brothers, to confess at the same time, your merciful forgiving love.

We give You thanks, most merciful Father, for your Son Jesus Christ Who has shown us the wisdom of the Beatitudes. Make our hearts meek, humble and poor so that we may know Him in the strength and power of His Resurrection and share His suffering.

We thank You, just and merciful Father, for having given up your Son for us, to the sadness of the Agony and the anguish of Calvary. Teach us to watch with Him in contemplation of your love: "My God, My God, why have You abandoned me?"

We thank You, Holy Father, for taking us deeply into the death and Resurrection of your Son by recreating us and daily giving us the Eucharist. Send your Spirit of love so that we may be united to Christ and be an eternal offering to the praise of your Glory.

We thank You, Holy Father, for having called all men to eternal life and to the knowledge of your Holy Name. Let us be intercessors through your only begotten Son, and priests of Christ Jesus to all our brothers by proclaiming the Gospel to them.

We thank You, Holy Father, for having raised up your Son Jesus through the power of the Holy Spirit. Teach us to recognize His presence in every event and in every person.

We thank You, Holy Trinity, for living in our hearts. Pour forth on us your loving Spirit so that we may live in Jesus and allow Him to pray to the Father in us.

Annex I

KINGFISHER MY SOUL

The pearl of great price is hid.
Dive deep, dive deep,
Kingfisher, my soul,
Dive deep, and seek.
Perchance thou findest nothing at first;
Kingfisher, my soul,
Persist, persist;
Dive deep, dive deep and seek.
They who know not the secret will laugh
And will make thee sad;
But lose not thy courage,
Kingfisher, my soul.
The pearl of great price is there, hid.
Faith will find the treasure,
And what is hid will reveal.
Dive deep, dive deep,
Kingfisher, my soul,
And seek and seek.
And seek...!

Dom Henri Le Saux

Annex II

THE ONE THING NECESSARY: TO MEDITATE

O Thou Who hast come unto the depths of my heart,
Grant me to be attentive only
To the depths of my heart!

O Thou Who art my guest in the depths of my heart,
Grant me to penetrate
The depths of my heart!

O Thou Who art at home in the depths of my heart,
Grant that I may sit in peace
In the depths of my heart!

O Thou Who alone dwellest in the depths of my heart,
Grant that I may dive and lose myself
In the depths of my heart!

O Thou Who art all alone in the depths of my heart,
Grant that I may disappear in Thee,
In the depths of my heart!

When I reached the depths of Thee,
Oh! what became of me?
Oh! what became of Thee?

When I reached the depths of myself,
There was no more of Thou nor I

There where nothing is,
There indeed is all.
Go deep into this secret
And thou to thyself shalt disappear:
Then only in truth THOU ART!

Dom Henri Le Saux

Annex III

SELF-SURRENDER

Saint Thérèse Couderc wrote down these lines Sunday, June 26, 1864.

Now, what is self-surrender? I well understand the full extent of the meaning of the word self-surrender, but I am unable to express it. I only know that it is very extensive, embracing the present and the future.

Self-surrender is more than being dedicated, more than giving one's self, it is even more than abandoning one's self to God. Self-surrender, then, is dying to everything and to one's self, no longer to be concerned with one's self but to keep it always turned towards God.

Self-surrender, again, is no longer to seek one's self in anything, either spiritually or physically, that is, no longer to seek self-satisfaction but solely God's good pleasure.

It should be added that self-surrender is also that spirit of detachment which prefers nothing, neither people, nor things, nor time, nor place, but which adheres to everything, accept everything, submit to everything.

Now, this might be thought to be very difficult. That is wrong: nothing is so easy to do and nothing so enjoyable to practise. It all consists of making once and for all a generous act while saying with all the sincerity of one's soul: "My God, I want to be wholly yours, deign to accept my offering." All has been said and done. From then on, one must be careful to stay in this state of soul,

187

and not to draw back before any small sacrifices that may help one's growth in virtue. One must recall that act of SURRENDER.

I pray to Our Lord to give an understanding of this word to all those souls desirous of pleasing Him, and to inspire them with such an easy means of sanctification. Oh! if it could be understood beforehand what sweetness and peace is tasted when no reservation is made with the good Lord! How He communicates with the soul that seeks Him sincerely and has been able to abandon itself. Let anyone try it and he will see that here is true happiness to be sought in vain elsewhere.

The self-surrendered soul has found paradise on earth since it enjoys that sweet peace which is part of the happiness of the elect.

Guide for a ten-day experience

We propose four high points of prayer a day. Each hour includes directions to help one to pray, and a prayer theme drawn from Holy Scripture. The Roman numerals refer to part IV, the Arabic numerals to the first three parts.

FIRST DAY

SECOND DAY

THIRD DAY

1st hour:	10	p. 31		11	p. 34
2nd hour:	VIII	p. 140		12	p. 36
3rd hour:	13	p. 36			
4th hour:	14	p. 38		15	p. 40

FOURTH DAY

1st hour:	IX	p. 142		X	p. 144
2nd hour:	XI	p. 146		16	p. 43
3rd hour:	XII	p. 148		17	p. 45
4th hour:	XIII	p. 151		18	p. 47

FIFTH DAY

1st hour:	19	p. 49		20	p. 51
2nd hour:	21	p. 53		22	p. 55
3rd hour:	XIV	p. 152		23	p. 57
4th hour:	24	p. 59		25	p. 61

SIXTH DAY

1st hour:	XV	p. 154		26	p. 64
2nd hour:	27	p. 66		28	p. 68
3rd hour:	29	p. 70		30	p. 72
4th hour:	XVI	p. 156		31	p. 74

SEVENTH DAY

1st hour:	32	p. 75		33	p. 77
2nd hour:	XVII	p. 158		34	p. 79
3rd hour:	35	p. 81		36	p. 83
4th hour:	37	p. 86			

EIGHTH DAY

NINTH DAY

TENTH DAY

Printed by
Imprimerie H.L.N.
Sherbrooke (Québec) Canada